OVER THE WALL

SUNY series,
Religion and American Public Life

William Dean, editor

OVER THE WALL

Protecting Religious Expression in the Public Square

FRANK GULIUZZA III

STATE UNIVERSITY OF NEW YORK PRESS

The author gratefully acknowledges permission to reprint material from the following publications:
Frederick Mark Gedicks. *The Rhetoric of Church and State*, (Durham, NC: Duke University Press, 1995). Reprinted by permission of the publisher.
Frank Guliuzza III, "The Supreme Court, the Establishment Clause, and Incoherence," in Luis E. Lugo, *Religion, Public Life, and the American Polity* (Knoxville: University of Tennessee Press, 1994). Reprinted by permission of the publisher.
Frank Guliuzza III, "Religion and the Courts," (book review) 58 *Review of Politics* 398 (1996). Reprinted by permission of the publisher.
Paul Kurtz (ed.). *Humanist Manifestos I & II* (Buffalo: Prometheus Books, 1973). Reprinted by permission of the publisher.
Douglas Laycock, "'Nonpreferential' Aid to Religion: A False Claim About Original Intent," 27 *William & Mary Law Review* 875 (1986). Reprinted by permission of the publisher.
James McBride, "Paul Tillich and the Supreme Court: Tillich's 'Ultimate Concern' as a Standard in Judicial Interpretation," 30 *Journal of Church & State* 245 (Spring, 1988). Reprinted by permission of the publisher.
Michael McConnell, "Religious Freedom at a Crossroads," in Geoffrey R. Stone, Richard A. Epstein, Cass R. Sunstein (eds.). *The Bill of Rights in the Modern State* (Chicago: University of Chicago Press, 1992). Reprinted by permission of the publisher.
Richard John Neuhaus, *The Naked Public Square* (Grand Rapids: Wm. B. Eerdmans Publishing Co., 1984). Reprinted by permission of the publisher.
Michael Perry. *Love & Power* (New York: Oxford University Press, 1991). Reprinted by permission of the publisher.
Kathleen Sullivan, "Religion and Liberal Democracy," in Geoffrey R. Stone, Richard A. Epstein, Cass R. Sunstein (eds.). *The Bill of Rights in the Modern State* (Chicago: University of Chicago Press, 1992). Reprinted by permission of the publisher.
Donald Swanson, "Accommodating Religion in the Public Schools," 59 *Nebraska Law Review* 2 (1980). Reprinted by permission of the publisher.
John M. Swomley. *Religious Liberty and the Secular State* (Buffalo: Prometheus Books, 1987). Reprinted by permission of the publisher.
Oliver Thomas, "Comments on Papers by Milner Ball and Frederick Gedicks," 4 *Notre Dame Journal of Law, Ethics & Public Policy* 451 (1990). Reprinted by permission of the author.
Mark Tushnet. *Red, White, and Blue: A Critical Analysis of Constitutional Law* (Cambridge, MA: Harvard University Press, 1988). Reprinted by permission of the author.

Published by
State University of New York Press, Albany

© 2000 State University of New York

All rights reserved.

Printed in the United States of America.

For information, address State University of New York Press,
State University Plaza, Albany, NY 12246

Production, Laurie Searl
Marketing, Dana Yanulavich

Library of Congress Cataloging-in-Publication Data

Guliuzza, Frank.
Over the wall : protecting religious expression in the public square / by Frank Guliuzza III.
p.   cm.—(SUNY series, religion and American public life)
Includes bibliographical references and index.
ISBN 0-7914-4449-X (hc : alk. paper) —ISBN 0-7914-4450-3 (pbk. : alk. paper)
1. Religion and politics—United States. 2. Church and state—United States. I. Title. II. Series.
BL65.P7 G85 2000
322'.1'0973—dc21   99-041434

10 9 8 7 6 5 4 3 2 1

Contents

Acknowledgments

There are a number of people I want to recognize and publicly thank for their help with this book. I am grateful for the education and attention I received from Michael Horan and Kenyon Griffin at the University of Wyoming. Richard Cunningham, a philosopher at the Southern Baptist Theological Seminary, first encouraged me to pursue a doctorate. The late Dale Moody, also of Southern Seminary, demonstrated vividly that one's scholarship could fit within the context of one's ministry. Although it has been many years since I finished the graduate program at the University of Notre Dame, the genesis of this book is my doctoral dissertation, "Beyond Incoherence: Making Sense of the Church-State Debate." Therefore, I want to acknowledge the contribution of Donald P. Kommers, who directed the dissertation, and the members of my committee: John Robinson, David Leege, and John Roos. I know that this essay is substantially different from the dissertation, but I remember that these gentlemen were quick to warn me when my argument was headed in the wrong direction. I hope that they will be pleased with the course this research has taken. Too, I want to thank several scholars who read and commented on portions of the book: Stephen Monsma, A. James Reichley, Allen Hertzke, Luis Lugo, James Skillen, Susan McKay, and Mark and Jodella Dyreson. Dr. Monsma and Dr. Reichley participated with me on a panel at the First National Conference of Christians in Political Science. During the round table, I presented much of the argument from chapters 4 through 7, and profited from the spirited exchange that they helped provoke. Dr. Hertzke commented upon a draft of chapter 3 at the same conference. Dr. Lugo and Dr. Skillen reacted to material in chapters 4 and 7 when it appeared as an essay in the book *Religion, Public Life, and the American Polity* (edited by Professor Lugo and published by the University of Tennessee Press in 1994). Dr. McKay and the two Dr. Dyresons are good friends whom I met at Weber State who spent many hours reading the manuscript. I cannot thank them enough for their time and effort. I am also grateful to the editors of the

Review of Politics. A portion of the material in chapter 6 was previously published in Volume 58 (Spring, 1996) of the *Review*. They are kindly permitting me to include it here—as is the University of Tennessee Press. I have presented several other chapters as papers at various political science conferences. I apologize for omitting the numerous panelists, discussants, and attendees who have commented extensively upon this study. I am grateful for their help, and I do offer the usual disclaimer: any mistakes or errors in judgment are my own.

There are also some people in my life without whom I would surely be diminished. Kathy Guliuzza is my wife, my partner, and my best friend. More than anyone else, Kathy helps me to see my strong points and many weaknesses. Matt and Tim are my foster children. They have given me a great gift—the unspeakable joy of parenthood. Randy Guliuzza is more than my brother. He is a very dear, close friend. My sister Robin Parkins perpetually reminds me to be mindful of love for, and loyalty to, my family. Until I met Kathy, my mother, Mary Guliuzza, was the most important person in the world to me. I will always cherish the early years of my life when Mom and I would stay up late into the night talking, planning, and dreaming about the future. My father, Frank Guliuzza, Jr., understood the value of education and preached his gospel with the fervor of any missionary. He taught me that to be true to one's values is more important than the approval of the crowd. He continues to show me that one need not be prominent to be a great man.

I have also been blessed with some very special friends who are persons of enormous talent, integrity, and passion for justice: Kyle Pasewark, Mark and Jodee Dyreson, Gary Malecha, Dan Reagan, David Barrett, Susan Burgess, Kathryn MacKay, Lyall Crawford, Bruce Baum, Neil Berch, Betsy Norton, Peter Vernezze, Elizabeth Ryan-Jeppsen, Kevin and Margaret Goins, Bret Kincaid, Alan Gibson, Frank Hickman, and the late Mark Theesen, to name but a few. I want to thank my colleagues in the Department of Political Science and Philosophy at Weber State University, under the direction of my chairs, T.R. Reddy and Rod Julander, for their faith in me. Twice the department held my position when I went to teach at Vassar College and the University of Minnesota, Duluth. They have made it possible for me to enjoy a rich professional life. Too, my friends in the Department of Political Science at the University of Minnesota, Duluth (UMD), were welcoming when I came and gracious when I returned unexpectedly to Utah. My colleagues at UMD helped make it possible for me to get this project started.

Finally, I want to thank the members of the churches where I have pastored (or ministered): Victory Baptist Chapel (Three Oaks, Michigan), Vassar Road Baptist Church (Poughkeepsie, New York), Calvary Baptist Church (Ogden, Utah), Northern City Baptist Church (Duluth, Minnesota), Swan Lake Baptist Church (Alborn, Minnesota), Mt. View Baptist Church

(Layton, Utah), and First Baptist Church (Brigham City, Utah). I am particularly appreciative of Rev. Robert Stockland at Northern City who encouraged me to present much of the material in this book as an eight-hour series on "religion and politics" to the members of his congregation. No doubt Bob was using the presentation to develop the gift of patience in his flock.

I have read some acknowledgments that are quite poetic, even emotionally gripping. Lacking the ability of these authors to communicate poetically, or to fully reveal the depths of my emotions in print, I simply want you to know that you are all very important to me, and I thank you.

Religion and Politics: Defining the Debate

Consider the following hypothetical, but certainly plausible, political exchange: you opened your newspaper one morning and read that Senator Burns publicly announced his opposition to foreign aid. "If I get my way, and, in the Senate, I *do* get my way, we're not gonna waste another nickel bankrupting our economy by helping foreigners as long as we've got our own troubles here in the United States." When asked what he meant by foreign aid—whether he was talking about economic aid, military assistance, or emergency relief for those who are hungry, dying from disease, or the victims of disaster—Burns replied, "I mean *all of it*, of course. Not another nickel, I tell you!"

In her next press conference, President Wayne responded to Burns. "It is imperative," noted the president, "that we do whatever we can to protect foreign aid. You don't realize it until you sit in the Oval Office, but foreign aid is in America's best interest. First, foreign assistance helps our economy by propping up other potential trading partners. A few dollars invested in foreign aid comes back several fold in new markets for American products. Second, foreign aid contributes to political stability. It is one of the best sources of leverage we have to accomplish our foreign policy objectives."

At this point, President Wayne became simultaneously cautious and yet passionate: "We . . . will . . . *never* go along with the Senate's plan . . . to eliminate emergency foreign aid. It is not right! Each night, before I go to sleep, I ask Almighty God to continue to bless America. I am convinced that there are a couple of clear-cut reasons why God allows America to flourish. First, because this is a place of religious freedom—people can worship and honor God, and they can freely preach the gospel. Second, because America is a *giv-*

1

ing nation. There is no crisis in the world which finds us unready to feed the hungry, give drink to those who thirst, clothe the naked, and do our level best to set the captives free. When we retreat from our commitment to religious freedom, and when we lose our compassion for those who suffer at home and abroad, then, I tell you, I fear that God will be finished with America!" Accordingly, the president announced that she would bring religious leaders into the White House as staff-level advisors. Further, she instructed her legislative liaison team to work with these newly appointed religious leaders to draft legislation that would create, as a matter of *domestic* policy, a benevolence fund called "Operation Care," administered by the religious leaders, and distributed at their discretion, to meet emergency situations anywhere in the United States or across the globe.

Quite apart from the positive or negative implications of the policy, at what point, if any, are President Wayne's actions unacceptable? Professors and students of constitutional law, and religion and politics, might find it educational to look closely at her proposal.

That she is within her authority as president to oppose Burns' legislative plan for foreign aid will not trigger substantial debate. Further, she will not raise many eyebrows for listing her "secular" objections to the senator's plan: She believes that the bill to cut foreign aid constitutes bad economic and political policy.

She is likely, however, to engender much more alarm when she departs from her secular justification for foreign aid. In a moment of incredible personal religious candor, Wayne has not only expressed her faith in God—not surprising since this is something almost every contemporary president does as a matter of course[1]—but she has disclosed that these *beliefs* help shape her *policy* decisions. In this instance, she believes that if it chooses not to perpetuate the foreign aid program America will find itself outside God's will. Wayne's comprehensive defense of foreign aid—one that includes both secular and sacred reasons for her position—will cause some to bristle. Although they might well agree with her position on foreign aid, they will argue that only secular justification and argumentation is permissible in the public arena. Further, they are sure that her invocation of God's will violates the Constitution's requirement of separation of church and state.

An even greater number, including those who agree with the president philosophically and theologically (they are even *pleased* that she was willing to invoke the name of God), will find frightening her executive order to hire religious leaders (working as religious leaders) to serve as official agents of the United States government and assigned to draft and administer emergency aid. They support the goal of protecting foreign assistance; they are sure, however, that her solution is violative of constitutional law.

The hypothetical example illustrates some of the various ways *religion* can intersect with *politics*. In fact, it suggests the ways religion *must* interact with politics. If one announces, at a gathering of colleagues, that he or she intends to talk about "religion and politics," or that the university will sponsor a lecture about religion and politics, it would be wise either to clarify precisely what topics might be discussed or plan to stick around for a long, long time.

Hopefully, the story reminds us that there are several debates within the larger discussion about the intersection of religion and politics. Among them are how to best include (or to exclude) religious dialogue from the political marketplace of ideas, and the thorny problem of how to interpret the religion clauses of the first amendment. Professor Kenneth Wald notes that he wrote his important book *Religion and Politics* to "show that religion is more important in American politics than most Americans realize but in different ways than they commonly imagine."[2]

Over the Wall: Protecting Religious Expression in the Public Square enters the extensive, and often heated, debates over both religious expression in political debate, and the appropriate relationship between church and state. Unfortunately, most of the participants treat them as two separate debates. Those who study religion and politics will offer some minimal commentary about the church-state debate, but that is all.[3] Similarly, those who are experts in constitutional law, and who study the Supreme Court's haphazard treatment of the first amendment's establishment clause, do not deal extensively with the impact of the church-state debate upon the larger question of religion and politics.

In *Over the Wall*, I bring the two debates together. The book, first, amplifies the argument advanced by those who claim that, increasingly, there is evidence to demonstrate that religious people are not taken seriously in the marketplace of political ideas. That does not mean that religious people, particularly evangelical Christians, are not participating actively in politics.[4] Somewhat paradoxically, however, while religious believers are becoming ever more active in politics and political debate at the same time, they are taken less and less seriously. Many academic and cultural elites maintain that religious-based argument is presumptively out-of-bounds in dialogic politics. This reaction to religious-based political expression is evidence of a concerted effort, though one that comes from multiple perspectives, to produce not simply a secular *nation*, but, indeed, a secular *society*.

Second, the book describes the linkage between those who want to secularize and privatize public space with those who insist that the Constitution's establishment clause requires "separation"—separation of church from state, and separation of religion from that which is not religion. Third, it argues that if one is serious about ending secularization, inasmuch as it impacts upon religious-based political participation, then one must look for a different approach to the establishment clause than that offered by the Supreme Court in *Everson v Board of Education* (1947)[5] and *Lemon v Kurtzman* (1971).

Finally, the book considers the alternative approaches proffered in the literature, and by those on the court, and selects one: "authentic neutrality." It concludes with the claim that, by modifying the court's approach to the establishment clause, there will be a substantial reduction in the negative consequences of secularization and separation. Thus, my contribution is to link the process of "secularization" with the Supreme Court's penchant for "separation," and to argue that should American policymakers desire to do something about the former, we need to reevaluate the latter.

ONE

Religious Expression in the

Marketplace of Ideas: Why the Fuss?

❦

Religion and politics: what's all the fuss about? Why are we even having this discussion? Is it fair to conclude that religious people are ostracized, as some scholars claim,[1] from political participation and political debate? Is religious expression, broadly defined, unwelcome in the marketplace of ideas? Addressing these questions will take us to the genesis of the Constitution's religious liberty clauses, and from there to an examination of the factors that have affected the level of political participation by religious people—concentrating particularly upon evangelical Christians[2]—throughout the nation's first 150 years and then in the twentieth century.

If it is true that religious people are politically active, then why is there such concern in the recent academic literature? I hypothesize that, although religious believers are becoming ever more active in politics and political debate, many academic and cultural elites dismiss religious-based argument from dialogic politics. If I am correct, then the frequency of political activism by religious believers does not mean that they are taken seriously, or even welcome in the marketplace, by many academic and cultural elites.

THE DEVELOPMENT OF RELIGIOUS LIBERTY IN THE UNITED STATES

Although historians and constitutional scholars often diverge when interpreting the founding of the nation,[3] there is a general consensus that many men

5

and women braved dangerous passage to America to escape religious persecution. They also agree that, once they came to the New World, many of these same religious refugees persecuted others who practiced different religious traditions. The persecuted rapidly became the persecutors.[4]

The history books are replete with examples of religious intolerance by those in colonial America and even after the successful revolution against Great Britain. Although many of those who settled the Atlantic coast colonies were seeking greater religious freedom for themselves, they felt no compulsion to extend that freedom to others. They often required religious tests for public office, compelled citizens to swear their allegiance to the Christian faith, forced religious dissenters to flee, and even executed religious heretics.[5] Donald Swanson writes:

> The religious cruelties and lack of religious freedoms that existed
> in the Old World provided a primary impetus for the migration to
> the New World. When the minority sects arrived in the New
> World and found themselves in a position of dominance, many of
> them could not resist the temptation to set up their own systems
> of church-state integration.[6]

There was a strange mixture of sentiment for religious liberty and at the same time (and generally by the same people), a tendency to merge church and government. The Puritans in Massachusetts are an excellent example of this apparent paradox. In principle, they insisted upon a church free from state domination, but in reality they could only accept religious freedom if church conformed to the expectations of those holding political power. Max Sevelle and Darold Wax note:

> For what the framers of the Westminster Confession and of the
> Cambridge Platform intended was exclusively the freedom of their
> own Congregational churches from interference by the state. For
> them there was only one true church: that was the Congregational
> Church as they knew it; for them, this church (or these churches)
> represented God's own idea of how churches should be constitut-
> ed for the worship of Him. Any other ideology, any other way of
> worship, would be a gross misinterpretation of God's wishes; to
> tolerate other forms would be to tolerate devilish threats to the
> work of God Himself.[7]

Yet during this period of religious intolerance, and as a direct result of the persecution, one finds planted the seeds of religious liberty and toleration. These seeds would eventually bloom into the freedoms guaranteed by the first amendment. Although they fell short of the liberties finally secured by the Constitution's establishment clause and free exercise clause, these state and colonial laws provided the foundation for the first amendment. For instance, Roger Williams' charter to found Rhode Island recognized the complete separation of church and state.[8]

In 1649, the Maryland Assembly passed the toleration act that provided "no person professing to believe in Jesus Christ shall be in any way troubled in his religion."[9] Unable to find asylum anywhere in the colonies but Rhode Island, the Quakers moved west and settled primarily in Pennsylvania where religious liberty was granted to all who would acknowledge God.[10]

The movement toward constitutionally recognized religious liberty received its greatest boost as a result of the conflict over the established church in Virginia. Because of the persecution suffered at the hands of the Congregationalists in New England, Baptists formed a number of communities in the south. In Virginia, however, only the Anglican Church was legally recognized. Baptists, Quakers, and Presbyterians actively opposed the establishment of the Anglican Church and the impact of such an establishment upon their own religious efforts. The question eventually became not only one of disestablishment of the Anglican Church, but how far disestablishment should go, and whether such disestablishment meant total separation of government from any particular church.[11] The question was resolved when the state legislature considered two competing bills for religious liberty: Patrick Henry's bill, which would have required Virginians to support financially their own churches, and Thomas Jefferson's bill which permitted no state-initiated financial support. Jefferson's bill, the far more separationist of the two proposed pieces of legislation, prevailed and became law in 1786.[12]

The push for religious liberties culminated in the opening clauses of the first amendment. They require that *"Congress shall make no law respecting an establishment of religion"* (the so-called "establishment" or "no establishment" clause) *"nor prohibiting the free exercise thereof"* (the so-called "free exercise clause").[13]

Not surprisingly, the first amendment's religious liberty clauses have engendered substantial debate. The bulk of the attention given to the religious liberty clauses by jurists, scholars, legislative leaders, and the public is reserved for the establishment clause.[14] This makes sense. The establishment clause is one part of the Constitution that demands clarification. What precisely does it mean that Congress can pass no law "respecting an establishment" of religion?

The various analyses of the establishment clause fall into two larger groups: a broad interpretation and a narrow interpretation. The broad interpretation would read the clause to mean: "Congress shall make no law *respecting religion*."

Sometime ago, I watched an episode of the television drama *Picket Fences*. In this strange program, cows were carrying human fetuses to term for mothers who were unable to have children. Once law enforcement officials discovered that "Old MacDonald had a cow"—and the cow was giving birth to a son—all sorts of legal and ethical questions were debated in this little Wisconsin community. At the end of the episode, the sheriff's daughter was left confused about her faith. She went to see the wisest person in town—Judge Bone. She asked the judge whether or not he believed in God. The judge cut her off. He told her that there was no way she was going to get him to *establish religion* by offering an opinion in his chambers with respect to the existence of God. This illustrates how broadly one might take the language in the first amendment: no law "touching" religion.

Alternatively, the narrow interpretation of the clause would require that "Congress make no law establishing *a* religion." In the *Picket Fences* illustration, the judge might have argued two things. First, he was not "establishing" anything by offering an opinion about his faith. He was simply giving his thoughts as the wisest person in town about the existence of God. Second, his comments, even if offered in chambers, would not elevate any single religion.

Important perspectives in this regard can be derived from studying the intentions of the framers of the Constitution respecting the establishment clause. My analysis of the framers' intentions has led me to three conclusions: first, the historical debate regarding how best to interpret the religion clauses will not be resolved directly. The quest to discover the original intent behind the first amendment religion clauses is attractive. The historical debate carries with it an automatic explanation for the Supreme Court's incoherent case results.[15] Separationists, those who favor the broader interpretation of the establishment clause, and accommodationists, proponents of the more narrow reading, believe they can use history to explain the court's inconsistent analysis. Unfortunately, their varied interpretations of the historical data are 180 degrees apart. The framers of the first amendment could not have required simultaneously strict separation of church and state—no law "touching" religion—and meant merely to secure the federal government from establishing a *national* church.[16]

Second, the prohibition against "establishment" only affected the national government. It would not impact upon the states until the 1940s when the court interpreted the fourteenth amendment's due process clause to incorporate the first amendment and to make it binding on the states.[17] At the time of the Revolution, ten of the thirteen states had established churches. In fact, one state, Massachusetts, maintained an official relationship with the Congregational Church until 1833.[18]

Third, the prohibition against "establishment" did not affect the interaction between religion, religious people, and politics. There is serious dispute in the scholarly literature over whether or not the Framers wanted to terminate "financial" accommodation by government toward religion. As I suggested above, some argue that the first amendment was designed to end anything *touching* religion. Clearly, they hold, the Constitution would permit no financial support for religion.[19] Others argue that Congress not only *intended* to offer financial support for religion, they quite frequently did just that—for example, government-supported chaplaincy programs and funds for missionaries to "educate and civilize" Native Americans.[20] The best evidence suggests that regardless of the framers' position with respect to "financial" accommodation, they did not want to terminate "ideological" support for religion. Law professor Douglas Laycock argues that the ideological accommodation of religion was not a good thing, but he acknowledges that it reflected the Protestant Christian consensus in eighteenth-century America:

> In 1791, almost no one thought that government support of Protestantism was inconsistent with religious liberty, because almost no one could imagine a more broadly pluralistic state. Protestantism ran so deep among such overwhelming numbers of people that almost no one could see that his principles on church taxes might have implications for other kinds of government support for religion. The exclusion of non-Protestants from pronouncements for religious liberty was not nearly so thorough or so cruel as the exclusion of slaves from pronouncements that all men were created equal, but both blind spots were species of the same genus.[21]

Thus, ample evidence shows that religious believers participated in the formation and the administration of early local, state, and national government under the Constitution.[22] Several decades after the founding, Tocqueville acknowledged the importance of religious faith to the American people in his thorough study of American politics.[23] The Supreme Court, approaching the twentieth century, identified America as a "Christian nation."[24] Even if the United States was intended to be a "secular" nation,[25] political scientist Kenneth Wald notes that America draws from a rich tradition of religious symbolism. This tradition provides a framework for America's collective goals and aspirations:

> At the core of the rich and subtle concept of a civil religion is the idea that a nation tries to understand its historical experience and national purpose in religious terms. In the same way that religion may endow the life of an individual with greater meaning than mere existence, so a civil religion reflects an attempt by citizens to give their nation transcendent value. The nation is recognized as a secular institution, but one that is somehow touched by the hand of God. British author G.K. Chesterton recognized this tendency in the United States, which he referred to as 'a nation with the soul of a church.'[26]

THE FALL AND RISE OF POLITICAL
ACTIVISM AMONG EVANGELICAL CHRISTIANS

In the late nineteenth and early twentieth centuries, political activism by Protestant Christians reflected the schism between theological liberals and theological conservatives. Broadly speaking, the "liberals" believed in the perfectibility of humankind before the return of Christ. Thus, they plunged into the performance and administration of good works—the "social gospel."[27] Conservatives while not abandoning their responsibility to care for the poor, hungry, naked, and downtrodden, preferred to reestablish the "fundamentals" of the faith within the church.[28]

It is important to note that both groups were motivated by their respective theological positions. To their credit, their predominant motivation was to better America by articulating values and encouraging public policies that they believed consistent with their understanding of Christ's admonitions. Their political rhetoric and activism, no matter how strident, did not correlate with an effort to "establish" the Christian faith.[29]

Following World War I, there emerged a substantial disillusionment with the liberal theologian's claim that humankind can, over time, grow past its penchant for evil.[30] This disillusionment offered an opportunity for conservative Christians to preach their particular message of hope.[31] However, any aspirations the fundamentalists may have harbored that they would shape public debate were crippled by the performance of William Jennings Bryan, (viewed through the lenses of H. L. Mencken) at the 1925 Scopes "Monkey Trial."[32] As a result, for nearly fifty years, conservative evangelical Christians largely abandoned the political world to concentrate upon a pure, undiluted message of salvation.[33]

What prompted the reawakening of this evangelical and fundamentalist sleeping giant? Some dug in their heels opposing the burgeoning civil rights movement. Others became vocal at the open rebellion of America's youth in the late 1960s and early 1970s—one popularly characterized by sexual promiscuity and illegal narcotics. A number reacted against the forceful opposition to the war in Viet Nam.[34] However, the watershed event that served as a catalyst for political activism among conservative Christians was the Supreme Court's 1973 decision, *Roe v Wade*.[35] Like their counterparts in the early part of the twentieth century, conservative Christians in the latter part of the century became simultaneously outraged and frightened by the direction they saw America heading. Their anger and their fear prompted their reentry in grassroots politics.[36]

Thus, conservative evangelicals justify their political activism as consistent with their theology. It is no longer a question of "doing either the gospel" (e.g.,

the functions of the church—worship, discipleship, evangelism, and benevolence) *or* engaging in the duties of citizenship. Both are seen as part and parcel
of doing the gospel.[37] Not surprisingly, there is strong connection between their
conservative theology and their political and social conservatism.[38]

After *Roe*, born-again Christians did get involved in politics. They came
out in support of one of their own, Democratic candidate Jimmy Carter, during the 1976 election.[39] Sensing an opportunity for victory in 1980, conservative interest groups made overtures toward several Christian leaders. The
ensuing relationship between these various members of the "New Right" in
American politics helped to catapult names like Jerry Falwell and Pat
Robertson into national prominence.[40] Christian television shifted away from
what was previously an almost exclusive emphasis upon evangelism and discipleship toward shouldering the responsibility for informing believers about
political truth and urging them to get into the game.[41]

Pat Robertson got into the game in 1988 when he announced that he
was convinced that it was God's will for him to run for president.[42] Although
Robertson did not secure the Republican Party nomination, he became a mas-
ter at grassroot politics. In six short years since his failed bid for the
Republican nomination, Robertson's Christian Coalition had shaken the
foundation of the old, established Republican Party. During the 1994 primary and convention season, the media ran several stories reporting that the
"New *Christian* Right" had captured the G.O.P in several states.[43]

Additionally, Robertson's *700 Club* still reaches an audience of millions
with a daily news summary and copious political commentary. Christians
responding to pleas by Robertson on the *700 Club* routinely swamp the
Capitol or White House switchboards with calls. His Regent University trains
graduate students in government, public policy, media, and produces lawyers
who are well-trained and ready to litigate.[44] His American Center for Law and
Justice—the ACL*J* (ready to do battle with the ACLU)—has proven itself at
the highest appellate court levels including victories before the United States
Supreme Court.[45]

WHY DO RELIGIOUS PEOPLE CONTINUE TO BE CONCERNED?
DIGGING BENEATH THE SURFACE

This range of political activism prompts some to say, "What's the fuss? You're
back in the politics business." The political activism undertaken by evangelical leaders might be categorized into three types. First, "prophets" participate
in political life from outside the system and challenge social and public policies they find to be repugnant. In addition, prophets understand their calling

as providing a challenge to the church if they perceive that believers are becoming too close and comfortable with the world. Second, "politicians" are different from prophets in that they enter fully into the political process and are accountable, directly or indirectly, to the public. Third, "players," are neither prophets nor kings (politicians) but are would-be kingmakers. The player best describes the activism of evangelicals beginning with phase one (e.g., the formation of the Moral Majority), and phase two (e.g., Pat Robertson's aborted efforts to become a politician that culminated in the Christian Coalition). Attorney Oliver Thomas argues that, rather than suffer in American public life, religion flourishes. It permeates public life:

> In short, the notion of a naked public square devoid of religious influence has no significant basis in fact. Certainly, there are isolated anecdotes and court cases demonstrating that religion does at times receive short shrift in the public arena—the absence of adequate references to religion in social studies textbooks being the most dramatic example. The overwhelming weight of evidence, however, is to the contrary. . . . A more accurate assessment would seem to be that religion enjoys a prominent, and some would argue favored, role in American society.[46]

If one digs beneath the surface, however, one will discover a far more unstable place for religious expression in the public square. There *are* indeed isolated anecdotes and court cases that *do* demonstrate that religion often receives short shrift in the public arena. Furthermore, there is a difference between the kind of religious expression that characterizes those politicians who wear their faith on their sleeves for public consumption—giving evidence of what many call America's "civil religion"[47]—and authentic religious expression. More religion does not correlate with "taking religion seriously."[48]

What a growing number of scholars are telling us is that the complex relationship between religion and politics has been damaged. The problem, they maintain, is that the two institutions do not fully interact in contemporary American society. Specifically, religious voices are neutralized and are thus restrained from many parts of American public life. Even though religion permeates the political and social environment, it is abrogated effectively by the actions of many cultural and intellectual elites.[49]

This concern is not a new one. Earlier in this century, Reinhold Niebuhr, John Courtney Murray, and Jacques Maritain were among those who sounded the same alarm.[50] Today, however, the warning comes with increasing intensity. A wide range of scholars from within political science, history, law, sociology, theology, including Mark Tuhnet,[51] Harold Berman,[52] Robert Bellah,[53] R. J. Neuhaus, A. James Reichley,[54] Paul Vitz,[55] Kenneth

Wald, James Davidson Hunter and Os Guiness,[56] Frederick Mark Gedicks,[57] Ronald Thiemann,[58] Franklin Gamwell,[59] Michael Perry, and Stephen Carter argue that the problem is unique and much worse. Even though they may not always tackle the issue from the same perspective and frequently proffer different solutions, each of these experts call upon citizens and policymakers to recognize and restore the relationship between the two venerable institutions.

TWO

The Pathway to Secularization

There exists in America today, a group of scholars (from a wide range of academic disciplines and none of whom are affiliated with the so-called Religious Right) who share the concern that religious expression is given short shrift in the public square. They argue that the abundance of what might be called "public religion" does not mean that religion receives serious consideration in the public square. Furthermore, they note that although religion permeates the political and social environment, it is at best trivialized and often demonized by the so-called cultural and intellectual elites—the very people who pride themselves on open-minded inquiry.[1]

If the claim of these scholars is valid, and if those in academic and intellectual communities do target religious expression, how is this manifested? Opposition to religious expression is exhibited in three ways—by what we may term trivialization, open bigotry, and secularization through privatization.

THE "TRIVIALIZATION" OF RELIGIOUS EXPRESSION

It is staggering to fathom the general contempt with which religion and religious people are held on college and university campuses. Peter Berger notes that there is "bemused contempt about the 'superstitions' of religious fundamentalists" within "the milieu of the 'new knowledge class.'"[2] This contempt might be understandable if intellectuals had reached their conclusions after serious study, but often scholars react to "religion" without employing the careful inquiry they devote to their own areas of expertise. Consequently, it is not uncommon for academics to casually dismiss religious argument as

15

unworthy of discussion. Moreover, they are quite content—even smug—about their capability to put believers in their place.[3] Law professor Michael Perry holds that it is often too generous to speak of this presumption as simple "misunderstanding," or "lack of clarification." Perry argues:

> "Misunderstanding" is, in some cases, too weak and polite a term. As David Tracy has written, in our society religion is "the single subject about which many intellectuals can feel free to be ignorant. Often abetted by the churches, they need not study religion, for 'everybody' already knows what religion is: It is a private consumer product that some seem to need. Its former social role was poisonous. Its present privatization is harmless enough to wish it well from a civilized distance. Religion seems to be the sort of thing one likes 'if that is the sort of thing one likes'."[4]

Perry's argument suggests two characteristics of the hostility toward religion common to many intellectuals. First, they either dismiss religious faith as something that is antimodern, irrational, and simply a crutch for those who need it. Somewhat paradoxically, intellectuals assume that religious believers realize that they suffer from an addiction to the irrational—that they are aware that their handicap requires a crutch. Further, at the very least the believers should be "rational" about expressing their irrationality. For instance, one should think in terms of this syllogism:

> *I know my life would hold no meaning without my belief in God. Hence, my belief serves as a crutch for my particular handicap.*

> *I know, too, that my belief is irrational and intellectually unsophisticated—it offends others who do not share my handicap.*

> *Therefore, when I am expressing my faith in God, through, for example, prayer, or the observance of holy days, I am very aware that I am acting irrationally and offending those who are intellectually sound.*[5]

Second, many critics of religious expression lump all religious faiths together. Despite the fact that there are substantial differences in the truth claims offered by various faiths—differences that are often impossible to reconcile intellectually—religion, regardless of expression, is still religion.

Thus, people are placed into two larger categories: One is either "religious," or one is not. But, rest assured, though the cast of characters and rituals may change from faith to faith, the "religious" people and their respective religious faiths are, at their core, the same.[6]

The twin tendencies to dismiss religious faith as irrational and to lump all religious beliefs together are symptomatic of what political scientist Kenneth Wald terms "modernization theory." This theory maintains that "contact with modern institutions inevitably erodes religious sentiments." Put simply, modernization is the process of bringing the best features of Enlightenment thought into practice. It is built around modern education—particularly in science and technology. It tears down primitive institutions like small, isolated communities in favor of large cities. Word of mouth is replaced by modern communication. Rugged individualism and limited government are supplanted by a burgeoning bureaucratic state. Modernization impacts upon almost every aspect of one's life. Certainly, Wald notes, its reach will include and trivialize "primitive" religious faith:

> Modernization is built upon the notion that people can under-stand nature and master it through science and technology. The "demystification" of the natural world—the sense that people rather than unseen gods shape human destiny—undermines belief in the supernatural. When held up to the scientific standards of proof and evidence, religious claims and, therefore, religious faith may falter.[7]

What Professor Wald is really describing is the failure of moderniza-tion, along with Marxism, to throw the knockout blow to religion in the United States. Moreover, it is important to note that despite the evidence he presents that religion is flourishing in America, Wald, too, is concerned about the fragility of religious expression in public life. Furthermore, the proponents of modernization cited by Professor Wald *are* precisely those intellectual elites whom I am describing. Even if most Americans do not, consciously or uncon-sciously, subscribe to the notion that modernization will cripple religious faith (and Wald offers some explanations why they do not), many within the acad-emy *are* persuaded. And, though modernization has yet to thoroughly secu-larize American society, that does not mean that it has no converts. Its apos-tles, prophets, evangelists, pastors, and teachers are often the ones preaching in colleges and universities across the United States.[8]

Recently, the reaction to religion by some of the cognitive elite has entered, at the risk of exploiting a well-worn term, its own "postmodern" phase.[9] While many scholars still cling to the modernization theory and its emphasis upon science and technology,[10] others start with a new reference point. They dispute the claim that science will facilitate nirvana.[11] For these scholars science is neutral. It can be used as a tool for the eradication of small pox. It can be used to increase the production and distribution of wheat. Yet, simultaneously, science can produce weapons of mass destruction. Science can create diseases that move, unchecked, throughout the population. Even when the results of science are not inherently evil—as, for instance, in the capabili-ties offered to would-be parents through in-vitro fertilization—they are often fraught with ethical, theological, and even legal concerns. Thus, since science can no longer be their "god," these scholars have reconsidered the human spiritual dimension.[12]

This postmodern (or, postscientific Enlightenment) emphasis upon spirituality is a welcome phenomenon to some religious believers because they believe their own faith is rational. For example, many apologists for biblical Christianity assert that their faith makes better sense than alternative forms of theism, atheism, humanism, and a whole host of other "isms."[13] Instead of deifying science, as do many modernists, the spiritual postmodernists employ the scientific method and other tools of rational inquiry to determine the veracity of competing truth claims. Thus, in the minds of some academics, this spiritual postmodernism is greatly preferred to modernization theory.[14]

Unfortunately, this postmodern breakthrough has not resulted in the kind of healthy quest for truth, applying the tools of rational inquiry to competing religious truth claims, that it might have—precisely because "rational inquiry" is at the heart of the enlightened "modernization" rejected by the postmoderns. Instead, scholars have, once again, trivialized religious faith by abandoning the tools of rationality and lumping various kinds of religious expression together. Rather than use science, logic, historiography, or the rules of evidence applied in a courtroom to inquire as to whether Buddhism can be defended as more rational than Islam, or whether Christianity is a valid extension of Judaism, or whether Mormonism is a valid extension of Protestant Christianity, or if Shirley MacLaine's assertion that she "is God" is at all plausible, many of the spiritual postmodernists just jettison them all together. Religion, they argue, is primarily myth, and myths are not tested rationally.[15] So, instead of establishing a series of religious claims that can be distinguished and evaluated, the spiritual postmodernist would follow the modernist, albeit for different reasons, in grouping all religious claims together.[16]

Unlike the modernist, however, the spiritual postmodernist, would not usually castigate one's myth. Most myth, whether Buddhist, Islamic, Christian, Jewish, Mormon, or New Age, has value to the postmodernist. It is a healthy part of one's "spiritual" development just as eating vegetables and exercising are good for one's physical development.[17] Yet the emergence of a generic interest in "spirituality" does, ironically, permit an evaluation between the larger categories of religious believers. Now one *can* choose between better or worse religion.[18]

Unlike the modernist, this kind of evaluation is not based upon the tools of rational inquiry. Like the modernist, however, one might argue that the criteria for evaluating religious faith generally squares with those with a decidedly secular world view. What makes for the good society? Where do we want to be as an enlightened people? This list can include several things: opposition to racism, sexism, and homophobia; promotion of multiculturalism, economic and political justice, artistic and creative development, and the like.[19]

Thus, good religion—religion that satisfies the need to develop the "spiritual" dimension of one's life—should teach those values that are consistent with these more secular objectives. Bad religion, on the other hand, runs counter to the goals of an enlightened society. It is exclusionary; it is often dogmatic; and it purports to teach accurately the difference between right and wrong, or truth and falsehood. Good religion talks of a "higher power," "ultimate concern," "genuine warmth," "the light" or "the force" that is behind the human perpetual upward evolution. If one chooses to personalize this force, one might refer to a heavenly parent named "A. Loving God." Bad religion introduces a judgmental dimension to the God who is love. Bad religion shackles its followers with a compulsion to evangelize and the duty to live holy and just lives. Good religion is fulfilling; it benefits the individual and society. Bad religion, for a whole host of reasons, is counterproductive for the community.[20]

Therefore, it is easy to trivialize or even express open hostility toward bad religion. But there is no need to panic. Bad religion has been exposed; its days are marked. Fortunately, the postmodernist asserts, bad religion can be replaced by good religion.[21]

ACCEPTABLE BIGOTRY?

Additionally, many academics feel comfortable about their attitudes toward religion—and their expression of those attitudes. I have many friends in the academy who would not tolerate offensive and discriminatory language in their presence, if the target of the diatribe, dialogue, or even thoughtless joke, was a person of color, a woman, a gay or lesbian, or one who is physically challenged. Well enough. Freedom of speech, and its accompanying responsibilities, permits, and might even *oblige*, one to speak out on such issues. However, those same open-minded friends and colleagues not only fail to rise to the defense of a religious person under verbal derision (with the possible exception of anti-Semitism),[22] they also openly participate in the ridicule. Professor Berger likens this bigotry by academics to the worst intolerances of religious fundamentalism:

> I happen to live two blocks from the Charles River; when I hear the word "fundamentalism," I think of my academic colleagues and neighbors whose unbending convictions and self righteous intolerance of heretics are fully up to ayatollah standards (though, thank God, they lack ayatollah means of enforcement).[23]

Two examples from my own experience teaching at a state university in Utah come to mind. In Utah, the presence of the Church of Jesus Christ of Latter Day Saints (the Mormon Church) is ubiquitous.[24] As a result, those who are non-Mormons, and who feel like they are very much out of the majority's culture, often feel it necessary to target the dominant local group for gratuitous verbal abuse. A few years ago, my department had a work-study student, a very faithful Mormon, whom I'll call Helen. One day several members of the department, in the presence of the student, launched into a mockery of Mormonism that could, at best, be described as mean-spirited. They were not engaging in the diatribe to hurt Helen. My suspicion is that they did not even *think* of Helen as occupying the same room. Had Helen been African American, or openly gay, or Asian, they would have noticed. Helen was none of these things. She was a student who was devout, and, although everyone knew it, either they forgot or else it did not matter: Even Helen must benefit from these words of wisdom. Even Helen would see the accuracy of their hostile critique of her church. What could Helen do? Although she wanted to respond, she felt like she was no match for the others. Furthermore, she worked *for* these folks—no small deterrent to her entry into the fray. So, she did the only thing that the she could do. With tears welling up, she walked out of the room.

I caught up with her a moment later, and we agreed that it was unfortunate that a group so protective against harassment of people because of their skin color, gender, or sexual preference could see no obvious inconsistency in deriding people because of their religious faith. Later, when I spoke about the incident with some of those in the department, they were genuinely embarrassed and sorry that they had been so insensitive to Helen. I did not sense, however, that they regretted their comments directed against all members of the Mormon Church. I am sure that they would, if pushed further, distinguish their behavior from the examples of bigotry expressed by racists, sexists, homophobes, and the like, that they find so loathsome.

The second incident is somewhat similar. I was eating lunch with a group of professors including a sociologist (I'll call him Walter). Walter started recounting his experience looking for an apartment prior to his arrival in town. It seems that Walter, while living back east, contacted a landlord in Utah. The landlord set up an appointment with Walter who flew out to househunt. When Walter went to the apartment to meet with the landlord, he saw a line of several people waiting to look at the unit. Walter went to the back of the line, although he thought that waiting was a waste of time. To his credit, the landlord arrived on time, acknowledged the crowd, and asked, "Is Walter here?" Walter went with him to look at the apartment. When they were away from the others, the landlord looked at Walter and said, "I just have one question for you: Are you one of those *fucking Mormons?*" Walter assured him that he was not, and the landlord offered him the apartment on the spot and dismissed the other hopefuls waiting outside. I was amazed not only at the facts of the story but at Walter's pleasure in telling it. The bigotry of the landlord was certainly outrageous, but Walter's complicity in the event, apparently without any shame or remorse, was just as stunning. From every conversation I had shared previously with Walter, I would have bet a small fortune that, when confronted with such raw, savage bigotry, he would have, at the very least, walked away from the apartment.

I do not want to overgeneralize from these two cases. One might argue that the religious climate in Utah is so very different that bigotry is an acceptable means of self-defense. My two stories do not exhaust the examples of smart, well-meaning members of the academic community in Utah who engage openly in religious bigotry. It was alleged that just a few years ago some faculty members at the University of Utah would ridicule the dominant local faith when recruiting new professors. Some would drive candidates past the LDS Temple in downtown Salt Lake City and tell the visitors that this was "Utah's version of Disneyland."[25]

Is this behavior justified because of Utah's unique religious climate? One might offer just such a defense for religious bigotry, but it is unacceptable— just as a similar defense for gratuitous gay-bashing by heterosexuals would be for those living in San Francisco, or a defense of racism by whites in South Africa. But the intolerance is not just in Utah. I have had dinner conversations with friends at academic conferences and listened as the conversation turned into a verbal spanking of Christians. As with the case of Helen, those telling their story 1) are oblivious to the the fact that I am there; 2) are insensitive to how I might feel about their remarks; 3) judge that, regardless of how I might feel, I need to hear them anyway; or, 4) assume that I am one of *them*, and, therefore, as "one of the good ones," I am not really like those other evangelicals who are the targets of their rancor. If someone changed the subject and made the exact same argument substituting a racial or ethnic minority group, my friends would have been, justifiably, quite outraged. In each of these examples, what is the message? That the same rules which we have come to value as a means of protecting and validating other kinds of targeted groups simply do not apply to religious groups or individuals.

"But some religious groups are so hateful and dangerous," one might remark. I agree. By all means, then, launch a barrage at all religious believers— the kind of barrage that, if leveled at any other group, would cause the academic community to rise up in anger. But do not stop with the religious believer. Some black separationists preach a message of hate; they are, in my view, dangerous.[26] The same might be said of some militant gays and lesbians—

those who, in the name of peace and tolerance, will, among other acts of violence, physically assault churchgoers on their way to worship, or interrupt a
service and savagely desecrate an altar.[27]

As with other forms of prejudice and bigotry, bigotry against religion
and religious expression has a wide range of consequences. Many in the academy are quick to assign most cultural problems to some sort of "ism": racism,
sexism, ageism, nativism, classism, homophobia, paternalism, jingoism, and
the like. It seems like the threshold for what constitutes one of these "isms" is
fairly low.

Yet simply to identify a particular "ism," to speak about a problem of
intolerance and discrimination, misses some of its complexity. One can speak
about discrimination using terms like "prejudice" or "bigotry" or "racism"
almost as if they were part of a continuum that denotes different levels of
severity. Much like the difference between sunburn and skin cancer, there is a
difference between prejudice and racism—the former is painful, the latter is
deadly.

Perhaps this differentiation is artificial, but recently I have heard others
make the same distinction. They usually argue that racism is more than prejudice or bigotry. It is prejudice plus power.[28] It is one thing if Archie Bunker
does not like his neighbors, the Jeffersons, because they are African
Americans. That is prejudice. It is another if Archie has the power to act upon
his prejudices to do physical harm to the Jeffersons, or to cost them their
house or a job. That is racism.[29]

With respect to discrimination against religion, the same continuum
applies. When a group of kids laughs at an individual's religious garment, or
they snicker at a hairstyle required by one's faith, that is prejudice. When the
same group corners and subsequently assaults a Jehovah's Witness in an alley
to indicate their displeasure with his or her message, or they burn down the
house of a family of Orthodox Jews, leaving a swastika on their lawn, then that
is more than prejudice. We just have not come up with the appropriate "ism."

Are academics guilty of the same behavior? In the illustrations I provided above, the story about Helen is a clear example of prejudice. Walter's
story is something more. It is tantamount to racism. The landlord who refused
to rent to Mormons was a bigot, and he coupled his bigotry with power. As a
result, he denied people access to housing. Academic bigotry against religion
becomes a problem to the extent that it infringes upon rights and liberties—
whether the liberties of one individual or of an entire community.

One additional story should illustrate that at the colleges and universities we can couple our prejudices with an (un)healthy dose of power. A close
friend of mine was a graduate student at an important state university. One
day he was in his department's office, and he observed his chairperson open-

ing the dossiers of candidates for a position in the department. My friend noticed that, occasionally, the chairperson would grunt and toss a dossier into the trash without submitting it to the normal review process before the department's search committee. When my friend inquired as to why certain candidacies were aborted, the chairperson responded that he got rid of those applicants who had attended a Bible college or a theological seminary. Now this was not a department of religion seeking an expert on Islamic thought. In that case, at least, one might assume that a devout Christian, presumptively, would not be likely to fit the job description. Nevertheless, since one can be an expert in something one does not believe in, even under these conditions, the chairperson's assumption would be invalid, although he might not realize it. In this situation, there appeared to be no such mitigating factors. What had motivated the chairperson's actions? Was there something about attending Bible college that, systematically, rendered candidates unfit for the position? The chairperson said he did not even *look* at their qualifications. He simply "did not want *those people* in the department." He did not like Christians (or certain types of Christians). Therefore, he made the decision, unilaterally, to give their candidacies no consideration whatsoever. Undoubtedly, his decision to indulge his bigotry greatly affected some people's careers. That is equivalent to racism. My hope is that this type of overt, egregious discrimination—with this level of consequences—is rare, but certainly it was not an isolated occurrence.[30] For these and other unfortunate applicants, discrimination by the university would be very difficult to prove since, often, scores and scores (if not hundreds and hundreds) of extremely qualified applicants compete for teaching positions at colleges and universities.

Is it even possible to look at the hiring practices of these institutions and see whether or not religious applicants get a fair shake? That is precisely what affirmative action officers do with regard to race and gender. When it comes to religion, however, appeals for fairness and diversity tend to fall on deaf ears.[31]

SECULARIZATION THROUGH PRIVATIZATION

Many intellectuals trivialize religious expression or target it for open hostility. Further, they are comfortable with their bigotry toward religion. Finally, and perhaps most disturbing, when it comes to religious expression in the marketplace of ideas, the quest for "secularization" among many cultural and intellectual elites prompts the "privatization" of religious belief and expression.[32] The late Leo Pfeffer, that eminent defender of religious freedom, defined secularism:

> A view of life or any particular matter based on the premise that
> religion and religious considerations should be ignored and pur-
> posely excluded; a system of social ethics based upon a doctrine
> that ethical standards and conduct should be determined exclu-
> sively with reference to the present life and social well being with-
> out reference to religion.[33]

One way to "secularize" moral and political debate is to insist that one's
religious beliefs, and moral and political arguments emanating from those
beliefs, should remain private.[34] Theologian Stanley Hauerwas maintains that
this presupposition—that "morality" remain in the "private sphere"—has
formed our public rhetoric and institutions.[35] Similarly, Professor Perry claims
that the secularists' objective is to marginalize and privatize questions of
human authenticity.[36] Stephen Carter argues that privatization is precisely the
message that modern American civilization is sending to religious people.[37]

The movement to privatize religion begins with the presumption that
America is a "secular" society. Many in the religious community would want
to agree with that premise. America *is* a secular *nation*, not a sectarian one.[38]
Its government is secular and does not adhere officially to the teachings of any
religious faith. Proponents of privatization mean more than that, however.
Their claim is that America is a secular *society*. First, as the illustration below
depicts, they distinguish between the "private" space in the larger society and
the "public" space.

PRIVATE SPACE (sexual choices, marriage, travel, career, family)
PUBLIC SPACE (education, police protection and military, social problems)

The private space includes all those activities that people engage in that
are, essentially, private—sexual choices, marriage, travel, career, family. The
public space, or the civil society, includes all those activities that involve members of the community collectively—education, policing and military, social
problems (like health care, benevolence, and care for the aged).

Until recently, there was little question that religion fell into both the
private and public realm. As the illustration indicates, on one hand, most religious questions were *private* matters—the choice to believe or not believe,
whom to believe in, participation in religious services, financial support for
religion, and the like. Simultaneously, however, "religion," or the tapestry that
emerged from the collection of individual choices, was generally thought to
have a role to play in tackling the problems that plague the civil society—education, social problems, and the like.[39]

> PRIVATE SPACE (religious choices)
> PUBLIC SPACE (religious approaches to social maladies)

In fact, in 1787, as Professor Harold Berman notes, the role of government in the civil society was rather narrow when compared with the role of religion. Religion shouldered the largest share of the burden for education, relief for the poor, health care, and other forms of social welfare.[40] Moreover, "religion played a guiding role, and government an implementing role, in family law and criminal law."[41] Within the last half century, there has been a concerted effort by some intellectual elites to claim the public space for the state and to wrest it from other institutions including religion. I offer that argument very cautiously. It is one thing to make an observation that government has emerged as the dominant force in solving social problems; it is another to assert that government expansion at the expense of a public role for religion is the product of a grand design. Consequently, I will tread down this pathway very softly.[42]

For a variety of reasons that I will discuss in the next chapter, there are those who believe passionately that it is preferable for the public space, or the civil society, to be secular. It is secular institutions that should take on society's problems. And, by constitutional decree, the one institution that *must* be secular is the state. Therefore, as the illustration below depicts, the state monopolizes all the public space available.[43] Religion is relegated to private space.[44]

> PRIVATE SPACE (sex, marriage, travel, career, religious beliefs and actions)
> PUBLIC SPACE (social problems dealt with, largely, by the state)

Berman notes that, in each of the areas of civil society mentioned above, the government has replaced religion's primary role. "In the twentieth century, we see a complete reversal of the respective roles of religion and government in American social life," Berman observes. "Defined in terms of their social functions, these two have radically changed their meaning."[45] Public education is almost totally secularized. Health care is no longer primarily a religious concern. Relief of poverty is a governmental concern. And, perhaps most important, family life and the criminal law now no longer reflect religious beliefs.[46] Consequently, Professor Berman argues that religion has become "privatized." It is increasingly less important in the public arena:

> In short, religion has lost most of its importance as a way of
> addressing publicly the major social problems of our society. It has
> become increasingly a matter of the private relationship between

the believer and God. Worship remains collective, and the churches continue to play an important part in the individual lives and
the interpersonal relations of their members; but the occasional
gatherings of fellow worshippers make only a minor contribution
toward solving social needs.[47]

And, as religion is thoroughly privatized, the civil society becomes more and
more dependent upon the state. Berman concludes:

> As religion has become increasingly a private matter, the social
> responsibilities of government have become magnified. Society
> has become increasingly identified with government. Divorced
> from religion, government has become increasingly political, so
> that the words government and politics, or government and state,
> have become synonymous. The state, as the great Polish Nobel
> Prize winning poet Czeslaw Milosz has said, threatens to swallow
> up the civil society.[48]

Thus, part of the effort to produce a secular society has been the successful strategy to reduce the role of religion—along with other private charities—and to substitute government as the driving force to tackle the problems plaguing the civil society—in fact, to dominate the civil society. But the
effort to "secularize" public space goes so far as to impact upon the kind of
argument and persuasion that is acceptable in the public square.[49]

It is not as though religious people are forbidden from participating in
the political arena or public debate. The first amendment's free speech clause
protects against that.[50] I concur with Oliver Thomas,[51] Kenneth Wald, and
others, that religious people are involved in politics. They are motivated to do
so by their religious faith, and, often, because they become swept up in the
trappings of "civil religion" that permeate American political and cultural life.

The pressure to privatize religion is more subtle than an overt restriction on political participation.[52] Remember: I am distinguishing the treatment
religion receives by intellectual elites from the public at large. Citizens who are
religious are welcome to the political debate as *citizens*. They can bring whatever intellectual arrows that are in their quivers to the fray—with one exception. Increasingly, religious argument is unwelcome.[53]

Two stories, one actual and the other hypothetical, help illustrate the
contention that religious folk can participate in political debate as long as they
check their religious arguments at the door. Once they introduce these religious arguments, they are not to be taken seriously.

Professor Stephen Carter recounts an experience he had when speaking
at the law school at the University of Notre Dame. At a reception that followed his speech, two law students told him how their fellow students mocked

them when, in class, they opposed abortion. Although they were Catholic students at a Catholic university, they were told by their peers that they could not justify their arguments by referencing their religious faith. Carter notes that had they simply couched their moral arguments in secular terms, "these students believed they would have been welcomed into the classroom's version of the public square."[54]

And, Richard John Neuhaus posed this hypothetical story to illustrate the separation of religious argument from public debate:

> We witness a son who routinely abuses his aged mother and, without consulting the law books or moral philosophy, we *know* that is wrong. If pressed on why we think it wrong, however, we could likely provide reasons that we think should hold up to public scrutiny. Among other reasons and maybe foremost among them, most Americans would likely invoke biblical injunctions about the honor due parents. But, according to current doctrine, that reason is not publicly admissible.[55]

Even when political action, or even a political movement, is founded upon, and galvanized by, religious belief, there is a tendency for intellectual and cultural elites to view it through secular eyes. The nonviolent civil rights movement of the 1950s and 60s, largely under the direction of Dr. (and Reverend) Martin Luther King, Jr. provides an excellent example. To fully understand the civil rights movement, one cannot remove it from its openly religious moorings. However, Stephen Carter notes that it was easy for the academics and the media to subsume the goals and the results of the movement "under the umbrella of secular argument."[56] Dr. King is regarded as a great champion for civil and human rights. He is hardly ever regarded as a minister, whose understanding of Jesus' teachings compelled him to take action against political, economic, and social injustice.[57]

THREE

What Motivates the Quest for "Secularization"?

⸙

In the first chapter, I observed that there is a small cottage industry of scholars (e.g., law professors, social scientists, historians, and theologians) who
maintain that there is an unhealthy containment of religion away from many
parts of American public life.[1] At first glance, their argument might appear
unpersuasive to some, for religious people leave sizeable footprints all over the
political arena. But how big are those footprints, actually? Some insist that
religious believers not only flourish in the political realm, but they have actually captured the one of the dominant political parties in the United States.[2]
Other political activists even praise conservative Christian activists for providing a *model* for engagement in grassroots politics in the United States.[3]
Still, as I suggested in the previous chapter, the argument that religion receives
shortshrift in the political arena is not as far-fetched as it might first seem. Its
advocates do not hold that religion has in fact been *banished* from public life;
their claim is that religious expression *suffers* in the hands of America's intellectual elites. These elites often "trivialize" religious expression; they either are
unaware of, or manage to justify, their bigotry toward religious expression (it
is treated differently from other kinds of prejudices); and their quest to "secularize" the public square prompts the call to "privatize" religious belief and
expression. When limited to these specific claims, the argument that religious
expression is on shaky grounds in the public arena becomes quite plausible.
The purpose of this chapter is to explore *why* there is an effort to secularize
the public square.

    In the previous chapter, I offered Leo Pfeffer's definition of secularism.
Pfeffer's definition is helpful because it contains two separate definitions in

29

one, and within them, one can find multiple motives for secularization. I will discuss two. The first is a "religious" or quasi-religious motive. One definition of secularization is "[a] view of life or any particular matter based upon the premise that religious considerations should be ignored and purposely excluded."[4] The second motivation for secularization might broadly be defined as "politically" based: a system of social ethics should be predicated upon the present life and determined without reference to religion.[5]

Remember the old maxim "There are two things one does not discuss in polite company: religion and politics"? The advocates of secularization must have not received this sage advice because, as I will argue below, quite consistent with Pfeffer's definitions, the two principal reasons for secularization and privatization are indeed the assertions that religious expression fosters bad "religion," or that religious expression fosters bad politics.

"RELIGIOUS"/QUASI-RELIGIOUS MOTIVES FOR SECULARIZATION

In the preceding chapter, I contended that there are those in the academic community who do not like religion—at least as it is generally expressed in America. I also suggested that, while their reasons for dismissing religion out of hand are often not very good, they are at least sufficient for self-persuasion.

One motive for secularization is, ironically, religious or quasi-religious. There are those intellectuals who, almost as a matter of religious faith, aspire to push religious expression from the public arena. This philosophy is reflected in the first part of Pfeffer's definition. It asserts that, as part of an overarching *view of life*, one should ignore and *purposely* exclude religion. It presumes that one has had an encounter with "religion," and has, deliberately and thoroughly, rejected it as important for one's life. In essence, one's *religious* belief, in this instance, is to *exclude* religion.

This portion of Pfeffer's definition speaks for a lot of folks who believe strongly in the human race's "perfectibility," "inherent goodness," "authority," or "harmony with nature," and who are sure that religion, as it is most generally expressed, is a serious threat to these concepts. Similarly, it speaks for many who believe that humankind's destiny can be fulfilled only if rational, scientific argument remains unpolluted by religious gibberish.[6]

These apostles for modernism or, for lack of a better term, *secularized humanism*, are very committed to eradicating the influence of religious argument on political debate. They are on the offensive, and among their important strategies are the "privatization" of religious faith and the "secularization" of public discourse. My contention is that these motives for secularization are *religious*.[7]

Consider the following arguments:

First, and quite obviously, there are intellectuals—adherents to the philosophies of secularism or humanism—who openly reject religion as having any value for their lives. Professor John Swomley offered a definition of "secularism" that is remarkably similar to the first part of Pfeffer's. "Secularism," notes Swomley, "is the philosophy that religion is *not relevant to life*."[8] Additionally, Swomley defines the term humanism as "putting human values ahead of material and institutional values. It can also be defined as making humans the measure and center of everything instead of God."[9]

Like Pffefer's, these definitions are very comprehensive in their scope. Secularism and humanism, as defined by Swomley, are overarching philosophies. They indicate that their adherents have considered the case for religion and have rejected it as "irrelevant" (or as violative of their belief that humankind should be "the center of everything"). I will maintain that when one allows the two philosophies to merge in one's own consciousness, and adheres to secularized humanism or secular humanism, then one is truly making a religious argument.[10]

Secularized humanism can be expressed in two forms. First, one might belong to a formal group, the American Humanist Association, for example, that teaches a secularized form of humanism. I will call those who fall into this category *H*umanists. Likewise, one might subscribe to the tenets of secular humanism and advocate secularization but belong to no formal groups or organizations. I will call these folks *h*umanists.

Whether *H*umanist, or *h*umanist, their quest for secularization is a manifestation of their philosophical or religious beliefs—much the way evangelization or proselytizing is a manifestation of the beliefs of many evangelical Christians, or Mormons, or Jehovah's Witnesses. One can legitimately make the argument that "religious" belief motivates both the Humanist and the humanist.

With respect to the Humanist, the case is pretty easy to make. The movement, such as it is, does have many of the formal characteristics of an organized religion.[11] In fact, they themselves refer to the movement as "*religious* humanism." Humanists have a statement of faith articulated in the *Humanist Manifesto I*, written in 1933, and the *Humanist Manifesto II*, authored in 1973.[12] The Preface to the first *Humanist Manifesto* proclaims:

> In every field of human activity, the vital movement is now in the direction of a candid and explicit humanism. In order that religious humanism may be better understood we, the undersigned, desire to make certain affirmations which we believe the facts of our contemporary life demonstrate.[13]

Those Humanists who adhere to the *Humanist Manifesto* have a belief about the origin of the universe: "Religious humanists regard the universe as self-existing and not created."[14] They have a viewpoint about eschatology: "Humanism asserts that the nature of the universe depicted by modern science makes unacceptable any supernatural or cosmic guarantees of human values."[15] They have a viewpoint regarding a traditional faith in God:

> As in 1933 [date of the *Humanist Manifesto I*] humanists still believe that traditional theism, especially faith in the prayer-hearing God, assumed to love and care for persons, to hear and understand their prayers, and to be able to do something about them, is an unproved and outmoded faith. Salvationism, based on mere affirmation, still appears as harmful, diverting people with false hopes of heaven hereafter. Reasonable minds look to other means of survival.[16]

Humanists also have a belief regarding their place, vis-à-vis the traditional religions, in contemporary society:

> Today man's larger understanding of the universe, his scientific achievements, and his deeper appreciation of brotherhood, have created a situation which requires a new statement of the means and purpose of religion. It is obvious that any religion that can hope to be a synthesizing and dynamic force today must be shaped for the needs of this age. To establish such a religion is a major necessity of the present.[17]

Furthermore, humanists, like other religious believers, have congregations, a mission, and a vehicle for sharing their message.[18] The "Humanist Society," or the American Humanist Association, is made up a relatively small number of people; it does, however, have about fifty chapters nationwide. The American Humanist Association published the *Humanist Manifesto I* in 1933 and the *Humanist Manifesto II* in 1973. It produces a journal, *The Humanist*, and a number of those in "The Humanist Society" have been powerfully influential—Sir Julian Huxley, John Dewey, and B.F. Skinner to name a few.[19]

Francis Schaeffer, the late Christian apologist, observed that these men (Huxley, Dewey, Skinner, and others) understood early on "that their world view, and the Christian consensus that dominated American culture, were two total concepts of reality standing in antithesis to each other."[20] They realized these very different concepts would give birth to two different conclusions both for individuals and for society, government, and law.[21] Their mission, therefore, was to supplant the hold Christianity had on society with their own rationalistic worldview. John Dewey wrote, in 1934, "I cannot understand how any realization of the democratic ideal as a vital moral and spiritual ideal in human affairs is possible without surrender of the conception of the basic division to which supernatural Christianity is committed."[22]

More to the point of this discussion, Humanists are passionate secularists. Their strategy for sharing the secularization is twofold. First, it is to eliminate any public financial support for religion. The *Humanist Manifesto II* states, "It [the state] should not favor any particular religious bodies through the use of public monies."[23] Second, it is to use public education to purge the effects of Christian theism. Paul Blanshard wrote:

> I think that the most important factor moving us toward a secular society has been the educational factor. Our schools may not teach Johnny to read properly, but the fact that Johnny is in school until he is sixteen tends to lead toward the elimination of religious superstition.[24]

John Dunphy was even more candid when, in a 1983 issue of *The Humanist*, he wrote:

> I am convinced that the battle for humankind's future must be waged in the public school classroom by teachers *who correctly perceive their role as the proselytizers of a new faith; a religion of humanity* that recognizes and respects the spark of what theologians call the divinity in every human being. *The classroom must and will become an arena of conflict between the old and the new—the rotting corpse of Christianity, together with all its adjacent evils and misery, and the new faith of humanism,* resplendent in its promise of a world in which the never-realized Christian ideal of 'love thy neighbor' will finally be achieved.[25]

Do all humanists embrace these beliefs? As with any religious organization, it is unlikely that each of its members subscribes to the tenets of its faith, its mission, or the method of accomplishing that mission. Not all Baptists, Methodists, or Episcopalians believe and follow their denominations' teachings. Not all Catholics subscribe to and live by the teachings of the Roman Catholic Church. Undoubtedly, not all humanists agree with the philosophy and mission described above.[26]

Likewise, however, as with any religious organization, the *membership list* does not exhaust those people who subscribe to the worldview and live by its commandments. Not everyone who believes the essential teachings of the *Baptist Faith and Message*, for example, is a Southern Baptist in good standing. Certainly not all those who would describe themselves as "Christians" are churchgoers or even churchmembers. Christianity represents for them a belief system that is worth living by. By the same token, although humanism might well be comprised of few members, those embracing its belief system are myriad. Their unofficial "membership" list includes many rationalists, atheists, and humanists who share the same worldview: rejection of the supernatural, belief in the all-sufficiency of human reason, belief in human perfectibility, and commitment to supplant the Bible's teachings regarding the fall of the human race into sin, the deity of Christ, and his resurrection.[27] These "members" are conveniently categorized, by critics, as humanists or "secular humanists." Francis Schaeffer noted:

> In the last sixty years the consensus upon which our culture was built has shifted from one that was largely Christian (though we must say it was far from perfect) to a consensus growing out of the Enlightenment. . . . I have described this consensus as secular humanism. The Enlightenment world view and the world view of secular humanism really are essentially the same, with the same intellectual heritage.[28]

Unfortunately, the Supreme Court is often indirectly referencing the proponents of this alternative consensus when it speaks of "non-believers" or "non-religion."[29] Although they might stand opposed to all existing recognized religious faiths, nonbelievers in fact represent a competing religious position.[30]

Some humanists might not even be aware they are articulating a religious position. Swomley, in the very chapter of his book *Religious Liberty and the Secular State* in which he attempts to distinguish secularism from religion, makes a number of notoriously *religious* statements. One example is his claim that modern science has *triumphed* over religious beliefs. Note that Professor Swomley does not limit the scope of this victory to a repudiation of those beliefs once harbored by people of faith which have been empirically falsified by science (e.g., "the earth is flat" or "the sun revolves around the earth"). Swomley asserts that modern science has triumphed over a worldview that includes heaven and hell, and the power of God and Satan over the human condition:

> The development of modern science has given us a world view that has *destroyed* the three-dimensional view of heaven above, the earth below, and hell beneath the earth. It has also *released us from the cosmic forces that at one time were believed to rule or direct the world. In turn, this means that we cannot blame our human condition on God or a devil. It is humans that have created the war system and racial segregation. It is humans who can eradicate cholera, black lung, syphilis, and cancer.*[31]

This sounds very much like a sermon one might hear in any number of churches next Sunday morning. It sounds much like the homily presented by Gene Hackman's character, *Rev.* Scott, in the film *The Poseidon Adventure*, or

Spencer Tracy's Colonel Drummond in the movie *Inherit the Wind*, who claimed that the advances of modern science and technology come with a cost: we must abandon the pleasant poetry of Genesis!

Swomley is wrong. Modern science has most definitely not given us a worldview that has "destroyed" the three-dimensional view of heaven, earth, and hell. Nor has science "destroyed" intelligent faith in "the cosmic forces" that are believed to rule or direct our world. But, with respect to the political and constitutional environment, whether Professor Swomley's cosmology (or theology) is correct or incorrect is not significant. His claim is a religious statement—a faith statement unable to be verified or disproven factually.

It is unfair to argue that all statements critical of religion are, in and of themselves, religious statements or indicative of one's worldview. If, for example, Joe remarks, "Religion is bunk," he is not necessarily articulating a religious statement. Nor does the assertion tell us Joe's underlying religious philosophy. Rest assured, however, Joe has an underlying religious philosophy. To discover his ultimate conviction(s), one must unearth what Joe thinks is not "bunk." Joe might believe "religion is bunk;" that statement could tell us that he believes that there is no God, so he must live his life accordingly. Joe might also believe that "religion is bunk;" by that claim Joe may be trying to tell others that it is his relationship with Jesus Christ, apart from the trappings of religion, that restored his fellowship with God. There is something that is ultimately important to him which might well be considered Joe's "religious" truth claim.[32]

It might appear to some that I am drawing close to the theologian Paul Tillich's notion of religion, and that therefore what constitutes one's "ultimate concern" should be the criterion to evaluate whether a critique of religion (or one's overt hostility to religion) is religious in nature.[33] Maybe that is not such a bad idea. Using Tillich's criterion, secularized Humanism or even secularized humanism as expressed in Pfeffer's and Swomley's definitions, surely would be a religious belief.[34]

In *United States v Seeger*,[35] the court embraced the concept of "ultimate concern" in order to determine if an individual's beliefs, even devoid of a reference to deity or the traditional trappings of organized religion, might be judged as the equivalent of a religious belief under the free exercise clause. If the court were to apply the same criterion to evaluate the establishment clause, then evidence which indicated that a program promoted a humanist worldview in the classroom would be grounds for a constitutional challenge.[36]

Professor James McBride recognizes the quandary stemming from the court's confused definition of religion and offers an imaginative resolution.[37] He argues that the court misinterpreted Tillich's definition of religion in *Seeger*. "Tillich's 'ultimate concern' cannot be reduced to an affective attitude alone,"

notes McBride. "If Tillich's notion is to be spared violence, the Court must recognize that there exist two poles in 'ultimate concern': objective as well as subjective."[38] What makes 'ultimate concern' ultimate, McBride maintains, is:

> Not only the affective attitude of the believer but also the object of
> belief which transcends the form and contents of the empirically
> observable world. Tillich refers to this essential transcendent char-
> acteristic of the holy as the 'Unconditioned,' i.e., that which lies
> beyond the conditions of phenomenal existence.[39]

Therefore, McBride reasons, Tillich felt secular humanism to be deficient, not because it had forgotten its religious character, but because by applying Tillich's concept of "ultimate concern," it is at best a "quasireligion." It fails
to advance any truth claims about the objective nature of the transcendent.[40]

McBride leaves us in the unenviable position of perpetuating, or "establishing," a philosophy that is admittedly deficient; he leaves us unable to bring
religious influences to bear upon the state. Thus he returns America to a far
more restrictive criterion for evaluating religion under the free exercise
clause.[41] Perhaps it is better to run the other direction. It is preferable to apply
the court's broad interpretation of religion to both the free exercise clause and
establishment clause than it is to narrow the definition of religion in order to
protect secularism.

Like their organized counterparts, many *h*umanists want to extricate
religion from public debate and policymaking. Swomley, for one, believes that
this objective has already been achieved. What is the goal of secularization?
Swomley argues that it is to destroy the shackles placed on America by religious faith, generally, and by Christianity, particularly, to free up knowledge.
Secularization, he claims, has exposed the shortcomings of Christianity:

> Secularization is a historical process to which many movements
> have contributed, including the Protestant Reformation, which
> sundered a united or monolithic church; the industrial revolution,
> which urbanized and organized people around another set of val-
> ues; Marxism, which exposed the church as a class and power
> structure; as well as the two world wars and the cold war, which
> showed the church as the handmaiden of nationalism and Western
> culture.[42]

And, notes Professor Swomley, this objective has been largely accomplished.
The "process of secularization," Swomley observes, has *destroyed* the "so-called
Christian era" and has freed science, education, art, and politics from confor-
mity to theological dogma and ecclesiastical hierarchies.

As I observed in the previous chapter, among those wanting to secularize the public square there are some motivated by an open hostility toward

religion. Frequently, their hostility is an outward expression of their own philosophical or perhaps even religious beliefs. Therefore, their quest for secularization is a manifestation of their religious faith—much the way evangelization is a manifestation of the beliefs of many religious groups.

One remaining issue concerns the level of success Humanists and humanists have had in their quest for secularization. Richard Neuhaus suggests that it depends entirely upon whether one is talking about *H*umanism or *h*umanism. If one is discussing the impact of *H*umanism, then Neuhaus thinks it is not much. People have been willing historically to accept the Humanists' passionate pleas for secularization. When it was drafted in 1933, "relatively few people shared the [*Humanist M]anifesto's* robust confidence that a vital public ethic could be maintained without the taint, so to speak, of religion."[43] By the time the *Humanist Manifesto II* was drafted in 1973, "that confidence and that animus seemed to have declined even further."[44] Though their rhetoric continued to be passionate, Neuhaus argues that those organized champions of secular humanism had largely lost their clout:

> The signers of Humanist Manifesto II made up a reunion of survivors against this century's assaults upon unbelief. Those under seventy were in a distinct minority. From the geriatric wards of America, academics emeritus gathered to unfold the grand old banner one last time. Religionists who rage against the "secular humanist conspiracy" appear to be beating up on old people who might more kindly be left to their dreams of a brave new world that was not to be. . . . The Humanist Manifesto, with its vulgar apotheosis of supposedly rational man and its dogmatic dismissal of religion as superstition, is not likely to fare well in a public referendum.[45]

If one is talking about secular *h*umanists, however, then Neuhaus warns that one will reach a different conclusion. Though there might not be an organized conspiracy, secularized humanism has been successful in capturing the public debate:

> Exaggerations aside, however, those who attack secular humanism are not so wide of the mark as some of their critics suggest . . . it cannot be denied that the variant [of humanism] called secular humanism has had a pervasive and debilitating effect upon our public life. Without ever having put them to a vote, without even subjecting them to democratic debate, some of the key arguments of what is called secularism have prevailed. There need not be a conspiracy in any coherent or calculating sense for ideas and prejudices to insinuate themselves into our thinking and acting. They become part of the conceptual air we breathe.[46]

Professor James Davidson Hunter charts the growth of secularism, or secular humanism, in America. "The secularist camp," notes Dr. Hunter, "represents the fastest growing community of 'moral conviction' in America." In 1952, they made up only two percent of the population. By 1972, secularists comprised five percent of the population. By 1982, they reached eight percent, and by 1990, they constituted more than ten percent of the population.[47] Like Neuhaus, Hunter argues that it is no exaggeration to talk in terms of a "secular" America—not legal or constitutional secularization, but, rather, ideological secularization:

> As the portion of the "secularist" and liberal religious population has grown, so too has an awareness of the secularistic nature of contemporary American public culture. Some on the religious right, of course, claim that there is a conspiracy afoot, that "secular humanists" and their ideological allies now "control" the major institutions of American life. While no serious scholar would accept that assessment at face value, most recognize the secular character of public life and the fact that there is a growing constituency who favor these circumstances. Based on mountains of empirical evidence, drawing from the work of Max Weber, Emile Durkheim, and Robert Bellah, one could argue quite plausibly that a secular humanism has become the dominant moral ideology of American public culture and now plays much the same role as the pan-Protestant ideology played in the nineteenth century.[48]

"Political" Motives for Secularization

There are those among the intellectual elite who, for what almost seem to be "religious" reasons, want to squelch religious expression in the public square. That is consistent with the first part of Pfeffer's definition of secularism: our view of life compels us to ignore or purposely exclude religion. Overt hostility against religion hardly explains the phenomenon entirely, however. Many elites are not hostile toward *religion*. They simply find that *religious expression* conflicts with constitutional and political values and policies they cherish.

If you recall, Pfeffer's definition for secularism contained two parts. The second part defined secularism as "a system of social ethics based upon a doctrine that ethical standards and conduct should be determined exclusively with reference to the present life and social well being without reference to religion."[49] The second part of Pfeffer's definition might help to identify other motives for secularization. Here Pfeffer did not speak of making a conscious decision to ignore or purposely exclude religion. To embrace this sub-definition of secularism, one need not reject religion as important for one's life. It only suggests that a system of social mores and ethics should focus upon this world and not make reference to religion. Thus, quite apart from one's attitude toward religion personally, one would contend that religious expression should be isolated from public dialogue. In other words, while there are, perhaps paradoxically, religious motives for secularization, there are other motives ("secular" motives?) for secularization. Although religion can inform one's personal life, one should not bring it to bear on questions of social and political policy.[50]

In this section, I will discuss these "secular" motives and contrast them with the religious motives for secularization addressed above. While there are a number of defenses used to justify the larger goal of secularization, they are generally placed under the umbrella of protecting the political arena from religion and its polluting effects. The first is a determination made by some scholars who defend "classical liberalism" that the political environment should be shielded from division.[51] When religious expression calls the social order's normative framework into question, it damages the liberal political order. Second, albeit substantially related, is the quest to protect cultural and political "pluralism." Since pluralism requires that diverse ideas be welcome in the public arena, religious expression because of its dogmatic nature is perceived as threatening. Finally, is the ardent desire of a growing number of political philosophers to safeguard rights and liberties, to prioritize rights, generally, over the "good"—the political philosophy identified as "contemporary liberalism" or "progressivism."[52]

There are a number of political philosophers concerned about perpetuating "liberal" premises in America. They are not referring to the more contemporary understanding of liberalism generally defined as "the advocacy of government programs for the welfare of individuals"[53] and a staunch defense of individual liberty. By liberalism, they mean that which is often called "classical liberalism."[54] The premises of classical liberalism included "freedom of the individual from interference by the state, toleration by the state in matters of morality and religion, laissez-faire economic policies, and a belief in natural rights that exist independently of government."[55]

Many proponents of classical liberalism presume that there must be a normative skeleton from which to flesh out society, and that people with diverse perspectives must be able to identify and embrace the skeleton. Political theorist Stephen Holmes maintains that "in a liberal social order, the basic normative framework must be able to command the loyalty of individuals and groups with widely differing self understandings and conceptions of personal fulfillment."[56]

How can the liberal social order best protect the basic normative framework from assault by groups and individuals with differing self-understandings and conceptions of personal fulfillment? Legal theorist, Bruce Ackerman's call for "neutral" politics contributes one illustration.[57] Ackerman believes that opponents in a political exchange should justify their political choices only on the basis of moral propositions they both share:

> My principle of conversational restraint does not apply to the questions citizens ask, to the answers they may legitimately give to each other's questions: whenever one citizen is confronted by another's question, he cannot suppress the questioner, nor can he respond by appealing to [his understanding of] moral truth; he must instead be prepared, in principle, to engage in a restrained dialogic effort to locate normative premises both sides find reasonable.[58]

For that reason, some contemporary proponents of classical liberalism add one additional premise: that all laws must have a secular purpose; they must be justified in secular terms.[59] Holmes notes that liberal theory should "steer clear of irresolvable metaphysical disputes."[60] Legal scholar Kent Greenawalt argued in 1988 that it is *contrary* to the premises of liberalism for citizens and leaders to rely on their religious convictions to justify publicly their political choices.[61]

Greenawalt distinguished between relying upon religious conviction to *formulate* political convictions and using religious conviction to *justify* political argument.[62] Unlike Ackerman, who maintains that political dialogue should emerge from the shared premises of the participants, Greenawalt claimed that individuals will enter into political debate operating from premises that are not shared. They come to the table with conclusions they have reached predicated upon their personal convictions—including religious convictions. And, he argued, it is unfair to limit political participants from relying upon their personal and moral convictions to *formulate* their beliefs.[63] However, once one uses those same religious convictions to *justify* a particular political argument, he or she has crossed an important line. In "public" or "open" political discourse, then, one should not rely upon religious premises or reasoning. Greenawalt noted, "public discourse about political issues with those who do not share religious premises should be cast in other than religious terms."[64]

Greenawalt claimed that his argument is not predicated upon the persuasiveness, or lack thereof, of religious argument. Quite obviously, a religious justification for one's position on abortion, nuclear armament, or world hunger, will be more or less persuasive depending upon the religious convictions of one's audience. Greenawalt moved beyond the strategic implications of religious-based argument in his contention that a religious justification is inappropriate in a liberal society, period:

> The government of a liberal society knows no religious truth and
> a crucial premise about a liberal society is that citizens of extreme-
> ly diverse religious views can build principles of political order and
> social justice that do not depend upon particular religious beliefs.
> The common currency of political discourse is nonreligious argu-
> ment about human welfare.[65]

Therefore, noted Professor Greenawalt, religious argument used to articulate
"public justifications for political positions" is, likewise, inappropriate:

> The liberal ground rules for public political dialogue are more con-
> straining than the principles relevant to how private citizens make
> political choices, and religious convictions should figure much less
> prominently in public justifications for political positions than
> they may in the development of the positions themselves.[66]

Professor Greenawalt revised the argument slightly in his 1995 book,
Private Consciences and Public Reasons. This work is far more comprehensive
(he takes on many more comers), and there is a subtle difference in his position. Previously, Greenawalt held that one could formulate and reach conclusions predicated upon one's religious beliefs, yet should not use religious arguments to articulate those conclusions. Now he has added another step. One
can use religious belief to formulate conclusions, and policymakers might even
take action predicated upon those faith-based conclusions. One still should
not use religious convictions when articulating policy preferences in dialogic
politics.[67]

Two immediate concerns with Professor Greenawalt's argument come
to mind. First, it hardly seems to further the objectives of liberal democracy
by permitting policymakers to withhold their bona fide reasons for taking
action. Suppose congressman X is a leading opponent of restrictions on abortion. His position earns him the support of many prochoice advocates. What
if, however, they were to learn that congressman X opposed restrictions on
abortion because he felt it was an effective method for limiting population
increase in the African American community? It is certainly possible that this
revelation, the racist convictions that serve to undergird his political action,
might prompt many supporters of the prochoice position to seek another
champion. Similarly, if an opponent of affirmative action learned that his or
her senator were motivated to kill set-aside programs in committee because
the senator was an avowed racist, it might well prompt him or her to look
elsewhere on election day. The convictions that motivate political action *are*
important. It does not further liberal democracy to limit their articulation in
the marketplace. Too, those classical liberals calling for secularization in the
marketplace seem to believe that liberal democracy is an end in itself. It is of

such importance that it needs to be shielded from dialogue that might prove to be threatening. Thus, by limiting certain kinds of expression, in this case religious expression, they permit no outside checks to liberalism and liberal democracy.[68]

— Law professor Michael Perry offers an even more extensive critique to those proponents of liberalism like Ackerman and Greenawalt who advocate secularization. First, limiting advocacy in a political conversation to shared normative premises effectively privileges some premises. Professor Perry speculates that were he to have a political dialogue with Professor Ackerman the "proportion of Ackerman's relevant beliefs that I would share would be larger, perhaps much larger, than the proportion of mine he would share."[69] Why? Because Perry's beliefs include religious convictions about human good. Therefore, Ackerman, notes Perry, would "get to rely on all or most of his relevant beliefs, including his most important relevant beliefs, while I would get to rely on only some of my relevant beliefs, *not* including the most important ones: my religious convictions about human good."[70]

Second, although very much akin to the first argument, limiting the right of advocacy to those who advance nonreligious arguments means that some are asked to abandon their right to advocate on a whole host of public issues including abortion, capital punishment, economic justice, the essential meaning of equality under the law, and nuclear proliferation. This is a critical diminishment of individual liberty. Perry asks:

> Why should one person be asked to forgo "public advocacy" of her position on the grounds that her advocacy would appeal to controversial religious premises about human good, when another person is invited to engage in public advocacy of his position because his advocacy appeals merely to controversial secular premises about human good?[71]

Third, it is often difficult to distinguish between a secular justification and a religious justification. In the previous section, I argue that many appeals for secularism are decidedly religious in their character. Professor Perry speaks to this difficulty:

> How is the distinction between personal moral questions that are secular in character and those that are religious to be administered if, as I later suggest, the relevant "religious" convictions—religious beliefs about human good—are, like many "secular" convictions, fundamentally about what it means to be truly, fully human . . . and if such religious convictions are not even necessarily theistic in character? Buddhism is, in the main, nontheistic. Are Buddhist convictions "religious" or "secular"?[72]

Fourth, it seems that in our society, "liberalism" has been defined synonymously with "moral pluralism." I will discuss pluralism below, but to the extent that pluralism and liberalism are used interchangeably, then proponents of liberalism have a problem. It may be that those engaged in political argument share *no* normative premises. Ackerman acknowledges this possibility and remarks, "As you and I discover that we disagree about more and more things, perhaps we will find that the exercise of conversational restraint leaves us nothing to say to one another about the basic problems of coexistence."[73] Granted, one's religious biases may affect the quality of the political conversation about abortion, capital punishment, economic justice, the essential meaning of equality under the law, nuclear proliferation, and the like. So would antireligious biases. However, the ends of liberalism are furthered by holding a conversation about these topics rather than abandoning their discussion.[74]

In addition to the effort expended to safeguard "liberalism," there are those scholars who want to protect their unique understanding of "pluralism." Pluralism, when used as a model to explain "who governs" in America, is defined as "a theory of government that attempts to reaffirm the democratic character of society by asserting that open, multiple, competing, and responsive groups preserve traditional democratic values in a mass industrial state."[75] It is often juxtaposed with elite theory. Thus, the term "pluralism" can be used both to *explain* who holds power in America, and to *articulate* a preferred model (e.g., pluralism is preferable to elitism).

In our ongoing discussion, however, I am not just talking about various interest groups competing to make public policy. I am referring to what Professor Perry calls the "*morally* pluralistic character of American society" where "many beliefs about human good are widely, deeply, and persistently disputed."[76] Still, even in this context, the term pluralism might be offered to *explain* that which has happened in America—the expansion of religious and cultural pluralism in America at the expense of Protestant hegemony—or to *articulate* a preferred political objective.

One can offer two observations about moral pluralism. First, the term remains very much a way to articulate a political objective rather than simply a means of explaining cultural changes in America. When viewed as political objective, pluralism requires that diverse ideas be welcome in the public arena. The holders of these ideas should compete to influence public policy and, hopefully, the give and take between diverse ideas will propel the society forward.[77] Second, the definition of moral pluralism has changed. Traditionally, whether one discussed interest group pluralism or moral pluralism, the concept did not mean that there were no winners and no losers. Different interest groups compete to affect public policy. Typically, somebody wins and somebody does not get their way. Likewise, when various ideas are introduced into the marketplace, some will be embraced and others rejected. Pluralism, however, notes Neuhaus, has now become a synonym for pervasive confusion. The notion is often used to argue that no normative ethic can be imposed in our public life and, in practice, it means that public policy decisions reflect a surrender of the normal to the abnormal, of the dominant to the deviant.[78] And, he suggests, pluralism is a jealous god and, when it is established as a dogma, there is no room for other dogmas. "The assertion of other points of reference in moral discourse becomes," argues Neuhaus, "by definition, a violation of pluralism."[79] Religious expression, because of its dogmatic nature, is perceived as threatening to pluralism.

Professor Stephen Carter presents a case study that serves nicely to illustrate how the goal of perpetuating "pluralism" is often at odds with religious expression: the confrontation between the City of New York and the Ancient Order of Hibernians.[80] The Hibernians put on New York City's famed annual Saint Patrick's Day parade. In 1992, the city took legal action against the Hibernians because "it refused to allow a group of gays and lesbians of Irish descent to join the march."[81] New York claimed that the Hibernians violated the city's human rights law which prohibits discrimination on the basis of sexual orientation. Why did the Hibernians refuse to include the group? Carter notes, "The Hibernians, by their charter, follow the dictates of the Roman Catholic Church, which considers homosexuality sinful."[82] The Hibernians prevailed in court, and did so again in 1993 when New York City attempted to deny them the permit necessary to stage the parade preferring to give it to another group that would include the group of gays and lesbians.

Although the Hibernians used the free exercise clause and the free speech clause in court, this was not the usual religious liberty confrontation.[83] New York City did not take action to oust the Hibernians in order to short-circuit their religious freedom. The city threatened to deny the permit because the Hibernians refused to include all points of view. Furthermore, the Hiberians insisted that they were right to do so. Each time the Hibernians, or some similar group, prove successful in court, the contemporary understanding of moral pluralism takes a beating. Pluralism cannot tolerate what it views to be intolerance. Pluralism cannot accept those who insist that their position is predicated upon absolute truth.[84]

The quest to protect pluralism is, in some ways, similar to the attempt to safeguard classical liberalism. In other ways, however, it is very dissimilar. The proponents of classical liberalism assume that there is a normative ethic that overshadows and influences dialogic politics. The proponents of moral pluralism deny that there is a normative ethic. Further, they insist there should *not be* a normative ethic—excepting, perhaps, pluralism. Both, however, are wary of religious argument in the political arena. Those advocating liberalism

are afraid that religious justifications for public policy will bruise the normative ethic. Proponents of pluralism are afraid that those who argue from a religious perspective will impose one.

There is a third group of scholars who want to secularize the public
square. These are advocates of *contemporary* liberalism or progressivism.[85]
Their political philosophy prompts their demand for secularization as a means
of protecting fundamental rights and liberties.

Contemporary liberalism has emerged out of a more general theory of
constitutional rights and liberties, and the role of the Supreme Court in protecting rights and liberties. As students of the Constitution are aware, the
Supreme Court's jurisprudence can, roughly, be divided into three historical
phases. The Marshall Court and arguably the Taney Court were determined
to fortify the national government in its perpetual struggle with the state governments.[86] From the last quarter of the nineteenth century and through the
first third of the twentieth century, the primary concern of the court was the
protection of property and laissez-faire economics.[87] Finally, since the late
1930s, the court has emphasized defining and protecting individual rights and
liberties. Henry Abraham and Barbara Perry explain:

> The post 1937 Court was radically different from that of the first
> four decades of the twentieth century—faced as it was with an
> agenda of increasingly complex economic, political, and social
> pressures and problems, both domestic and international. . .
> Gradually the Court thus embarked upon a policy of paying close
> attention to any legislative and executive attempt to curb basic
> rights and liberties in the "noneconomic" sphere. . . . As of this
> writing (mid-1993) the Rehnquist Court (1986-) has, in general
> continued its predecessor court's jurisprudence.[88]

The evolution of a "modern" Supreme Court, a judicial body that
emphasizes individual rights and liberties, coincided nicely with the emergence of contemporary liberalism as an important political theory. What are
the particulars of this political theory with respect to rights and liberties,
and how does "contemporary liberalism" differ from the kind of "classical
liberalism" discussed above? Political philosopher, Michael Sandel, defines
the former:

> The version of liberalism with which I am concerned is prominent
> in contemporary moral, legal, and political philosophy. Its central
> idea is that government should be neutral on questions of the good
> life. Since people disagree on the best way to live, public policy
> should be "independent of any particular conception of the good
> life, or of what gives value to life."[89]

Sandel notes that one important component of this contemporary version of liberalism is the claim that "right" precedes "good" in two specific ways: first, individual rights cannot be relinquished for the sake of the general good. Second, the principles of justice that identify these rights cannot be predicated upon any particular vision of the good life.[90] Sandel observes:

> What justifies the rights is not that they maximize the general welfare or otherwise promote the good, but rather that they comprise a fair framework within which individuals can choose their own values and ends, consistent with a similar liberty for others.[91]

What is the difference between classical liberalism and the more contemporary version that Sandel identifies? Their respective positions toward religious practice and belief help distinguish the two. Whereas classical liberalism has traditionally been thought to promote religious liberty, contemporary liberalism, under the guise of protecting religious freedom, works to limit the scope of religious expression through privatization.[92] Sandel argues:

> It may be helpful to examine the political theory of contemporary liberalism and to describe its stance toward religious practice and belief. In one respect, the liberal tradition seeks to secure for religion the most favorable conditions; given its emphasis on toleration and respect for conscience, liberal political theory promises the fullest religious liberty for each consistent with a similar liberty for all. In another respect, however, liberalism limits the reach of religion; its insistence that government be neutral among competing moral and theological visions, that political authority be justified without reference to religious sanction, would seem to confine religion to private life and to resist a public role.[93]

Maybe if we strip the political motives down to their core, we will discover another, less lofty political rationale for secularization. I have friends in the political science "community" who, if they are reading this work, must be very frustrated by this point. Their concern is not with the theoretical defenses for secularization. They study practical politics, and, they would argue, if one looks behind the theory, one will find a basic, real world, political motive for secularization and privatization. What, they would want to know, is the bottom line? Why are many in the legal and political community such thoroughgoing champions for the cause of secularization? If it is possible to reduce what, I think, are some fairly complex motives down to a simple justification it would be this: that many American intellectual elites are political liberals who link religious-based argument with the political right, and they stringently oppose the policies advocated by the so-called religious right.[94]

One might ask, "Why strip religion from the public square? Why don't those on the political left just include religious arguments in their own political discourse when it is appropriate?" Good question—particularly when one considers that, until recently, those on the political left did not regard religious arguments as taboo. For more than a century, the public rhetoric of religion was "largely the property of liberalism"—from the abolitionist movement, through the "social gospel" movement of the late nineteenth century and early twentieth century, through the civil rights movement in the 1950s and 60s.[95]

What changed the nature of religion's public rhetoric? Several things. First, "modernization" (discussed in the previous chapter) diminished the appetite many intellectual elites once might have had for religious argument. Second, Christian fundamentalists and evangelicals, many of whom had eschewed the secular political arena for nearly a half-century, were convinced that secular society was indeed on the road to self-destruction. Thus, they began to enter into the political fray armed with religious argument for conservative social and economic policy. Third, with the Supreme Court's decision in *Roe v Wade*,[96] the Roman Catholic Church, long quick to enter political debate to effectuate social justice, puts its considerable influence behind the prolife movement—a cause, notes Carter, "that the left considered an affront."[97] As a result, those on the political left have, largely, abandoned religious political argument, and the right has gladly stepped in to fill the void.[98]

It is, of course, incorrect to claim that those on the political left have fully abandoned religious-based political argument. There are politically liberal Christian evangelicals, and American Roman Catholic bishops have spoken out on what are typically regarded to be liberal causes—for example, a nuclear freeze. However, these arguments are generally welcome in the public square. "There is much depressing evidence," argues Carter, "that the religious voice is required to stay out of the public square only when it is pressed in a conservative cause."[99]

For the most part, however, and in direct response to the proliferation of public religious rhetoric by the religious right, those on the political left have moved to banish religion to the private sphere to protect the public sphere. Professor Carter argues that not only has this effort to secularize the political arena proven to be counterproductive for those on the left with respect to electoral politics,[100] but also it "has led us astray."[101]

One might posit one final practical question: if religious believers and religious-based argument are not welcome in the political marketplace, then what avenues of expression are available?[102] As I suggested in the first chapter, conservative evangelical Christians became active in politics and litigation, after sitting out for nearly a half-century, for several reasons: First, because they believed that the culture was moving rapidly away from one with a moral, "godly" foundation.[103] Second, because they have found that many institutions are increasingly hostile toward religious freedom. There are abundant examples of Christian students, educators, parents, employees, and political activists who are the targets of discrimination for exercising their faith.[104] Third, because they are alarmed by the ever-increasing reach of government into virtually every religious institution. Fourth, and perhaps most important, because they wish to insure the public proclamation of the gospel in the marketplace of ideas.[105] Politically active Christians *are*, as critics of religious-based dialogue accuse, resisting the status quo, but they are doing so within the framework of a system that gives them the right to speak, to run for office or endorse candidates, and to vote.

It is probably quite obvious that I greatly respect Stephen Carter's efforts to expose trivialization of religion and religious expression. His book *The Culture of Disbelief* has proven quite influential within the Academy and to a more general audience. He calls upon the larger community to accept religious speakers as legitimate critics of culture. What is somewhat troubling about Professor Carter's argument, however, is that after he makes his case convincingly, he engages in a lengthy diatribe against the abuses of the so-called Christian Right. What is it that they do that he finds most problematic? It is their recent tendency to engage in what he calls "political preaching."[106] Unfortunately, the shrillness with which Carter launches into his case against political preaching does much to undercut his larger and more important thesis. Although it is certainly not his intention, he provides ammunition for those who are committed to silencing the so-called Christian Right, in particular, but also religiously-based political speech, generally.

As "critics of culture," conservative evangelicals, and other religious believers, could do several things:

1) They could withdraw from the secular-political world and concentrate on preparing souls for the next one. Of course, Professor Carter argues persuasively why this would badly impoverish the public square. To exercise this option, believers would fail miserably in their function to resist the established powers.[107]

2) They could resist by taking up arms in an attempt to purge and remake the state in God's image—a terrifying option that all but the most fervent extremists have opted to reject.[108]

3) They could resist passively and nonviolently. Like Ghandi or King, the church could speak out against the evils of the state and suffer—even welcome—arrest, torture, or death.

4)   They could resist by opposing, from within the political arena, what they find to be immorality or injustice practiced by the state. The Constitution guarantees that, as citizens, religious believers, even if motivated by their faith in God, have a right to engage in combat in the political arena: To concede that "if we can't join 'em—and we can't join 'em—then we can beat 'em."[109]

The work of Professor Carter, Professor Perry, Richard Neuhaus, Frederick Gedicks, Ronald Thiemann, and others confirms the obvious: only the third and fourth options are acceptable. Retreat from the important issues of the day means that, in particular, Christian believers will have abrogated Christ's commandment that his followers be salt and light to the world. Furthermore, they will have abandoned their crucial role as an outside critic of the state. The same is true for other religious people outside the Christian community. Alternatively, armed resistance is disastrous in a nation that purports to be "under law."

Whether through passive resistance, or all-out *political* "warfare," religious believers should resist unjust political leadership. In many countries, however, their alternatives are limited so as not to include the option of resistance from *within* the political process. And all Americans, particularly religious believers, should be thankful we live in a nation that recognizes and protects, as a matter of constitutional law, this fourth option. Many scholars sense that, even if it is in an embryonic stage, there is a danger of eroding those protections that make possible political resistance by Christians through active political dialogue and participation.

FOUR

Secularization and the Wall of Separation

The first three chapters advance two related arguments: First, even though religious people are becoming increasingly involved in politics, there is still plenty of bigotry against religious faith (particularly among intellectuals). This bigotry is manifested as a concerted effort to lasso religious expression, broadly defined, and place it in the *O.K.* (As Long As It's Kept Private) *Corral* and away from the secular marketplace of ideas. Second, there are several factors that motivate the quest for secularization by academic and cultural elites. Some genuinely believe, akin to a religious faith, that society is poisoned by antiquated religious expression. These "religious" secularists take their charge at least as seriously as do many religious missionaries. They want to share the good news of secularization. Others, including many people of faith, express more overtly "secular" motives. They want to protect classical liberal democracy, safeguard their understanding of moral pluralism, or even maximize individual freedom (an advance of a contemporary definition of liberalism), and one way to accomplish this goal is to keep religion away from politics.

In this chapter I shift the argument a bit. I want to make two points. First, many of the secularists identified above are ardent supporters of strict separation of church and state. They do not simply want to separate church from state, they want to perpetuate and protect the separation *doctrine* that was first articulated some fifty years ago. Second, the Constitution's language respecting religious liberty, as interpreted by the court, *requires* separation. Although some constitutional scholars talk about a progression in the court's interpretation of the establishment clause (e.g., from separation—to neutrality—to accommodation), the separation doctrine is still controlling.

LINKING "SECULARIZATION" WITH "SEPARATION"

There is a strong linkage, and perhaps not a surprising one, between the case for "secularization" of the political arena and the case for "separation" of church and state. While I recognize that the linkage is far from complete, and that, in many respects, the secularization debate and the church-state debate are two separate disputes, the overlap is substantial and noteworthy.[1] More than a few academic, legal, and cultural intellectuals—even those with various motives—share the same objective: to create and maintain a secular public society. To achieve the goal of secularization, they often advocate the same strategy. They move the debate from a political argument to a constitutional one. They interpret the religious liberty clauses of the first amendment to require the separation of church from state. Thus, the quest for "secularization" of the political arena becomes a quest for "separation" in the constitutional arena.

In fact, for thoroughgoing secularists, there does not seem to be a great deal of difference whether one is identified as a "secularist" or a "separationist." Their constitutional goals and strategies are interchangeable. They advocate the separation of church, or more accurately, religion from state. However, unlike those separationists for whom divorcing church from state would be an end in and of itself, for the secularist, separation is a means to a greater end: secularization. Their argument in public debate generally follows the same form:

1) They identify an important "objective." The objective might be to maximize religious liberty, to safeguard society from irrational religious superstition, to end the political consequences of religious divisiveness, to initiate political dialogue from shared moral premises, to shelter political debate from dogmatism, or the like.

2) They couple the desired objective(s) with the process of "secularization."

3) They link secularization with "separation."

One example of this pattern is available in Professor John Swomley's book, *Religious Liberty and the Secular State*.[2] Notice the pattern:

1) Swomley identifies the objective: maximizing religious liberty. He notes, "religious liberty is a crucial aspect of a free society. People must be free either to accept or reject religion or particular expressions of religion."[3]

2) Swomley then couples the desired objective with the goal of secularization. He asserts that the only way to guarantee religious freedom is in a secular state: "Given the fact of strong religious conviction and competing religious groups, religious liberty can be guaranteed only in a secular state."[4]

3) Swomley concludes the argument by linking secularization with separation. He maintains that "separation of church and state . . . is the essence of a secular state."[5]

Swomley's effort to link objectives with secularization, and secularization with separation, is not unique. The argument is oft repeated. Philosopher Robert Audi's case for secularization follows the same pattern.[6]

Audi has an objective. He wants to protect liberal democracy and fears that it is endangered by religious expression. Audi is particularly concerned that one group will try to dominate all others, and that when religious convictions are the basis of political disagreements, then it is less likely that the participants can agree to disagree—they are unlikely to resolve the dispute peaceably. Thus, Audi couples his objective with his case for secularization.[7] Does he, then, complete the argument by linking secularization with separation? Absolutely. Notice how closely he links the two:

> More specifically, I believe that just as we separate church and state institutionally, we should, in certain aspects of our thinking and public conduct, separate religion from law and public policy matters, especially when it comes to passing restrictive laws. The separation in turn implies the need for motivational as well as rationale purposes.[8]

He simply calls secularization "separation," and distinguishes between secularization, as it is commonly discussed in the political arena, and separation, as it is commonly discussed in the constitutional arena, by referring to the former as "motivational separation," and the latter as "institutional separation."[9] Make no mistake, however; like Swomley, Audi argues that secularization depends heavily upon separation—institutional separation:

> My claim is that a substantially weaker separation of church and state than I have defended is not fully consonant with the ideals of liberal democracy, at least as it is best understood.[10]

Professor Kathleen Sullivan's case for secularization, and, therefore separation, follows the same pattern. What is her objective? Professor Sullivan maintains that it is the same goal as those who founded the civil order: to protect liberal democracy from, among other things, the "war of all sects against all."[11] To attain this objective, she argues for a secular public moral order. She notes:

> Religious teachings as expressed in public debate may influence the civil public order but public moral disputes may be resolved only on grounds articulable in secular terms.[12]

How can America best ensure secularization? Secularization is inextricably linked with the Constitution's establishment clause:

> The bar against an establishment of religion entails the establish-
> ment of a civil order—the culture of liberal democracy—for
> resolving public moral disputes. . . . Public affairs may no longer be
> conducted as the strongest faith would dictate. Minority religions
> gain from the truce not in the sense that their faiths now may be
> translated into public policy, but in the sense that no faith may be.
> Neither the Bible nor Talmud may directly settle, for example,
> public controversy over whether abortion preserves liberty or ends
> life. The correct baseline, then, is not unfettered religious liberty,
> but rather religious liberty insofar as it is consistent with the estab-
> lishment of the secular moral order.[13]

One can even uncover the overt coupling of secularization and separation in the opinions of some of the justices on the Supreme Court. Consider
two examples: Justice Felix Frankfurter's concurring opinion in *McCollum v.
Board of Education* (1948),[14] and Justice John Paul Stevens' dissent in *Webster
v Reproductive Health Services* (1989).[15]

In *McCollum*, an 8-1 decision where the court struck down a "released
time" program in Champaign, Illinois, because it permitted religious teachers
access to their students on campus and during the school day, Justice
Frankfurter argued that one of the objectives in creating a system of public
schools was to foster a liberal, secular democracy free from the strife of competing religious sects:

> The sharp confinement of the public schools to secular education
> was a recognition of the need of a democratic society to educate its
> children, insofar as the State undertook to do so, in an atmosphere
> free from the pressures in a realm in which pressures are most
> resisted and conflicts are most easily, and most bitterly engen-
> dered. Designed to serve as perhaps the most powerful agency for
> promoting cohesion among a heterogenous democratic people, the
> public school must be kept scrupulously free from entanglement in
> the strife of sects.[16]

Frankfurter argued further that a secular public school system is the best way
to achieve the desired objectives:

> The public school is at once the symbol of our democracy (and
> secular public unity) and the most pervasive means for promoting
> our common destiny. In no activity of the State is it more vital to
> keep out the divisive forces than its schools, to avoid confusing, not
> to say fusing, what the Constitution sought to keep strictly apart.[17]

Finally he offered his prescription for secularization in public education. How can society best safeguard the secular character of the public schools? Through the separation doctrine:

> The preservation of the community from divisive conflicts, of Government from irreconcilable pressures by religious groups, and of religion from censorship and coercion however subtly exercised, requires strict confinement of the State to instruction other than religious, leaving to the individual's church and home, indoctrination in the faith of his choice. . . . Separation means separation, not something less.[18]

Frankfurter advocated a particular type of separation. He argued for what I will describe below: a strict, rigid separation of church and state.[19]

Did Justice Frankfurter's secularist spin on the separation doctrine win the day? Subsequent to the *Lemon* decision, in *every* case where government looks to be impacting positively or negatively upon religion, government is required to show that it has a secular purpose. Absent a secular purpose, the court will permit no further review of the legislation in question. That has been true whether the policy in question had a direct positive or negative impact upon religion— for example, Alabama's silent prayer legislation eventually dismissed as unconstitutional in *Wallace v Jaffree* (1985),[20]—or if it had an indirect impact upon religion—for example, Louisiana's balanced treatment act that required creation science be taught alongside evolution in public school science classrooms. Louisiana's statute was struck down in *Edwards v Aguillard* (1987).[21] Why? The court held that Louisiana's attempt to provide a secular purpose for the statute was, largely, a sham. Its purpose was to promote fundamentalist Christianity.

The post-*Lemon* decisions are based upon a different type of separation. As I will indicate in the next section, they are packaged under the label of "neutrality." They hold that if there is significant religious motivation for a particular public policy, then it violates the Constitution's establishment clause—which, in essence, requires the separation of church and state.

The *Webster* decision provides an illustration of the secularism-separation linkage in an abortion decision—a case not generally categorized with the court's establishment clause jurisprudence. In *Webster*, the court considered Missouri's law requiring physicians to test the likelihood of viability on fetuses over twenty weeks and prohibited the usage of public facilities for abortions unless to save the life of the mother. Missouri also affixed a preamble to the law which said, "life begins at conception and that unborn children have protectable interest in life, health, and well-being."[22]

Justice Stevens affirmed the softer definition of separation articulated in *Lemon*. He held that there is no identifiable secular purpose for Missouri's declaration about the beginning of life, and therefore the law violates the establishment clause. A religious purpose for public policy is unacceptable. Only secular motives are constitutional:

> I am persuaded that the absence of any secular purpose for the leg-islative declarations that life begins at conception and that con-ception occurs at fertilization makes the relevant portion of the preamble invalid under the Establishment Clause . . . the pream-ble, an unequivocal endorsement of a religious tenet of some but by no means all Christian faiths, serves no identifiable secular pur-pose. That fact alone compels a conclusion that the statute violates the Establishment Clause.[23]

Of course Justice Stevens' argument is greatly overstated. There are those who contend fervently that life, and therefore personhood, begins at conception based only upon the scientific and medical evidence.[24] More ger-mane to this discussion, his argument suggests that the distinction between "purpose," defined as "mission," and "purpose," defined as "motive," is murky. Is government required to show a secular mission (or objective) for legisla-tion which might impact on religion to pass constitutional muster,[25] or hav-ing offered a secular mission, must government prove that the motives for the legislation (with the secular mission) were fully secular? Stevens' interpreta-tion of the establishment clause permits only secular *motives* for any public policy—even those not generally thought to establish or hinder religion. The establishment clause, authored to protect religious freedom, becomes a tool not simply to prevent a marriage between church and the state but to protect and foster a secular society. Separation is, therefore, a vehicle to achieve sec-ularization.

THE SUPREME COURT AND THE WALL OF SEPARATION

There is no question that many scholars, jurists, and policymakers believe that separation is the best way to bring about secularization.[26] The illustrations from Frankfurter and Stevens suggest dramatically that there are justices on the high court who agree. Frankfurter, at least with respect to public educa-tion, was very candid about employing the separation doctrine to foster a sec-ular society. Justice Stevens' interpretation of the establishment clause permits nothing but secular-based public policy.

Are Frankfurter and Stevens isolated examples, or has the court's approach to the establishment clause generally, even if unintentionally, been designed to foster secularization? Professor Gedicks thinks the answer is obvious:

> The Supreme Court's religion clause jurisprudence is limited and
> controlled by the rhetorical resources of secular individualist dis-
> course. By confining religion to public life, secular individualism
> can subordinate religion to secularism in public life, or exclude it
> altogether.[27]

Is Professor Gedicks' charge accurate? One way to answer that question
is to see whether or not the court crafted the establishment clause to require
separation of religion from the state. To the extent that the establishment
clause has been interpreted to require separation, one indeed might make the
case that the court is, in many respects, the most important tool for fostering
secularization and privatization of religion in American public life. It is difficult to argue that the court redefined the establishment clause to mean separation, especially since "separation" is not how the court characterizes its own
treatment of the establishment clause. Instead, the court claims to have moved
away from separation and toward "benevolent neutrality."[28] In fact, several
scholars actually trace an evolution in the court's treatment of the establishment clause away from separation to neutrality, and others spell out the evolution within the court's definition of neutrality.[29]

The court is engaging in suspect advertising. The court has never interpreted the establishment clause to require "neutrality." Instead, its majority has
continued to offer a variation of the separationist jurisprudence it introduced
in 1947. If I am correct, then the conscious strategy to link secularization with
separation not only is plausible, it is extremely likely. And, even if there were
no conscious strategy among the particular justices, the linkage was accomplished nonetheless.

In the remainder of this chapter, I examine the court's treatment of the
first amendment's establishment clause. I maintain that, whether intentionally or not, the court has interpreted the clause in such a way as to perpetuate
this "wall of separation" (albeit sometimes high and sometimes low, often solid
and occasionally porous).

The court built its establishment clause jurisprudence upon two seminal pillars: the "separation" doctrine articulated in *Everson v Board of Education*
(1947),[30] and the requirement that there be a benevolent "neutrality" between
government and religion and nonreligion as in *Lemon v Kurtzman* in 1971.[31]
The distinction between the separation doctrine and the neutrality doctrine is
largely artificial, however. If one looks carefully at *Everson*, one will find that
Justice Black offered two separate definitions of separation: a strict, rigid definition of separation that is consistent with many of the dicta in the opinion,
and a softer, more pliable definition that is consistent with the results of the
decision. It is the second definition of separation, the softer definition, that

has evolved into the neutrality doctrine. Make no mistake, however; Justice Black placed both definitions under the umbrella of separation.

Thus, if one traces the major establishment clause cases during this developmental period (between 1947 and 1971), one will discover that sometimes the court employed the strict definition of separation. Other times it used the softer definition of separation. As the 1960s drew to a close, the court began to speak almost exclusively in terms of the latter definition of separation—the one now permanently misidentified as neutrality.

I look at three clusters of cases between the court's two seminal establishment clause decisions, *Everson* and *Lemon*. In these early, pivotal decisions, the court offers two different definitions for "separation"—a strict definition and a softer definition that is linked with the term "neutrality." In *Lemon*, the court embraced but one of the definitions of separation. It picked the softer definition, though it is a separationist conceptualization of the establishment clause nonetheless.

Cluster One: *Everson, McCollum, Zorach*

In a course in American government or constitutional law, one will generally learn that in *Everson* the court articulated the "wall of separation" metaphor holding that the Constitution requires the "strict separation" of church and state. *Lemon* later clarified the court's position by fully embracing the "neutrality" doctrine and developing a three-part test—namely the "secular purpose test," the "primary effects test," and the "excessive entanglement test," to determine government's neutrality toward religion. If one looks carefully, however, at three sets of cases decided between 1947 and 1971, he or she will see that the progression from "separation" to "neutrality" is not quite as clear as might be presented in the classroom.

The first cluster of cases, decided from 1947 to 1952, introduce and flesh out the separation doctrine. In *Everson*, the majority opinion does not equivocate on the issue of separation. The court held that the establishment clause imposes several restrictions upon the state: government cannot set up a church. It cannot pass laws which aid religion or prefer one religion over another. Government cannot influence a person to attend or not attend church. It cannot punish him or her for entertaining or professing a religious belief or disbelief. No tax can be levied by a state or the national government—no matter how large or small, or no matter what the tax might be called—to support religious activities or instructions. Government cannot, openly or secretly, participate in the affairs of any religious organization. Justice Hugo Black states that the establishment clause "was intended to erect a 'wall of separation' between Church and State."[32]

There is a problem with the *Everson* decision, however. As most students of constitutional law are aware, this is the case where Justice Black's
dicta do not square with the results of the decision. A New Jersey school board
was able to scale the wall of separation and reimburse parochial school students for riding on busses operated by the public transportation system.
Defending the results of the case, Black concedes that the ordinance might
make it easier and more attractive for parents to send their children to
parochial schools. It provides an indirect benefit to the religious mission of the
religious institution. For that matter, so do police and fire protection, sewage
disposal, and sidewalks. Cutting off church schools from these essential services, argued Black—services generally available to the community at large—
actually pits the state against the church as adversaries.[33]

How does Black resolve the dilemma? He argues that it is obviously not
the purpose of the first amendment to promote hostility between church and
state:

> That Amendment requires the state to be neutral in its relations
> with groups of religious believers and non-believers; it does not
> require the state to be their adversary. State power is no more to be
> used so as to handicap religion than it is to favor them.[34]

Thus the majority upheld the school board's reimbursement plan. To do so,
however, Black *simultaneously* defined the establishment clause to "erect a wall
of separation between church and state" and to require "the state to be neutral
in its relations with groups of believers and non-believers."[35]

It is hard to follow the logic of Justice Black's argument. At first glance,
he interprets the establishment clause to require both "separation" and "neutrality." A careful look at the opinion invites another interpretation. After
rationalizing the decision to uphold New Jersey's program, over vigorous dissent,[36] Black once again returned to the separation theme. He argued, "The
first amendment has erected a wall between church and state. That wall must
be kept high and impregnable. We could not approve the slightest breach."[37]
Since Black did not retreat from his separationist argument—rather, he sand-
wiched his discussion of neutrality between two passionate statements supporting separation—he might well have interpreted neutrality and separation,
in this context, synonymously. At the very least he seems to view neutrality as
a subcomponent of separation.

If there is any question that Black intended for the establishment clause
to require strict separation, he settled the issue one year later in *McCollum*.
Several statements affirm his commitment to separation. First, he argued that
both the majority opinion and dissenting opinions in *Everson* "agreed that the

first amendment's language, properly interpreted, had erected a wall of separation between church and state."[38] Second, he repudiated the traditional non-preferentialist argument that "historically the first amendment was intended to forbid only government preference of one religion over another and not impartial governmental assistance of all religions." Further, he distinguished separation, "a requirement to abstain from fusing functions of Government and of religious sects," from simply treating all religions equally.[39] Third, Black struck down the released time program in Champaign, Illinois, maintaining that the state cannot utilize its public school system to aid any or all religious faiths in the dissemination of their doctrines and ideals. His decision to nullify the Illinois program did not constitute unlawful hostility toward religion.[40] He concluded by reiterating the separationist theme:

> For the first amendment rests upon the premise that both religion and government can best work to achieve their lofty aims if each is left free from the other within its respective sphere. Or, as we said in the Everson case, the first amendment has erected a wall of separation between Church and State which must be kept high and impregnable.[41]

The last decision in the court's early trilogy of establishment clause cases, its decision to uphold New York's released time program in *Zorach v Clauson*,[42] might be more of a reaction to the ensuing protest following *McCollum*.[43] It certainly is enigmatic in light of the *Everson* dicta and the unyielding support for strict separation in *McCollum*.

Justice Douglas distinguished New York's programs from its counterpart in Champaign, Illinois, and argued that, rather than coercing students to get them to attend religious classes, "the school authorities are neutral in this regard and do no more than release students whose parents so request."[44] The court did not, he insisted, waver from its support for the separation doctrine. He noted that the church and state should be separated, that the separation must be complete and unequivocal, and that the first amendment permits no exception. "The prohibition," he said, "is absolute."[45]

From that perspective, however, Justice Douglas' reasoning starts to look like Black's in *Everson*—only, unlike Black's opinion, it is almost impossible to outline any coherent argument. First, Douglas departed from his commitment to strict separation. Early in the opinion he observed, "The first amendment, however, does not say that in every and all respects there shall be a separation of Church and State." Later he maintained, "The constitutional standard is the separation of Church and State. The problem, like many problems in constitutional law, is one of degree."[46] Surely, he argued, separation cannot be pushed to the degree that it would rob the church of police and fire protection, or disallow references to God in presidential addresses or prayers in our legislative halls? That scenario would leave the state and religion as aliens to each other—"hostile, suspicious, and even unfriendly." Next, he noted, "We are a religious people whose institutions presuppose a Supreme Being. . . . When the state encourages religious instruction or cooperates with religious authorities by adjusting the schedule of public events to sectarian needs, it follows the best of our traditions."[47] Therefore, in order to prevent hostility, he mandated that government must be neutral, even accommodating, to the religious needs of the people.

Douglas used three statements to support this shift. He argued that the state follows the best of our traditions when it cooperates with religion, "for then it respects the religious nature of our people and *accommodates* the public service to their spiritual needs." Later, he insisted that "the government must be *neutral* when it comes to cooperation between sects." Finally, he noted:

> We follow the *McCollum* case. But we cannot expand it to cover the present released time program unless *separation* of Church and State means that public institutions can make no adjustments of their schedules to *accommodate* the religious needs of the people. We cannot read into the Bill of Rights such a philosophy of hostility toward religion.[48]

Douglas' opinion constructed the following arguments:

1. *Everson* and *McCollum* were correctly decided. The establishment clause requires separation of church and state—strict separation of church and state.

2. The establishment clause cannot tolerate hostility.

3. Therefore, government must be neutral, or even accommodating, to circumvent hostility.

4. Neutrality is acceptable because strict separation does not mean strict separation. The requirement of separation of church and state, in any given situation, becomes one of degree.

Justice Douglas' analysis followed Justice Black's reasoning in *Everson* with some notable exceptions. First, Douglas *softened* "strict separation." *Zorach* tells us "strict separation" is one of degree. Further, we discover in *Everson* and *Zorach* that the establishment clause will tolerate "less than strict separation," or what others might call neutrality, in the name of strict separation. The more flaccid definition of separation, namely Douglas' definition, will become important as the court justifies its "benevolent neutrality" doctrine in future decisions. Ironically, Justice Douglas would be unable to accept some of the future excursions from strict separation that would emerge from his own softer definition.[49]

Second, Douglas, unlike any other separationist justice in the relatively brief history of the court's interpretation of the establishment clause, appeared to recognize that accommodation might be a legitimate subcomponent of neutrality. Thus he allows for a more generous level of neutrality. He even speaks of government accommodation toward religion. Unfortunately, like Black in *Everson*, he wrapped the whole package—neutrality and accommodation—and placed it under the tree of separation. While he recognized that neutrality and accommodation can fit together nicely, he failed to discern that neither accommodation nor neutrality squares with rigid separation. This analysis will become more critical below.

Third, and again rather profoundly, Douglas expanded upon what it means to be hostile toward religion. He expanded the previous definition of hostility—denying religious groups essential government services—to one that recognizes the possibility that government might actually prefer nonreligion to religion which, noted Douglas, would cut against the grain of America's best traditions.

Thus, even in the light of the early establishment clause trilogy, the troubled marriage between separation and neutrality, discussed above, still holds up. Though the court appears to clean up the inconsistencies evident in *Everson*, by endorsing strict separation in *McCollum*, the justices revert to ambiguity in *Zorach*. The establishment clause requires separation. To avoid hostility, the establishment clause requires neutrality. Therefore, either separation is defined to equal neutrality, or separation requires neutrality. As I shall indicate in the chapter 7, either conclusion is fatuous.

Cluster Two: *Engel* and *Schempp*

Ten years passed between the *Zorach* and the Bible reading and prayer decisions *Engel v Vitale*[50] and *Abington Township School District v Schempp*.[51] *Engel* reads very much like *McCollum*—a strident affirmation of the separation doctrine. The court overturned the New York state board of regents' prayer composed by state officials and recited daily in public schools. Writing for the majority, Justice Black said, first, that the prayer was an unconstitutional violation of the separation doctrine:

> The State's use of the Regents' prayer in its public school system breaches the constitutional wall of separation between Church and State. We agree with that contention since we think that the constitutional prohibition against laws respecting an establishment of religion must at least mean that in this country it is no part of the

business of government to compose official prayers for any group
of the American people to recite as a part of a religious program
carried on by government.[52]

Further, Justice Black strongly dismissed the charge that prohibiting religious
services in the public schools is to "indicate a hostility toward religion or
toward prayer":

> Nothing, of course, could be more wrong. . . . It is neither sacrile-
> gious nor antireligious to say that each separate government in this
> country should stay out of the business of writing or sanctioning
> official prayers and leave that purely religious function to the peo-
> ple themselves and to those the people choose to look to for reli-
> gious guidance.[53]

Although *Engel* speaks of strict separation, *Schempp* is couched almost
exclusively in terms of neutrality. In his majority opinion, which struck down
Bible reading and recitation of the Lord's Prayer in Pennsylvania and
Maryland, Justice Clark described the "wholesome neutrality" between government and religion.[54]

To test if a statute violates the wholesome neutrality, and thereby threatens a fusion of governmental and religious functions, Justice Clark proposed
to look at the purpose and primary effect of the enactment. To "withstand the
strictures of the establishment clause," argued Justice Clark, "there must be a
secular legislative purpose and a primary effect that neither advances or
inhibits religion."[55] The decision, noted Justice Clark, does not disallow classroom Bible study, for its literary or historic qualities, or forbid a general study
of religion, when presented as part of a secular program of education. But, he
observed, the exercises in question do not fall into those categories:

> They are religious exercises, required by the States in violation of
> the command of the first amendment that the Government main-
> tain *strict neutrality*, neither aiding nor opposing religion. Finally,
> we cannot accept that the concept of *neutrality*, which does not
> permit a State to require a religious exercise even with the consent
> of the majority of those affected, collides with the majority's right
> to free exercise of religion.[56]

Justice Brennan's concurring opinion supports Clark's plea for neutrality. Brennan noted, "I think a brief survey of certain of these forms of accommodation will reveal that the first amendment commands not official hostility toward religion, but only strict neutrality in matters of religion."[57] Further,
Brennan carefully distinguished between the restrictions placed upon governmental involvement with religion, in order to satisfy the first amendment's
neutrality requirement, and "hostility":

The State must be steadfastly neutral in all matters of faith, and never favor nor inhibit religion. In my view government cannot sponsor religious exercises in the public schools without jeopardizing that neutrality. On the other hand, hostility, not neutrality, would characterize the refusal to provide chaplains and places of worship for prisoners and soldiers cut off by the State from all civilian opportunities for public communion, the withholding of draft exemptions for ministers and conscientious objectors, or the denial of the temporary use of an empty public building to a congregation whose place of worship has been destroyed by fire or flood. I do not say that government must provide chaplains or draft exemptions, or that the courts should intercede if it fails to do so.[58]

One might make the case that *Schempp* actually represented a shift in the court's approach from "strict separation" to "strict neutrality."[59] That conclusion would be erroneous for several reasons. First, it ignores the impact and reasoning of *Engel*. It would be one thing if the court maintained a consistent separationist position in the first cluster of cases and then, ten years later, undercut the separation doctrine in favor of "neutrality." *Engel*, however, was decided just one year before *Schempp*; it deals with roughly the same constitutional questions; and the outcome was comparable. To treat the two cases as one cluster and look for them to form one coherent position simply makes better sense than to insist that they are distinct and that the court's doctrine evolved sharply in twelve months.

Second, even though the court speaks of neutrality in *Schempp* and not strict separation, look at how Justice Clark defines neutrality:

As we have indicated, the establishment clause has been directly considered by this Court eight times in the past score of years and, with only one Justice dissenting on the point, it has been consistently upheld that the clause withdrew *all* legislative power respecting religious belief or the expression thereof.[60]

By withdrawing *all* legislative power respecting religious belief or the expression thereof, Clark, like Black and Douglas before him, meshed separation and neutrality and made them one doctrine.

Third, Justice Brennan, whose concurring opinion in *Schempp* was so influential, did not forsake the separation doctrine in favor of strict neutrality. More than twenty years later, in *Grand Rapids School District v Ball*, Brennan adopted Justice Black's separationist argument to strike down a remedial and enhancement program operated by the Grand Rapids public school district.[61]

Cluster Three: *Allen, Walz,* and *Lemon*

A third cluster of developmental cases was decided between 1963 and 1971. In *Board of Education v Allen*,[62] the Court applied the *Schempp* test to a program of lending state-approved textbooks free of charge to all secondary school students, including those in private schools. It found that there was indeed a "secular purpose" and that "the primary effect" of the program neither advanced nor inhibited religion. Speaking for the court, Justice Byron White insisted that the "constitutional standard" is the separation of church and state. He conceded, however, "that the line between state neutrality to religion and state support of religion is not easy to locate." Separation of church and state, observed White, like most constitutional problems, is one of degree.[63] Justice White almost used separation and neutrality interchangeably, as the court started to fashion a new meaning for the separation doctrine.

In *Walz v Tax Commission*, Chief Justice Warren Burger's majority opinion upholding tax exemptions for religious property expanded upon the shifting definition of separation articulated in *Allen*. Burger cited the opinion in *Zorach* to argue that the first amendment does not say "that in every and all respects there shall be a separation of Church and State."[64] There are some general principles, Burger said, deducible from the first amendment, over which there is no debate:

> We will not tolerate either governmentally established religion or
> governmental interference with religion. Short of those expressly
> proscribed governmental acts there is room for play in the joints
> productive of a benevolent neutrality which will permit religious
> exercise to exist without sponsorship and without interference.[65]

He argued further that, "No perfect or absolute separation is really possible; the very existence of the Religion Clauses is an involvement of sorts—one that seeks to mark boundaries to avoid excessive entanglement."[66]

Like *Allen*, the majority in *Walz* attempted to limit the separation doctrine and square it with an acceptable standard of neutrality. In *Lemon*, the court finished administering its deathblow to strict separation. Chief Justice Burger distinguished parochial school aid programs in Pennsylvania and Rhode Island from *Walz*: the former is unconstitutional aid; the latter is not. The objective of the establishment clause, noted Burger, is to prevent the intrusion of either church or state into the precincts of the other and not to construct walls of separation:

> Our prior holdings do not call for total separation between church
> and state; total separation is not possible in an absolute sense.
> Some relationship between government and religious organiza-

tions is inevitable. Fire inspections, building and zoning regulations, and state requirements under compulsory school attendance
laws are examples of necessary and permissible contacts. Indeed,
under the statutory exemption before us in *Walz*, the State had a
continuing burden to ascertain that the exempt property was in
fact being used for religious worship. Judicial caveats against
entanglement must recognize that the line of separation, far from
being a "wall," is a blurred, indistinct, and variable barrier depending on all the circumstances of a particular relationship.[67]

There is little doubt that the last cluster of cases radically changed the
court's approach to the establishment clause. By the *Lemon* decision, strict
separation was all but out of the picture. Despite the severity of their language—the requirements pronounced in *Everson*, the majority opinion in
McCollum, and the dissent in *Zorach*—the separationists on the court did not
push the "high wall of separation" to its logical conclusion. The scope of strict
separation is obvious. Strict separation will tolerate *no* accommodation.
Government, arguably, could *not* provide police and fire protection to church
buildings—maybe not even to parsonages. Even if unequivocal separation did
not require a fireman to look askance at a blazing church building, the implications of strict separation are potentially ominous. The government could not
distribute hot lunches, provide educational equipment, medical or psychological treatment, or even diagnostic testing, to thousands of children attending
parochial schools. Government could not provide funding for church hospitals or child-care facilities. Military academies could not fund chaplains; soldiers would not be afforded religious comfort on the battlefield; Congress and
the Supreme Court could not open sessions with reference to God—whose
name, no longer the source of our trust, would be unceremoniously (since any
ceremony would smack of a government approved religious service) stricken
from our money.

Some strict separationists support *Everson*'s rhetoric and historical
analysis but refuse to wash neutrality out of the equation in favor of unbridled
separation.[68] In fact, the court has largely disengaged from strict separation.
Despite the fact that enforcing strict separation would provide the court with
coherence, strict separation is not a desirable option. It never could be—not
in the 1780s, nor two centuries later.

The shift did not mean, however, that the separation doctrine had been
abolished. Just as Justice Douglas had done in *Zorach*, the *Lemon* court softened the separation doctrine. The majority did not eliminate it. Not unlike
Plato's Socrates in "The Statesman"[69] who, though not a major actor in the
dialogue, remains in the background as an ever-present and dominant figure,
the "wall of separation" affects every establishment clause decision

The court, in the three clusters of cases between *Everson* and *Lemon*, actually fashioned two competing views of separation: "strict" separation, illustrated by Black's dicta in *Everson* and by the majority opinions in *McCollum* and *Engel*, and "softer" separation, illustrated by Douglas' opinion in *Zorach* and by the majority opinions in *Schempp* and *Lemon*. See the figure below for a depiction of the competing models of separation.

The essential difference is that, post-*Lemon*, the separation doctrine has a dual nature. When the court speaks of separation, and means strict separation, it says "separation." When the court speaks of separation, and the justices mean softer—or partial—separation, they say "neutrality."

COMPETING MODELS OF SEPARATION

"Strict"

Everson → *McCollum* → *Engel*

"Softer"

Zorach → *Schempp* → *Allen, Walz, Lemon*

Justice Lewis Powell's opinion in *Committee for Public Education v Nyquist*[70] illustrates the dual nature of separation. He started his analysis by noting Madison's commitment, shared by Jefferson and others, to strict separation. Madison was so jealous for religious freedoms, Powell said, that he hoped they would never become entangled in precedents. Powell noted, however, that despite Madison's admonishment and the "sweep of the absolute prohibitions" of the clauses, this nation is not, nor ever has been, "one of entirely sanitized separation between Church and State." Total separation has never been thought either possible or desirable.[71] As a result, he observed, the church-state cases have "presented some of the most perplexing questions to come before the Court. Those cases have occupied the concern and thoughtful scholarship of some of the Court's most respected former Justices."[72] Consequently, Powell argued, the court no longer meanders all over the map when adjudicating church-state cases. The constitutional standards are well defined:

> As a result of these decisions and opinions, it may no longer be said that the Religion Clauses are free of "entangling" precedents. Neither, however, may it be said that Jefferson's metaphoric "wall of separation" between Church and State has become "as winding as the famous serpentine wall" he designed for the University of Virginia. Indeed, the controlling constitutional standards have become firmly rooted and the broad contours of our inquiry are now well defined.[73]

In his introductory argument, Powell never spoke of neutrality. The context of his argument dealt with separation. Yet Powell applied *Lemon's* test for neutrality to evaluate New York's aid package, thereby putting neutrality into the context of this modified view of separation. He neatly bridged the gap between separation and neutrality.

The only substantial difference between Powell's "contemporary" approach, illustrated by his opinion in *Nyquist*, and Justice Black's original separationist argument in *Everson* is what each justice meant by "separation." Black spoke of strict separation; Powell referred to a less rigid type of separation. One might even argue that since Black spoke of separation and neutrality simultaneously, and authored the majority opinion in a case that upheld governmental aid to parochial schools, there is really *very little* difference between the *Everson* approach and the *Lemon* approach. Both are rooted in separation but end up defining the separation doctrine to require neutrality. As it turns out, cases like *McCollum* and *Engel* do not fit the pattern because of their doctrinal purity. The intensity with which they push the separation doctrine sets them apart from the general level of definitional ambiguity demonstrated by the court.

Thus, the evidence does support the argument that the court crafted the establishment clause to require the separation of church and state. It is not surprising to some scholars that there is a clear overlap between those who advocate secularization through the process of separation and the Supreme Court's establishment clause jurisprudence. The court is, in many respects, the most important tool not only for fostering the separation of church and state, but also for the more important objective: secularization and privatization of religion in American public life.[74] In fact, law professor Michael McConnell argues that a conscious quest for secularization provides the underpinning of the Supreme Court's treatment of the establishment clause:

> More significant was the Court's tendency to press relentlessly in the direction of a more secular society. The Court's opinions seemed to view religion as an unreasoned, aggressive, exclusionary, and divisive force that must be confined to the private sphere. When religions stuck to the private functions of "spiritual comfort, guidance, and inspiration," the Court extended the protection of the Constitution. But the Court was ever conscious that religion "can also serve powerfully to divide societies and to exclude those whose beliefs are not in accord with particular religions." The more important mission was to protect democratic society from religion.[75]

It is difficult to say whether the court actually led the modern quest for secularization, or if it was merely reacting to secularist philosophies articulated in the marketplace. Audi suggests it was the former. The tradition of separating church and state, he notes, "has contributed to secularization."[76] McConnell argues that the philosophy of secular liberalism, one that consistently critiques religious belief as suffering next to the scientific method, predates the court's entrance into the establishment clause arena in 1947.[77]

Regardless of which came first—the quest for secularization or separation—Professor Stephen Carter notes that the court's focus has shifted from looking at the establishment clause as a source of protection for religious liberty to making it a hammer with which to nail down a public philosophy of secularism:

> Thus conceived, the clause exists less for the benefit of religious autonomy than for the benefit of secular politics; that is to borrow from the test itself, the Establishment Clause was written to further "a secular legislative purpose," trying to erect around the political process a wall that is almost impossible to take seriously.[78]

The impact of the linkage between the court's establishment clause jurisprudence and secularization is not only evident, but also rather frightening. "The potential transformation of the Establishment Clause from a guardian of religious liberty into a guarantor of public secularism," argues Carter, "raises prospects at once dismal and dreadful."[79]

FIVE

The Consequences of Separation

In the preceding chapter, I maintain that the trivialization of religious expression, described earlier in this work, did not just happen. Many secularists are fervent partisans of the separation *doctrine* because they believe it to be the key to a secular state and society. And, during the past fifty years, the court has crafted the establishment clause to require the separation of church and state. Therefore, it is not surprising to some constitutional commentators that there is a clear connection between those who advocate secularization through the process of separation and the Supreme Court's establishment clause jurisprudence. The court is, in many respects, the most important instrument for not only fostering the separation of church and state, but also for secularization and the privatization of religion in American public life.

In this chapter, I examine some of the consequences of the separation doctrine—particularly as it has helped to foster a public policy of secularization. There are two "primary" consequences and two "secondary" consequences. By "primary" and "secondary" I do not mean to imply a level of seriousness. I use the two terms only to suggest that the secondary ramifications emerge from the primary consequences.

What are the primary consequences of the separation doctrine proffered by the Supreme Court? First, the separation doctrine has so undermined the stability of the first amendment's establishment clause that it is nearly impossible to make sense out of what the court has done subsequent to its holding in *Lemon v Kurtzman* (1971).[1] Although the court's confused treatment of the establishment clause has been well documented in other work,[2] I feature the more obvious inconsistencies.

Second, the court's treatment of the religious liberty clauses has fostered a perception of strict separation. Whether the Court speaks in terms of neutrality or separation, most Americans assume that the Constitution's requirements regarding religious liberty can be summarized in five words: *separation of church and state*. The problem with this sort of public perception is that it creates de facto separation where none is required, and it makes discussions like this one—a lengthy argument respecting the legitimacy of religious dialogue in the public square—quite a challenge. Why? Because most who believe that the Constitution requires the separation of church and state also believe that the Constitution safeguards against the influence of sectarianism on public policy.

What, then, are the secondary consequences of the court's confusing approach to the establishment clause? De jure or de facto separation works to silence the religious voice in the public square. As I mentioned in the first two chapters, there is a wide range of scholars who insist that religious expression is necessary for America's political and social health. In a nutshell, they teach that religion offers a standard from which to judge the integrity, honesty, and the justice of the state. It provides a necessary alternative to the state's course of action. Democracy itself, they argue, is predicated upon the existence of such an alternative. Secularization, however, intentionally silences the religious voice.

Finally, separation, whether de jure or de facto, has done serious damage to the individual rights of religious people. If you recall, in the first chapter, I maintained that the religious liberty clauses were intended to protect against the mistreatment of religious minorities. This sort of mistreatment still abounds. However, some of the horror stories are starting to turn around. It is often those in more mainstream religious faiths who are the target of persecution by government officials. More correctly, in an atmosphere where secularism has become the majority philosophy, religious expression itself is in the minority and has been duly targeted.

PRIMARY CONSEQUENCES OF SEPARATION

It Has Fostered Some Muddled Case Law

If there was ever a court case that was aptly named, it was *Lemon*. The decision, inasmuch as the court tried to provide a clear, consistent standard by which to interpret the establishment clause, was a failure.[3] As I suggested in the previous chapter, *Lemon* is extremely deceptive because it purports to shift the interpretation of the establishment clause away from "separation" in favor of benevolent "neutrality." It does no such thing. In *Lemon*, the court embraces a less severe brand of separation—a strain that had surfaced more and more frequently since *Everson v Board of Education* (1947).[4] The separation doctrine remains the doctrinal linchpin of the court's establishment clause jurisprudence.

The requirements articulated in the *Everson* dicta, and subsequently reaffirmed in *McCollum v Board of Education* (1948) and in *Engel v Vitale* (1962), forced the court into an impossible position. From the outset, as the results in *Everson* attest, the court was required to compromise the strict separation doctrine. The plea for neutrality constitutes just such a compromise in its interpretation of the strict separation doctrine rather than a distinct shift in the court's interpretation. Particularly in the post-*Lemon* era, the court is in a position to hold fast to the separation doctrine when it chooses, or modify the doctrine if a majority of the justices can be persuaded to do so. The court can wield the doctrine to disallow financial aid to sectarian institutions, or it can play with the doctrine to again permit accommodation when a majority sees fit.

Lemon fully locked the court into a case by case evaluation of legislation that aspires to nurture cooperation between church and state. It did arm the justices with a tool—the three-pronged test. The results, however, do not validate the success of the *Lemon* test. With respect to the establishment clause, it often has turned the court into a collection of pop-psychologists, mind-readers, and doctrinal schizophrenics.

For example, in *Lemon*, the court struck down both Rhode Island's salary supplement program for teachers of secular subjects in religious schools, and Pennsylvania's direct subsidies for expenditures in "nonreligious" subjects. The court did not conclude that the programs had no secular purpose, or that their primary effect was to advance or inhibit religious faith. It held that the programs violated the "excessive entanglement" test. Teachers might take the money to teach secular subjects and then turn around and proselytize in class. To reach this conclusion, the majority administered what one might describe as a "psychological evaluation" of the teachers' motives. Although Pennsylvania teachers testified, to the satisfaction of the district court, that they did not interject religion into their secular classes, Chief Justice Burger's opinion challenged even the educators' subconscious motives:

> We need not and do not assume that teachers in parochial schools will be guilty of bad faith. . . . We simply recognize that a dedicated religious person, teaching in a school affiliated with his or her faith and operated to inculcate its tenets will inevitably experience great difficulty in remaining religiously neutral. . . . With the best of intentions such a teacher would find it hard to make a total separation between secular teaching and religious doctrine. What would appear to some to be essential to good citizenship might well for others border on or constitute instruction in religion.[5]

Since a teacher is unlike a book, noted Burger, and cannot be inspected only one time to test the depth of his or her beliefs and compliance with the first amendment, there must necessarily be excessive contacts between state authorities and the parochial school. These contacts cause excessive entanglement.[6]

One might ask why Burger's concerns warrant a judicially manufactured three-prong test. Alternatively, it might justify either 1) rejecting *all* government aid, in compliance with the *Everson* dicta, 2) likening salary supplements to police and fire protection so that the Pennsylvania and Rhode Island salary packages would square with *Everson*'s results, or 3) admitting that the *Everson* standard is untenable and permitting government to come up with a reasonable standard for accommodation. Instead, Burger tries to harmonize the court's previous holdings—decisions that confuse the concepts of "separation" and "neutrality" and to use them to fashion a workable doctrine.

Lemon was not the last time the court engaged in pop-psychology and mind-reading. In *Wolman v Walter*, the court upheld an Ohio program giving state money for speech, hearing, and psychological *diagnostic* services for students in nonpublic schools, but held that *treatment* programs must take place somewhere away from the nonpublic school facilities.[7] Justice Blackmun's opinion reiterates the court's concern over who is more likely to transmit sectarian views. In this case, Blackmun pits teachers and counselors against diagnosticians:

> The nature of the relationship between the diagnosticians and
> pupil does not provide the same opportunity for the transmission
> of sectarian views as attends the relationship between teacher and
> student or between counselor and student.[8]

The issue is not whether or not Blackmun was correct in his speculations regarding student-adult relationships. It is, rather, what possible difference does it make? Government aid is government aid. It is easy to see how both thoroughgoing separationists and those who support government accommodation of religion would be angered and confused by the court's reasoning.

In *Grand Rapids School District v Ball* (1985)[9] and *Aguilar v Felton* (1985),[10] Justice Brennan simply repeated many of the same arguments presented in *Lemon* and *Wolman* to justify the court's decision to strike down legislation benefiting parochial school students. The Grand Rapids program hired public school teachers to teach nonpublic school children in courses that would supplement the basic core curriculum—art, music, and physical education. *Aguilar* concerned New York's usage of Title I money to provide remedial programs for nonpublic school children taught on Saturdays by public school teachers in public school classrooms. Brennan questioned the teachers' ability to divorce themselves from their religious mission under any circumstances. Further, he surmised that the supervisory programs necessary to enforce against religious dissemination meant that excessive entanglement was unavoidable.[11]

In several other decisions the court exhibits dubious analysis. For instance, in the 1984 decision *Lynch v Donnelly*,[12] Chief Justice Burger reasoned that, since a creche sponsored by Pawtucket, Rhode Island, was part of a Christmas display that contained other secular symbols of Christmas, the creche had been transformed into something secular.[13] That reasoning is certainly questionable enough, but just five years later, in *Allegheny County v ACLU*,[14] the court struck down a nativity scene displayed inside the Allegheny County courthouse. Justice Blackmun distinguished the case from *Lynch* claiming that, because the display was indoors, located in a prominent place, and without the other trappings of the season, it gave the impression that the state was endorsing Christianity.[15] In the same case, the court upheld an outdoor display of a 45-foot Christmas tree standing next to an 18-foot menorah. Blackmun argued that the Christmas tree was suitably secular, and by positioning the menorah next to the tree—with the tree more than twice the size of the menorah—the county would not give viewers the impression that the government endorsed either Christianity or Judaism.[16]

If one compares the two sets of cases—those which articulated and implemented the psychological coercion test, and the decisions regarding public display of a crèche at Christmas—one might conclude that the court had considered branching off into different career paths. Justice Scalia suggests as much in 1992:

> I find it a sufficient embarrassment that the Establishment Clause jurisprudence regarding holiday displays, has come to "require scrutiny more commonly associated with interior decorators than with the judiciary". . . . But interior decorating is a hard-rock science compared to psychology practiced by amateurs.[17]

Finally, consider Chief Justice Rehnquist's behavior in the case *Bowen v Kendrick*.[18] For years prior to *Bowen*, Associate Justice Rehnquist had thoroughly repudiated and rejected the three-prong test of neutrality formulated by the court in *Lemon*. At one point, Justice Rehnquist argued passionately:

> The three-part test represents a determined effort to craft a workable rule from a historically faulty doctrine; but the rule can only be as sound as the doctrine it attempts to service. The three-part test has simply not provided adequate standards for deciding Establishment Clause cases, as this Court has slowly come to realize. Even worse, the *Lemon* test has caused this Court to fracture

into unworkable plurality opinions, depending upon how each of
the three factors applies to certain state action. The results from
our school services cases show the difficulty we have encountered
in making the *Lemon* test yield principled results.[19]

How can Rehnquist's rejection of *Lemon* be more unequivocal?

Yet it was Chief Justice Rehnquist who authored the majority opinion
in *Bowen*, in which the court upheld the Adolescent Family Life Act
(AFLA),[20] legislation that gave federal funding to organizations, even religious groups and churches, that would promote abstinence to teenagers. In
reversing the lower court, Rehnquist mechanically employed the *Lemon* test.
He observed that the AFLA had a secular purpose. Its services do not advance
religion—any advancement is "incidental and remote." And, because there has
been a long history of cooperation between government and charities, there
was no excessive entanglement—despite the evidence that suggested that
some ministers were using the counseling sessions to evangelize the
teenagers.[21] Rehnquist's opinion actually served to *fortify* the *Lemon* test in
church-state jurisprudence.[22]

It probably does not come as any great surprise to learn that the court's
establishment clause decisions are all over the constitutional map. For
instance, the court held in *Everson* that communities can provide bus transportation for parochial school students to get to and from school. Nearly thirty years later, the court determined that the school districts cannot provide bus
transportation to parochial school kids to take field trips to local museums.[23]
Granted, transportation to and from school and transportation for field trips
are not the same thing, but the distinction must seem perplexing to all but the
most serious constitutional scholar—or to the proponent of strict separation.

Similarly, the Court held in *Board of Education v Allen*[24] that school boards
can lend textbooks to parochial school children. However, later, applying the
three-part test in *Lemon*, the majority forbade lending equipment to the
schools.[25] Rehnquist once observed caustically that the district might lend a student attending a parochial school a history textbook with a map of, say, George
Washington's crossing the Delaware. They could not, however, lend the school
the same map to place inside a history classroom.[26] Again, there is a significant
difference between lending materials to students, and giving them directly to
religious schools, but it is likely a distinction lost on most of the public.

As I indicated above, in *Wolman*, decided within six years of *Lemon*, the
court held that diagnostic testing (for hearing, eyesight, and the like) could be
conducted on parochial school children and on parochial school grounds. But,
should the tests uncover a malady that required therapy, the therapy must be
administered off campus—in a trailer parked somewhere down the street.[27]

Since 1962 the court has made it abundantly clear that public schools cannot set aside a period devoted to prayer—either in the classroom[28] or more recently during graduation exercises.[29] This prohibition includes even government-sponsored silent prayer.[30] But members of Congress are constitutionally permitted to hire their own chaplain to lead members in daily prayer.[31] Additionally, public schools cannot make time and space available for students to pray or read the Bible in the classroom, but the same schools can make classroom space available for Bible clubs to meet and pray after school.[32]

Finally, the court has rigidly forbidden after-school or weekend programs fostered by communities to address the remedial needs of parochial school students or to provide these students with enrichment programs otherwise available to kids in the public schools.[33] At the same time, the court upheld programs that give money to churches who counsel and teach teenagers against promiscuity—even where there is substantial evidence that the pastor or church worker is clearly using the counseling sessions to evangelize or proselytize.[34]

Although there might be nuances to each of these examples—nuances that justify the various decisions—the perceived pattern evident in the post-*Lemon* decisions is *inconsistency*. Moreover, a careful reading of the establishment clause cases reveals the suspect nature of the analysis behind the decisions. Often the justices' reasoning was so counterintuitive that these inconsistent results were inevitable.[35]

Just how bad are the court's establishment clause decisions? It is not simply that the decisions are analytically suspect. Stephen Pepper argues that they are "in significant disarray."[36] Mark Tushnet finds the constitutional law of religion to be "incoherent."[37] Leonard Levy calls some decisions "disastrous."[38] Gerard Bradley states that "these counterintuitive judicial commandments are also historically counterfactual."[39]

One might argue that the court's haphazard approach to the establishment clause is inconsequential. The justices are addressing a touchy issue, a sensitive area of constitutional law, and have, by and large, adeptly negotiated the potential landmines. That laudatory assessment is simply invalid. Professor Francis Lee correctly observes that pragmatic reasoning does not equate with principled or prudent reasoning:

> In fact, the voices of reason and common sense would defend the Court's actions regarding both free exercise and establishment clause as being realistic, politically sound, and at bottom, pragmatic. They may be all three, but a Court that is solely realistic, political, and pragmatic may have problems convincing the realistic, pragmatic, and political types that inhabit the halls of Congress and the White House that it is the Constitution, and not the

> Justices, speaking. They may fail—in fact in the realm of religion
> they *have* failed—to persuade. Consequently, they find their deci-
> sions in this area scorned by a majority of Americans and, not sur-
> prisingly, transformed into political issues. Such surely is the case
> with prayers in the public schools and possibly with the issue of aid
> to religious schools. These problems, rather than being resolved,
> seem to have been aggravated, even inflamed, as a result of the
> Court's ministering.[40]

Professor Carter accurately summarizes the reaction of a good many
scholars to the court's treatment of the establishment clause since *Lemon*.
"The embarrassing truth," notes Carter, "is that the Establishment Clause has
no theory; that is, the Supreme Court has not really offered guidance to tell
us when the clause is violated."[41] There does not seem to be a coherent theory to explain how the court *has* interpreted the establishment clause, much less
how the court *should* interpret the clause.

It Perpetuates the Strict Separation Myth

Although there is a debate among those in the academy, and those on the state
and federal courts, regarding the meaning and purpose of the establishment
clause, the separationists/secularists have already largely won the battle for
public opinion. For most Americans, "religious liberty" means the "separation
of church and state" which, in turn, obliges a secular civil society.

In the *Lemon* decision the court launched an interpretation of the establishment clause that has floated adrift in the sea of incoherence. Examining
the case law surrounding the first amendment's establishment clause reveals
an extraordinary lack of consistency. It is very little wonder why, when asked
about the first amendment's religious liberty clauses, people unthinkingly
express their belief that they require "separation of church and state." The
court's confusing interpretation of the establishment clause leaves nearly
everyone somewhat befuddled and looking for an easily identifiable doctrine.
Thus, the result of the *Everson-Lemon* doctrine has been to nurture the myth
of strict separation—a de facto separation if you will.

Stephen Carter suggests that many readers of his book, *The Culture of
Disbelief*, a work in which he advocates strongly welcoming religious expression into dialogic politics, will scratch their heads, wondering if all this talk
does not, in fact, promote public policy which is a colossal violation of the
Constitution.[42] Why the concern by Carter's readers and presumably the readers of this work? The court's jurisprudence has created a mindset that the
establishment clause requires strict separation of church and state. Although
theoretically the court retreated from the *strict* separation doctrine, it is hard
to overestimate the impact the "wall of separation" metaphor has had on the

thinking of the American public. The late M. Glenn Abernathy notes that "the 'establishment clause' of the first amendment has long since been rephrased in the general literature and the popular mind to become simply a guarantee of 'separation of church and state.'"[43]

Former Vice President George Bush unknowingly illustrated just how dramatically the separation doctrine has taken root during the 1988 presidential campaign. Bush related to his audience how he felt when, as a young fighter pilot, he was shot down during World War II:

> Was I scared floating around in a little yellow raft off the coast of an enemy held island, setting a world record for paddling? Of course I was. What sustains you in times like that? Well, you go back to fundamental values. I thought of Mother and Dad, and the strength I got from them—about God, and faith, and *the separation of church and state.*[44]

Perhaps candidate Bush was on to something when he afforded "separation of church and state" the same status in his mind as loved ones, God, and faith. I recall an exchange in one of my classes in civil liberties. We were discussing free exercise clause decisions—most notably *Reynolds v U.S.* (1879)[45] and *Sherbert v Verner* (1963).[46] In *Reynolds*, the court upheld, despite the religious liberty claim of the appellant, national legislation prohibiting polygamy in federal territories. Several decades later in *Sherbert*, the court determined that the government could not withhold unemployment compensation to one who refused to take a job that required her to work on Saturdays—a requirement that cut against her religious beliefs.

One student in the class argued that both decisions were wrongly decided simply because Congress can make *no law* that impacts upon religion—no exemptions, no exceptions. At first glance, it seemed his complaint was more logically located against the *Sherbert* decision than *Reynolds*. It was in the former case that the court required an exemption be given for religious Sabbatarians. Thus, consistent with his argument, no law means no exception—either for the polygamist or for the Sabbatarian.

But the student persisted in arguing that *Reynolds* was still wrong. Why? It turned out that he wanted to protect the state by isolating it from religion. Therefore, he actually required *total* exemption for religious people who were not making a financial claim against the state. If the believer wanted AFDC, drug rehabilitation, a Pell Grant, or, in the case of Ms. Sherbert, unemployment compensation, then he or she must play fully within the rules established by government. No exceptions or exemptions. Otherwise, however, the student wanted religious believers to operate almost as an independent entity within the United States. Not unlike foreign diplomats, religious folks would be under no obligation to follow national or state criminal law. Nor would they receive any of the public welfare benefits offered by society.

When his fellow students started to push his argument to its logical extremes, the more rigid he became. Hence, if the church building were on fire or the police witnessed a burglary in process at the church, too bad. The church needs to get its own fire department and police force. Similarly, the state could not require religious parents to give their children food, shelter, or health care. Government could not enforce child labor laws against religious believers or criminal laws against child abuse or even sacrificing children. Why was he clinging to a position that most of the students thought to be preposterous? Because, he insisted, he believed deeply in the "wall of separation between church and state." And, even if it meant going to such extremes, the high wall must be defended!

My suspicion is that most Americans have not quite made separation into a god, nor the wall metaphor into an altar at which to worship. Most would, I suppose, want to scale the wall, or climb over the wall, before it ever became as high as my student would have it. But I am convinced that most Americans genuinely believe along with my student and, apparently, former President Bush, that the wall of separation is fundamental constitutional language. Law professor Gerard Bradley observed, "'Separation of church and state' is right up there with Mom, apple pie, and baseball in the American iconography."[47] Bradley indicates that the public must be assured that "of course, God and Caesar remain in their respective domains."[48]

Thus, as incoherence goes hand-in-hand with de facto separation, de facto separation gives birth to the "secondary" consequences I will discuss more fully below. Not only, argues Professor Carter, does it make discussions like this one, where one talks about religious dialogue in the public square nearly impossible, it short-circuits a religious perspective on a whole range of policy issues.

The false notion of strict separation is particularly damaging in public schools where administrators, confused by the court, mechanically apply the separation doctrine. This conscious decision to refrain from "establishing religion" only serves to frustrate some religious parents who want their children exposed to their values sometime during the thirty-to-forty hour school week.[49]

How far has religion been extricated from public schools—both at the expense of political dialogue and individual liberties? Social scientist Paul Vitz examined the sixty-five social studies textbooks used by more than eighty-five percent of America's elementary school children. He looked for "primary" references to religious activity—prayer, church attendance, or participation in religious ceremonies, and "secondary" references, such as citing the date when a church was established. Vitz found a total absence of any primary references about typical contemporary American religious life and very few secondary references.[50] Charles Colson notes that Vitz's study reveals the extent of the policy of religious cleansing in the public schools. Often, religion is not permitted even as a way to introduce historical facts:

> Pictures of pilgrims and the first Thanksgiving were bountiful—
> without any mention of to whom thanks was being given. One
> mother told Vitz that her son's social studies book made no refer-
> ence to religion as part of the pilgrim's life. Her son told her that
> "Thanksgiving was when the pilgrims gave thanks to the Indians."
> When the mother called the principal of her son's suburban New
> York City school to point out that Thanksgiving originated when
> the pilgrims thanked God, the principal responded, "That's your
> opinion."[51]

SECONDARY CONSEQUENCES OF SEPARATION

It Helps Secularize the Public Square

In the first three chapters, I argued that religious expression has been trivialized and privatized in an effort to secularize the public square. That observation, while not at all unique to me, is certainly more significant than my simply having identified a group of disgruntled religious folks who feel that they are not taken very seriously in dialogic politics. Several scholars link freedom for religious expression with American vitality and even with national security.

Loren Beth, in his 1958 work *The American Theory of Church and State*, argued that there are eight broad classifications of church-state relationships: pure theocracy, mixed theocracy, total identification, total conflict, erastianism, totalitarianism, total separation, and partial separation.[52] Additionally, Beth noted that although these pure classifications seem more distinct on paper than they ever are in human history, they do exist and have greatly influenced the Western world since before the Christian era. Too, the first seven models do not fit the American situation.[53]

Most Americans would likely agree with Beth that at least most of the models do not square with religious liberty as expressed in the United States Constitution. But what about "total separation"? Surely it "fits the American situation"? Professor Beth rejected total separation for a couple of reasons. First, it is purely a theoretical idea because it is impossible to avoid conflict between church and state. "No state has every achieved it," noted Beth, "nor will any."[54] Total separation assumes that religion is pietistic and privatized, and, with the exception of some of the German pietistic sects and perhaps sometimes the Quakers, religion in Western civilization does not fit the model. Christianity, for example, seeks to guide the believers' actions as well as their spirit and soul. Unless religion were restricted "to so small an area of human activity that it would cease to be a real force in human society," it must inevitably come into conflict with the state.[55]

Second, Beth argued that total separation is just as undesirable as it as impossible. Total separation of church and state is a wholly ineffective means of safeguarding against totalitarianism—the most dangerous model for a democratic people.[56] Totalitarianism permits the state to determine which religions, if any, are permitted to exist. Totalitarians, as their name implies, attempt to control the total person—soul, spirit, body, and economic life— and, as a result, move to crush other institutions in their pathway. The state becomes the religion of the people and, as such, the object of reverence and the highest moral authority.[57]

Beth held that partial separation is the alternative that best protects the state from becoming a pure theocracy and simultaneously prevents the state from subsuming religion. Therefore it moves one step closer toward all-embracing governmental power. Religion may not be necessary to maintain the moral standards of the political community. The state can set those standards. Beth insisted, however, "if *freedom* is to exist in the community, some agency besides the state must be in a position to exert moral influence."[58]

Thus, contrary to those contemporary constitutional philosophers who want to distance religious expression from dialogic politics to safeguard liberal democracy,[59] Beth argued that democracy requires the existence of groups that are in a position to criticize the state not only on political grounds but also on moral grounds. Religion provides just such a critical voice. It offers the nation a moral foundation that claims to be higher than that of the state. Without competing standards for morality the state must articulate and enforce a moral position that most do not believe to be absolute and which could not be judged by reference to any other standard. Whether seen as offering an absolute standard of morality or merely a relative moral position that competes with the state, religion, argued Beth, occupies a crucial position in the society:

> If it represents absolute morality, and infallibility, it provides a definite standard by which to judge the morality of the state and the actions of the state; if it represents merely *another* standard of morality, it still provides a necessary alternative to the state's course of action. Democracy depends greatly on the existence of such an alternative and on the maintenance of the freedom of the citizenry to choose this alternative in preference to that of the state.[60]

"[Partial] separation of church and state, then," argued Beth, "regardless of its other virtues, may be regarded as a major bulwark of the liberal democratic state as opposed to totalitarian democracy."[61] But partial separation, even if embraced by the court, is at odds with the de facto total separation so predominate today. Other writers confirm the relevancy of the argument that Beth expressed nearly forty years ago. They recognize that religion offers an alternative moral agenda to that of the secular state, and it can admonish the government when necessary. Sociologist Robert Bellah, for example, reached many of the same conclusions articulated by Professor Beth. Bellah argues that religion inculcates moral values and commitments essential to the functioning of social life. Religion also gives social and political order a foundation—a divine order, a claim to truth.[62] A. James Reichley is even more direct. He claims that there is a direct link between religion or religious expression, and America's continued success as a free and democratic nation. He suggests that religious people benefit society at large by nurturing the moral values that helps a free society to humanize capitalism and give direction to democracy. "From the beginning of American history," Reichley argues, "religion and the practice of democracy have been closely intertwined."[63]

Law professor Mark Tushnet argues that, in addition to providing a necessary "prophetic voice" by serving as a necessary critic of culture, religious institutions operating in the public sphere are necessary intermediate institutions between individuals and the comprehensive state. How do they serve this function? Professor Tushnet notes that the nation-state was created by subordinating and eventually eliminating "from public life the influence of personal attachments to institutions operating on an other-than-national scale." Religion challenges the secular ruler's claim to unqualified loyalty.[64] Professor Carter's work supports the positions taken by Bellah, Reichley, and Tushnet. He claims that religious institutions help protect society from tyranny by both providing a necessary critical voice and by competing with the state for the allegiance of their adherents.[65]

Richard Neuhaus warns that restricting the autonomy of religious institutions and silencing their voice in the public square can have ominous consequences for America. He fears the "naked public square"—the vacuum created when spiritual truth is jettisoned from the political arena.[66] More than an invasion by a great foreign power, Neuhaus predicts, the effort to establish and maintain the naked public square will be the most likely reason for the collapse of American democratic society. Why? Precisely because of the reasons offered above: religion provides a check on the state and its authority over its citizenry.[67] Absent a religious voice and that necessary check, the state loses its reason to be democratic, fair, and to ensure rights and liberties. "Religion is the singular institution," maintains Neuhaus, "that both keeps the state under transcendent judgement and affirms the divinely given nature of the rights of persons, especially the most vulnerable, in society."[68] Furthermore, the vacuum caused by the reduction of religion would inevitably be filled, and totalitarian monism would be the consequence. Democracy, virtue, and security for individual rights and liberties assume normative truths by which political discourse and action are to be guided and judged.[69]

Why not safeguard religion from government intrusion, and religious minorities from persecution and coercion, by simply commanding complete separation of religion from the state and of religion from politics? Beth, Bellah, Reichley, Tushnet, Carter, and Neuhaus—scholars who are writing from multiple perspectives and who are not associated with extreme theological or political conservativism—tell us why not. First, it is impossible to fully separate religion from the state. Second, a religious voice in the public square and operating outside the actual realm of government is essential to shield democratic society from a totalitarian state.[70]

Although these scholars warn of the consequences should religion become extricated from the public arena, that is exactly what they say is happening. The public square is becoming increasingly secularized, either as a direct result of the court's confused treatment of the religious liberty clauses, or because of the perception that these clauses mandate strict separation, or both.

Professor Tushnet, from out of the confusion in the law of religion, has identified two principles that explain much of what the Supreme Court has done to emasculate religion: the reduction principle and the marginality principle. The reduction principle strips from religious belief anything that would distinguish it from other types of belief. The rituals of religious belief are treated like symbolic speech and tested by the standards developed in symbolic speech cases. Furthermore, the reduction principle applies similar rules to actions motivated by religious belief that govern in cases where speech is suppressed because of its effect on governmental interests.[71] The marginality principle holds that the law need only recognize religion to the degree that religion has no socially significant consequence. It will not do so if religion is socially significant. The marginality principle requires the state balance the interests of religion against its own regulatory interests.[72] The result has been the curtailment of religion's role in the public arena:

> Religion has no distinctive role to play in the shaping of public policy. Indeed, by treating individual preferences as outside the scope of political analysis, the liberal tradition excludes religion from public life. It then seeks a theoretical expression for what it has done. The reduction and marginality principles together provide that expression: religion is still largely private, and its intrusion into the public sphere is small and unimportant.[73]

The degree to which religion has been dismissed from the public sphere puts America on a dangerous pathway. Neuhaus maintains that America has crossed the line (described in chapter 2) that distinguishes between a secular state and a secular society. In many respects ours is now a secular society. The framers had a built-in flexibility that recognized the family, state, religion, and other mediating institutions. They supported the uniqueness of each and understood the necessary tension between the different institutions. Such toleration, notes Neuhaus, is no longer evident.[74] Neuhaus offers several reasons why we have become a secular society: the role of the schools in promoting secularization, the bias of the media away from religion and in favor of the secular society, the disdain that intellectual elites often feel for democracy, and the systematic undermining of religion by the state's appetite for all available public space.[75] Each suggest that those engaged in the quest for secularization profit extraordinarily by perpetuating either de jure or de facto separation.

It Thwarts Individual Rights and Liberties: Persecution Revisited

In the first chapter, I observed that many of those who came to America to escape religious persecution, once in power, became persecutors themselves. The religion clauses of the first amendment were written, in no small part, to protect religious groups and individuals from persecution. One of the consequences, however, of the court's approach to the establishment clause—with its incoherent case law and the emergence of de facto separation—has been an ever-increasing erosion of individual and group religious rights and liberties. Make no mistake about it: bigotry and persecution, some of the very reasons that prompted the framers to draft the first amendment, are still pervasive enough in American society to warrant its retention. Examples of persecution are contemporary, ongoing, and abundant.

For example, a former defense department supervisor, Donald Zimmerman, was barred in the late 1980s from federal employment for five years. Another worker in the office, Michael Pouy, was demoted and fined $1,000. What did they do? They were accused of continually harassing a Jewish co-worker with religious taunts over a two-year period. Pouy and Zimmerman allegedly told Wallace Weiss that he was a "Christ killer," the "resident Jew," and the "rich Jew." During an Easter pageant, the two co-workers reportedly told Weiss that he would have to hang from a cross for killing Jesus.[76]

With the number of racist and anti-Semitic groups on the increase (or at least coming out in the open), a large number of whom clothe themselves in quasi-Christian rhetoric, the brutalization Weiss faced is hardly isolated.[77] For instance, in the Florida panhandle community of Crestview, a Jewish family suffered harassment for their attempt to halt Christian prayers before football

games at the public high school. When Max Berlin, a senior at Crestview High
School, challenged the prayers in federal court, he was subjected to vicious hate
graffiti scrawled on the bathroom walls of the high school. One reported read,
"Max Berlin is one dead Jew. Hitler should have gassed you, too!" Further, the
family car was also vandalized and covered by Nazi swastikas.[78]

In January 1988, twins Athena and Theda Stivers reported to their
father John that their substitute algebra teacher was repeatedly quoting Bible
verses during the class period. When the Stivers, all professed atheists,
protested to the school board against what they felt to be the substitute
teacher's sustained proselytizing, the twins were called "Satanists," serenaded
with "Jesus Loves Me" by their fellow students when they entered a classroom,
and even sent home to avoid the abuse they received.[79]

One might argue that, particularly in the Berlin and Stiver examples,
the student athletes and the substitute math teacher, are simply exercising
their own rights under the free exercise clause and the free speech clause. I will
address that claim more fully below. There is a point, however, where the religious activities of a community, or even a single educator, are likely to engender conduct that exceeds simply offending religious minorities. Such conduct
is similar to the "danger of imminent lawlessness" rule in free speech cases.[80]
Even if the speaker is not personally engaged in unlawful conduct, the authorities can shut down the speech if it poses a danger of imminent lawlessness by
others. Similarly, whether or not the ballplayers or math teacher were directly violating the establishment clause, their actions posed a danger of severe
curtailment of religious liberty. This conduct crossed the line between offending or embarrassing to actually persecuting and coercing.

If the cost to one who refuses to participate in community-initiated or
community-endorsed religious activities, such as classroom prayer or a
pregame invocation, is that he or she is *offended*, then one must seriously question whether or not these activities, likely protected by the free exercise clause
or the free speech clause, should be forbidden by the establishment clause.[81] If,
alternatively, the cost to one who refuses to participate in community religious
activities is *persecution* or *coercion*, then it seems that the nexus between state
and church does violate those intentions upon which the establishment clause
is well accepted: to secure religious liberty and to stop the persecution of religious minorities.[82]

Constitutional historian Leonard Levy, in the footnotes of his book *The
Establishment Clause*, reveals how religious exercises in the public schools can
create behavior that extends beyond simply offending those who do not wish
to participate in the religious exercises. Levy recalls attending school in
DeKalb, Illinois, in 1935 to 1936. There was prayer in the public school, Bible
reading, and "some christological celebration of Christmas." He notes, "my

refusal to participate stigmatized me and unleashed latent anti-Semitism. I learned to associate religion in the public schools with . . . getting beaten up regularly because I was the 'Jew bastard' and 'Christ killer' who refused to pray in school."[83]

The more recent case of Rachael Bauchman illustrates the distinction between "offense" and "coercion/oppression." Ms. Bauchman is one of the few Jewish students at West High School in Salt Lake City, Utah. An honor student, she was selected as a member of the highly competitive choir at West High. While a member of the choir, she raised several objections to some of the practices of the Mormon choir director. First, she said that she felt uncomfortable with the number of "Christian songs" performed by the choir during rehearsal and public presentations.[84] Second, she questioned why the choir should sing two such songs for the graduation ceremony—"Friends" and "The Lord Bless You and Keep You."[85] Finally, she complained that the director would often have the choir sing in local Mormon churches, and, while the choir was on tour, the director invited several Mormon students to share their individual "testimony" to their audiences. "When we go into churches and sing 'Jesus is my Saviour, my King,'" noted Ms. Bauchman, "I can't identify, because Jesus is not my Saviour. I always felt like an outsider."[86]

In addition to threats and verbal harassment, the compromise offered by the school only served to marginalize Ms. Bauchman even further. The director offered to include several "Jewish songs" to the choir's repertoire, and he offered to allow her to skip out of rehearsal when the choir practiced Christian songs.[87] Ms. Bauchman's claim is not simply that she was offended by the inclusion of songs that made reference to Jesus. Her argument is that she was, essentially, coerced into singing songs that cut against her beliefs. No alternative was available unless she wanted to give up her spot in the prestigious choir—or remain as a part-timer. These unacceptable alternatives, coupled with threats and harassment, served to persecute Ms. Bauchman for challenging established choir policy which favored/established one religious faith.[88]

Undoubtedly, some of the persecution faced by Rachael Bauchman, Max Berlin, and the Stiver twins emanated not from their refusal to participate in religious activities, but rather from their efforts to put an end to those activities within their respective communities.[89] Thus, it is difficult to tell just how much of the backlash was due to their refusal to participate in the community religious exercises, the perpetual undercurrent of religious bigotry that will always find some outlet for its expression, the general outrage that emerges from the community when it feels pushed around or is otherwise challenged by dissenters, or from the dubious interpretation by the courts that prompted Bauchman, Berlin, and the Stivers to believe that they could and should put a halt to these "unconstitutional" religious activities.

The Weiss illustration suggests, however, that there is a substantial reservoir of religious intolerance in the American community—intolerance that is manifested at the expense of children in public school and at the workplace. As a result, religious minorities still very much need the protections afforded by the first amendment. Furthermore, Levy's account and Ms. Bauchman's case illustrate the price some undoubtedly continue to pay for standing up for their beliefs by simply refusing to participate in the community's religious activities. They provide substantial justification for carefully interpreting the establishment clause and for exercising extreme caution when bringing church and state too closely together.[90]

If these examples highlight the need for policymakers and the courts to remain sensitive to the religious liberties of Americans—and they surely do—then why raise serious objections to the status quo (the *Everson-Lemon* test)? Because, unfortunately, the application of the *Everson-Lemon* test, its progeny, and the emergence of de facto separation threatens religious liberty just as severely as would unrestrained accommodation.

For example, in *Grand Rapids v Ball* and *Aguilar v Felton*, the Court prevented parochial school students—who are required by the state law to attend school six to eight hours a day and whose parents must pay to support remedial and extracurricular programs in the public schools—from receiving these same benefits, benefits that their state and national policymakers felt should be available to all students, if they are provided by the community after school or on Saturdays.[91]

Furthermore, the perception that the establishment clause erects a wall of separation can cut deeply into the rights of those who, though required by law to attend school, wish to exercise their religious beliefs in ways that, perhaps unlike public prayer or Bible reading, do not foster *coercion* or *oppression*. One such example is the perpetual fight by some school boards and principals to keep religious groups or clubs off campus even though the Supreme Court upheld the right to equal access in 1990.[92]

Moreover, there are myriad examples of religious discrimination in public schools that are not argued before the Supreme Court. In fact, each instance that comes to trial might represent myriad others that never receive legal attention. These less notorious cases, the cases that are not frequently discussed before polling Americans regarding their views toward separation of church and state, reveal very real examples of religious discrimination: students and teachers who are told they are "breaking the law" when they exercise their religious beliefs.

In November 1988, James Gierke, a fifth-grade student at Spring Lake Elementary School in Omaha, Nebraska, finished all of his work in class. His teacher had instituted a class policy that pupils finishing their work could read a book of their choice for the remainder of the period. James picked up his Bible and started to silently read it. The teacher, when she became aware of what he was reading, came over and told James that "he was breaking the law." She instructed him to remove his Bible from the classroom and put it in his locker.[93]

A week later, the same thing took place. James tried to read his Bible after completing his work and his teacher ordered him to put the Bible in his locker. After lunch, he asked if he might retrieve his Bible from his locker. The teacher explained to him that the principal had told the faculty that "no Bibles were allowed in the school." She told him not only could he not read the Bible in class, despite the fact that other students could read materials of their own choosing, but he could not even bring it onto the school grounds.[94] Gierke's story prompted commentator Nat Hentoff to note, "Not even the child's locker could be a sanctuary anymore for the dangerous book. James was ordered to take his Bible home."[95] James' father called the school and asked why James was not only forbidden to read the Bible in class but also had to keep it at home. The principal said "that either a federal or state law commanded her to act as she had." The perplexed father told the principal that he had heard there was a Bible in plain view in the school library. Why could James not check that Bible out, he asked, and read it during his free time? The principal told Mr. Gierke that the Bible in the library was only for reference and it could only be checked out by the adults in the school.[96]

The Gierkes filed suit in U.S. District Court and, unfortunately, the case was settled before it went to trial. The federal courts did not have a chance to rule on the decision. In the meantime, one wonders how many children, in different communities, are told that reading a Bible on campus during their free time is "breaking the law." How many children are told that "no Bibles are allowed" in their school buildings?[97]

Sadly, just as it is likely that the persecution visited upon Berlin, the Stivers, Bauchman, and young Leonard Levy are not isolated instances, James Gierke's story is hardly unique. There are several other examples of discrimination against religious freedom in the public schools:

• A teacher in Colorado was forced to remove his Bible from his desk and to remove Christian literature from the class library even though books about Native American religions were permitted to remain on the shelves.[98]

• Science teacher John Peloza was told not to discuss "religious matters" with students—even if the students initiated the discussions. Peloza was also allegedly told that he must teach evolution as scientific fact (as opposed to introducing the subject as the predominate scientific theory of origins) in his biology classroom.[99]

- A public school math teacher, Lily Ellis, was prohibited from reading her Bible while performing her duties as a lunch-room monitor. Teachers frequently would read material of their choice while on monitor duty , and Ellis was told she could read anything she wanted—except the Bible.[100]

- One school district proposed a policy that would effectively forbid teachers from having any conversation or discussion dealing with religious topics—even among themselves.[101]

- A high school principal prohibited the class valedictorian, Susan Salem, from mentioning Jesus Christ in her valedictory address.[102]

- A Bible club in Texas was prevented from advertising its meetings on the campus community bulletin board if they made reference to Jesus or God.[103]

- In Nazareth, Pennsylvania, the after-school club, "Teens for Christ," was told that its picture would not be included in the yearbook.[104]

- In Illinois, students were *arrested* for gathering for group prayer around their school's flagpole.[105]

- Sam Eversole was told that he could not sing "Jesus Loves Me" in a school talent show because of its "religious nature."[106]

- Eleven-year-old Raymond Raines, of St. Louis, was allegedly sent to the principal's office for praying before lunch. The principal is supposed to have told Raines that "he must discontinue the practice."[107]

- In Maryland, a student was prevented from making a cross for his grandmother's grave in wood shop class. He was told that he could cut, sand, and varnish the two pieces of wood in class, but that he had to assemble the cross at home.[108]

- Professor Patricia Lines reveals that, in some school districts, student distribution of Bibles has been prohibited. She notes that in Florida one girl who gave a report to her class on the New Testament and distributed copies to her friends was taken to the principal's office. The principal confiscated all copies of the New Testament, including her personal copy, and told her that she could not quote the Bible in her book report. One Oklahoma child "caught bowing his head to pray before taking the math section of a standardized test," notes Lines, "was taken to the principal's office and ordered to write 'I will not pray in class' 500 times."[109]

Religious discrimination is not limited to the public schools however. Religious believers still have to fight to evangelize in public parks and on public sidewalks,[110] or to display their advertisements on the community bulletin board at the public library.[111] The small business administration recently denied a loan application for a Christian day care in Ohio.[112] On Ash Wednesday in 1993, a judge told a prosecutor that he had to clean the ashes from his forehead so that the jury might not be influenced by its knowledge of the prosecutor's religiosity.[113]

Marietta Bell, a real estate agent in Arizona, was told by the Arizona attorney general's office that she could not use the "fish symbol," an historically and universally recognized symbol depicting one's faith in Jesus Christ, in her real estate advertisements. Bell used the symbol to indicate that she is not ashamed of her Christian faith and to let those who do business with her know what they might expect from her. She learned that the Arizona fair housing authority actually published an "Advertising Word and Phrase List." In it, eighty-two words are considered "unacceptable" and forty-two are to be used with "caution," including words like Christian, Near Church, Catholic, Jewish, Mosque, Near Church(es), Near Temple, Near Synagogue, and the like. Thus, according to the attorney general, Ms. Bell was violating the law by using the fish symbol in her advertisements and on her business cards.[114]

Like James Gierke, Ms. Bell filed suit in federal court. As with the Gierkes, the Arizona attorney general settled the case before it came to trial. The settlement agreement acknowledges that the use of Christian symbols, like the "fish symbol," in real estate advertising, newspaper advertisements, in business cards, and flyers is not a violation of Arizona law.[115] Again, one wonders how many of these small battles must individual religious believers win before they can enjoy their basic freedoms of religion and speech? Too, one wonders how many religious people do not have the financial resources, the time, or even the gumption to take on their state's attorney general?

It is difficult to blame educators and local community officials who are led to believe that the Constitution demands absolute separation of church and state when they restrict religious liberties. It is probably a bit tougher to excuse the highest legal officers of particular states for making that same mistake. Whether de jure or de facto, it is most certainly time to scale the wall of separation between church and state. Just as it is unreasonable, however, to believe that uncontrolled accommodation between church and state will have no negative impact on churches and individuals, it is unrealistic to believe total separation has not fostered religious discrimination.

In an address delivered in early 1995, columnist Molly Ivins proclaimed that, while the Constitution's language did not include the phrase "separation of church and state," separation represented the vital spirit behind the law. It is imperative, noted Ivins, that Americans protect both the spirit and letter of the law—the wall of separation as it informs the actual language of the establishment clause—from an attack by those on the religious right.[116]

I disagree. As metaphors go, the "wall of separation" metaphor has been a flop. The consequences are just too severe to allow it to continue as the spirit that breathes life into the first amendment.

SIX

A Better Way?

Alternatives to the *Everson-Lemon* Doctrine

In the first several chapters, I have maintained that there are those committed to secularizing public debate in the United States. One of the most effective strategies available to proponents of secularization is to push for the "separation" of church and state in the constitutional arena. The battle over how to interpret the establishment clause is more than a contest among academics and judges. The consequences of separation are very real and, often, quite inauspicious. Therefore, it is time to search for an alternative approach that has the effect of securing religious freedom and more fully protecting a place for religious expression in the marketplace of ideas.

In this chapter, I look at several such alternatives already proffered by those on the bench and in the academic literature. Each of the alternatives is, arguably, vastly superior to the court's establishment clause and free exercise clause jurisprudence. The question is, will any of them take us beyond the incoherence fostered by the jurisprudence emanating from the "wall of separation"? Make no mistake about it. There are better ways to interpret the establishment clause than did the Supreme Court in *Everson v Board of Education*[1] and *Lemon v Kurtzman*.[2] In fact, several have already been offered by particular justices on the court and by those in the academic literature who reject, wholly or in part, the *Lemon* test.

In the first portion of this chapter, I consider some of the judicially crafted alternatives: Justice O'Connor's "endorsement test," Justice Kennedy's "noncoercion test," and Chief Justice Rehnquist's case for "nonpreferential accommodation." If the alternatives offered from the bench are not particularly wide ranging, is there a persuasive alternative available in the academic literature? In the second part of this chapter, I consider two very recent, and severely different, entries into the extensive church-state debate: Jesse Choper's book, *Securing Religious Liberty*, and Steven Smith's, *Foreordained Failure*.[3] While there are several alternatives proposed in the scholarly literature related to church and state,[4] Professor Choper offers a "comprehensive" thesis for securing religious liberty. Conversely, Professor Smith argues that all such efforts to articulate a constitutional principle of religious freedom are "foreordained" to failure.

ALTERNATIVES FROM THE BENCH

Unsatisfied with *Lemon's* three-part test, Justice O'Connor offered her own alternative in the early 1980s: the "endorsement test." In *Wallace v Jaffree*,[5] Justice O'Connor defined the endorsement test:

> Direct government action endorsing religion or a particular religious practice is invalid under this approach because it "sends a message to nonadherents that they are outsiders, not full members of the political community." Under this view, *Lemon's* inquiry as to the purpose and effect of a statute requires courts to examine whether government's purpose is to endorse religion and whether the statute actually conveys a message of endorsement.[6]

Note that Justice O'Connor does not jettison the *Lemon* test. The endorsement test is designed to give some analytic content to the purpose prong and the effects prong of *Lemon*. For instance, what does it mean that public policy, under scrutiny by the judiciary, must satisfy some secular purpose? What does it mean that its primary effect can neither advance or inhibit religion? O'Connor argues that they mean that government cannot convey a message of endorsement.[7]

Justice O'Connor argues, correctly, that the endorsement test is superior to *Lemon* because it recognizes that "the secular interests of government and religious interests of various sects and their adherents will frequently intersect, conflict, and combine."[8] For example, government should not be concerned that its efforts to criminalize murder might be held invalid under the establishment clause because they support the Bible's teachings against unlawful killing. The endorsement test, notes O'Connor, does not prevent government from acknowledging religion or even from considering religion when formulating public policy. What does the endorsement test do? It prohibits government from "conveying or attempting to convey a message that *religion* or a *particular religious belief* is favored or preferred."[9]

Justice Kennedy is also dissatisfied with *Lemon*. In his alternative approach, he argues that there is a fine line between the accommodation of religion and the establishment of religion. The line is crossed when the government either gives direct benefits to religion so that it establishes a state religion (or even religious faith generally), or if it "coerces" anyone to "support or participate in any religion or its exercise."[10] What constitutes coercion? Kennedy offers several examples: "Taxation to supply the substantial benefits that would sustain a state-established faith, direct compulsion to observance, or government exhortation to religiosity that amounts in fact to proselytizing."[11]

Kennedy's approach is a substantial departure from both *Lemon* and O'Connor's endorsement test. So long as government does not provide direct financial benefits to religion, or coerce someone to participate in activities that violate his or her religious freedom, government need not be wary of openly permitting a religious voice:

> If government is to participate in its citizen's celebration of a holiday that contains both a secular and a religious component, enforced recognition of only the secular aspect would signify the callous indifference toward religious faith that our cases and traditions do not require.[12]

Thus, for the court to squash the government's efforts to recognize the religious underpinnings of a holiday, notes Kennedy, is not neutrality, but a pervasive attempt to "insulate government from all things religious."[13] Government is not required by the religion clauses to accommodate religion in this way, but it is not forbidden to do so either.[14]

Kennedy's alternative might be characterized as a form of preferentialism. His noncoercion test permits the government to prefer religion to nonreligion just as long as, in exercising this preference for religion, it forbids coercion.[15]

Let me offer an illustration. In the state of Utah, July 24 is a legal state holiday—Pioneer Day. Pioneer Day celebrates the founding of Utah in 1847. It is a secular holiday, but it would be "refusing to acknowledge the plain fact, and the historical reality" that it is linked pretty closely with the history of the Mormon Church. The Mormons, under the direction of Brigham Young, were, arguably, the group that "founded" Utah in 1847. It would seem plausible for the state, according to Kennedy, to support the religious character of the holiday so long as the state did not coerce anyone into participating in the celebration. The state can prefer religion to nonreligion, and include religious symbolism, imagery, and argument along with secular symbolism, imagery, and argument.

Chief Justice Rehnquist, in his dissenting opinion in *Wallace v Jaffree* (and when he was Justice Rehnquist), articulated perhaps the most outrage toward *Lemon*.[16] He challenged the very foundations upholding the separation/neutrality doctrine articulated in *Lemon*: that government must be neutral in its treatment of religion and nonreligion:

> The Establishment Clause did not require government neutrality between religion and irreligion nor did it prohibit the federal government from providing non-discriminatory aid to religion. There is simply no historical foundation for the proposition that the Framers intended to build the "wall of separation" that was constitutionalized in Everson.[17]

Thus, the entirety of the court's post-*Everson* establishment clause jurisprudence, notes Rehnquist, is neither "principled or unified." Rather, the *Everson-Lemon* doctrine has, "with embarrassing candor conceded that the 'wall of separation' is merely a 'blurred, indistinct, and variable barrier,' which 'is not wholly accurate,' and can only be 'dimly perceived.'"[18]

If not the separation doctrine, or *Lemon's* test of benevolent neutrality, then what does the establishment clause require? Rehnquist argues that it forbids government from establishing a national religion, or from showing preference among religious sects or denominations. As Justice O'Connor observed, government will inevitably intersect with religion. Rehnquist not only concedes that such will happen, but that government's accommodation of religion is healthy. When government does accommodate religion, then it must be careful to do so without showing preference:

> Undoubtedly the spirit of the Constitution will require, in all these cases, that care be taken to avoid discrimination in favor of or against any one religious denomination or sect; but the power to do any of these things does not become unconstitutional simply because of its susceptibility to abuse.[19]

Rehnquist's nonpreferentialism does more than modify *Everson-Lemon*. It offers a clear-cut alternative to the three-prong test and, in fact, offers a clear alternative to the separation doctrine, period.

One important distinction between the positions held by O'Connor, Rehnquist, and Kennedy relates to the relationship between government and religion and nonreligion. O'Connor argues that the establishment clause must protect against the government's endorsement of religion over nonreligion. As I will argue more fully in the next chapter, this means that the policymakers must take two steps when evaluating whether or not a proposed policy violates the establishment clause. First, they must determine whether or not the policy favors one religion over the others. If they are sure that government has not endorsed a particular religion, then they are ready for the second step. They must determine that the policy does not endorse religion over nonreligion. If it does then, to safeguard against making the nonreligious feel like "outsiders," the policy will not withstand constitutional scrutiny.

Rehnquist, circa 1985, abandons O'Connor's two-part approach. He would treat nonreligion, or irreligion, as an alternative religious viewpoint. To satisfy the establishment clause, the government must be neutral—it must not give preference to any of the competing viewpoints. Rehnquist's understanding of the establishment clause is the most consistent with what might be called a real-world definition of neutrality.

So, looking at the various positions offered by the court, here is what we have:

THE POSITIONS PURPORTED TO BE OFFERED BY THE COURT:

the separation doctrine (Justice Black)
the neutrality doctrine (Justice Burger)
the endorsement test—to flesh out neutrality (Justice O'Connor)
Kennedy's noncoercion test (Justice Kennedy)
Rehnquist's nonpreferentialism test (Justice Rehnquist)

But, in reality, here are the various interpretations the justices have given to the establishment clause:

ACTUAL POSITIONS OFFERED BY THE COURT:

the separation doctrine	used when the court means to speak of *strict separation*
the neutrality doctrine	used when the court means to speak of *softer separation*
noncoercion	used when the court means to speak of *preferentialism*
nonpreferential accommodation	used when the court means to speak of *neutrality*

O'Connor's endorsement test is, of course, absorbed within the neutrality doctrine which, in reality, makes it a test for the "softer separation" described in chapter 4.

Essentially, that is it. When it comes to interpreting the establishment clause, these are the options provided by the court: Separation—strict or softer (spicy or mild?), preference, and neutrality.[20]

The way the court has interpreted the establishment clause is both deceptive and quite limited. There are several positions offered by the various justices on the court since 1947. The most important interpretations are that the establishment clause requires the separation of church and state (the separation doctrine), and that the establishment clause requires neutrality between government and religion and nonreligion. Judicial modifications have emerged from efforts to improve upon the neutrality doctrine—Justice O'Connor's endorsement test, Justice Kennedy's noncoercion test, and Justice Rehnquist's call for nonpreferential accommodation. Justice O'Connor's endorsement test is better than *Lemon*, but since it largely maintains *Lemon*'s purpose and effects prongs, it therefore perpetuates *Lemon*'s definition of neutrality. This definition is, as I noted above, simply the "softer" definition of separation introduced in *Everson*. Justice Kennedy's coercion test is better still. However, Kennedy offers what amounts to, in many ways, the "preference" of religion over nonreligion—a far more radical departure from the ideas of separation and neutrality that dominate modern establishment clause jurisprudence. Only Chief Justice Rehnquist's alternative, nonpreferential accommodation, is consistent with an authentic definition of "neutrality."

But, in fact, each of the interpretations, tests, or doctrines identified above actually masks a more basic meaning. When the court invokes the separation doctrine, it really means to speak of strict separation of church and state—the kind of separation articulated in *Everson*'s dicta, and, subsequently, in *McCollum v Board of Education* (1948),[21] and *Engel v Vitale* (1962).[22] When the court invokes the neutrality doctrine, it really implies the softer definition of separation that was introduced in *Everson*'s holding, and repeated in *Zorach v Clausen* (1952)[23] and *Abington Township v Schempp* (1963).[24] When Justice Kennedy offers noncoercion as the proper foundation for the interpretation of the establishment clause, he really permits a mild dose of preferentialism. When Justice Rehnquist advocates nonpreferential accommodation, he really is calling for neutrality as it is properly defined.

THE RELIGION CLAUSES AND JUDICIAL AUTHORITY

The alternatives to *Everson* and *Lemon* are not limited to the judiciary. If one surveys the vast literature that makes up the "church-state debate" in constitutional law, he or she will discover that, albeit for substantially different reasons, there is nearly unanimous criticism of the Supreme Court's treatment of the first amendment's religion clauses.[25] Those familiar with this literature can surely verify the observation that few constitutional scholars, if any, are fully pleased with the court's establishment clause and free exercise clause jurisprudence.

Two legal scholars, Jesse Choper and Steven Smith, are among the most recent participants in the church-state fray.[26] Although quite unintentionally, since neither is responding directly to the other, Choper and Smith provide their readers with a debate. They both acknowledge the shortcomings in the court's establishment clause and free exercise clause jurisprudence, but beyond that point of agreement, Choper and Smith part company about as seriously as two scholars can. Choper faults the court for providing no clear, consistent, single principle for adjudicating the religious liberty clauses. To remedy the situation, he offers one. Smith argues that it is precisely the quest *to* discover, and articulate, a constitutional principle of religious freedom that has left the religion clauses in shambles. He thoroughly rejects any continued efforts to do so.

Those who read either Choper or Smith, or, preferably, Choper *and* Smith, will recognize the importance of their respective arguments. My suspicion, however, is that few will find that either author has provided an acceptable solution to the ongoing church-state debate. What they might discover, surprisingly, is that Choper and Smith have said much about judicial authority—about both its necessity and the potential limits thereof.

Professor Choper's treatise is most ambitious.[27] His comprehensive approach to the religion clauses is made up of four principles: the "deliberate disadvantage" principle, the "burdensome effect" principle, the "intentional advantage" principle, and the "independent impact" principle.[28] His cohesive theory is a substantial departure from the court's holdings in *Lemon* and *Employment Division v Smith* (1990).[29]

The "deliberate disadvantage" principle would hold that government action that intentionally prejudices individuals because they do or do not have certain religious beliefs violates the free exercise clause unless the government can demonstrate a compelling interest. Choper notes that the principle is designed to protect against hostility visited upon religious groups in much the same way that the equal protection clause protects racial and ethnic groups.[30] It is worth noting, argues Choper, that the sort of overt discrimination covered under this principle is very rare, although the court did address just such an example in *Church of the Lukumi Babalu Aye, Inc. v City of Hialeah* (1993).[31]

While the deliberate disadvantage principle is pretty straightforward, the "burdensome effect" principle is far more elaborate. It tries to fashion a general theory for religious-based exemptions when discrimination against religious faith or action is not deliberate, but rather is an impact of what otherwise is a secular law enacted for neutral purposes.[32] In such instances,

Choper argues that the free exercise clause should require an exemption from the legislation if the following conditions are met: the violation has to be one that involves "extratemporal" consequences (the person believes that his or her "soul" is in jeopardy); that there is a clear, cognizable injury; that the belief is sincerely held; that there is a limited exemption for the parties in question rather than a total abandonment of the regulation; that an alternative burden can be imposed; and finally, if the state has no compelling interest.[33]

The "intentional advantage" principle permits government programs to deliberately favor religious interests or to provide exemptions because of religious beliefs, unless they violate the establishment clause. Such programs would only violate the establishment clause if they pose a significant threat to religious liberty or if they are discriminatory.[34] Essentially, a program would be held unconstitutional under the intentional advantage principle if it either coerces people to "violate their existing religious tenets, or to engage in religious activities or adopt religious beliefs when they would not otherwise do so," or if it compels people to "afford financial support either to their own religion or to that of others."[35]

Finally, Choper's "independent impact" principle, like the burdensome effect principle, evaluates the constitutionality of programs which, although having a nonreligious purpose, a general applicability, and independent secular impact, have the effect of benefiting religion. Such programs would still violate the establishment clause if they posed a danger to religious liberty as defined above.[36]

Participants in the church-state debate will quickly recognize that Choper's principles would dramatically change the landscape of the court's establishment clause and free exercise clause jurisprudence. For example, with respect to public schools, Choper's approach would retain the prohibition against vocal prayer and Bible reading, graduation prayers, and on-campus released time programs. Yet it would permit placing the Ten Commandments in public school classrooms, and introducing creation science courses in science classes (as well as laws *restricting* the teaching of evolution in science courses), while at the same time, it would prohibit off-campus released time programs. With respect to "official" acknowledgments of religion, the approach would retain Sunday closing laws and permit public displays of religious symbols during holidays. It would ban, however, paid chaplains (legislative, military, and prison) and prohibit the display of nativity scenes in a county courthouse. More important, it would permit a government to officially endorse a particular religion—"Christianity is our religion." Finally, with respect to financial accommodation offered to church-related institutions, Choper's approach would retain the types of prohibitions articulated in *Lemon* and its progeny, but it would also do away with property tax exemptions for religious groups and would prohibit the usage of financial aid for the blind at parochial schools or colleges.[37]

Thus, on paper, Choper is successful. He does articulate a comprehensive thesis for adjudicating all kinds of cases arising under the religion clauses. He integrates the establishment clause and the free exercise clause and yet protects their different functions. The theory raises more than a few concerns, however.

First, it is a good thing that Choper believes that an energetic role for the court is justified when it comes to religious liberty cases because the amount of oversight and ministering by the court required to apply Choper's comprehensive approach would be massive. Granted, some decisions would be made relatively easy. If a policymaking body were foolish enough to craft a law that discriminates against religion on its face, it is unconstitutional. If a law provides any financial assistance to a church or religious group, it too is generally unconstitutional—with a few exceptions (vouchers given to parents for usage in parochial schools).[38] But Choper's approach still requires substantial judicial micromanaging. For example, what constitutes "coercion"? And, consider the particulars of the burdensome effect test. The court must define "religion" by determining whether or not a belief has "extratemporal" consequences, and it has to decide if that belief is sincerely held. The court must determine the significance of a level of injury and make sure the government imposes an alternative burden on the recipient of any religious-based exemption. This is on top of the more traditional review of the program to determine whether or not it is justified by a compelling interest. The prospect of an increased role for the judiciary in interpreting the religion clauses hardly sounds attractive. As Professor Francis Lee observed, "these problems [in the realm of religion], rather than being resolved, seem to have been aggravated and even inflamed as a result of the Court's ministering."[39]

Second, Choper's approach is, in many respects, more of an illustration of his general theory of judicial review than it is a successful and workable alternative approach to the establishment clause and free exercise clause. My guess is that very few jurists and scholars will embrace Choper's alternative. That conclusion comes as no shock to the author. He agrees. Choper notes, "I know of no one—including me—who does not disagree with some, if not many, of the results my approach produces."[40] Particularly, Choper is concerned that his principles permit school boards to excise the study of evolution from the curriculum, governments to erect sectarian displays on public property, and, most disturbingly, they actually permit a government to officially endorse a particular religion. His concerns are understandable since he has fashioned an approach that, under the guise of interpreting the establishment clause, protects the authority of government to *establish* a religion! But,

notes Choper, he could think of no way to accomplish these ends and still protect his conception of the proper role of the court in exercising its power of
judicial review.[41] It is precisely that quandary that justifies a serious look at
Professor Smith's work.

Smith begins with a few pivotal observations. He notes that there is
plenty of scholarship addressing the Constitution's treatment of religious liberty, but on the whole, the scholarship suffers from a malaise because no one
is happy with the court's doctrines or decisions. Thus, generally, scholarly
writing in the church-state debate amounts largely to policy advocacy.
Everyone wants to tell the court what it should *do* about religious freedom.[42]

It is not as though the court cannot use the advice. Smith agrees that
the court's intervention has proven counterproductive. He notes that, in
Everson v Board of Education (1947), the court plunged into the religious liberty arena without considering either the historical meaning of the religion
clauses or the practical consequences of its intervention. However, Smith's
objective is not to offer another test or another theory for interpreting the
establishment clause and the free exercise clause. It is, instead, to rethink the
court's role in fleshing out religious liberty in the United States.[43]

The problem that plagues judges and constitutional scholars is precisely their quest to discover *the* single correct principle of religious freedom
embodied in the Constitution. Smith argues that this is the wrong objective.
First, seeking a single principle to define the meaning and scope of religious
freedom produces, in judges and scholars, a single conception of religious freedom. Thus, it fosters in them a tendency to see others as either "for" religious
freedom or "against" religious freedom instead of recognizing that, for the
most part, the competitors in the church-state debate are all "for" religious
freedom. They are simply providing different visions of religious freedom.[44]

A better quest is not to find and articulate the single principle, but
rather, which version of religious freedom a person believes in, "and the normative question is which version of religious freedom is most attractive or
sound, either generally or in a given context." Smith's effort is to identify and
respond directly to two approaches that judges and scholars employ "in an
effort to discern *the Constitution's* theory or principle of religious freedom": the
"originalist" approach and the "theoretical" approach.[45]

Originalism is an oft used tool to discover the single meaning of the
religion clauses. It is implemented by those who advocate strict separation of
church and state, and by those who insist that the Constitution permits, and
might even require, government accommodation of religion. Not surprisingly,
it makes up a large bulk of the literature in the church-state debate. Smith
argues that originalism will not yield a single principle of the establishment or
the free exercise clause. Why not? Surprisingly, it is not because scholars can-

not uncover the intentions of the framers, but because once these intentions are exposed, the honest scholar will concede that the framers did not intend to articulate a single principle of religious freedom.[46]

Smith argues that, at the time of the founding, issues like religious freedom generated two different types of questions: "first-order (substantive) questions," and "second-order (jurisdictional) questions."[47] He notes that, with respect to religious freedom, the framers did not attempt to answer the first order questions because of the irreconcilable differences between those who were traditionalists—folks who believed that religion is of value to the state and that to protect its development, government should support religion—and the voluntarists—folks who agreed that religion is vital to the political and social order but who rejected the idea of government support for religion often because they felt that such support would be harmful to the cause of religion. Since they did not agree which position should prevail, they avoided first-order questions. They adopted no substantive principle or theory of religious liberty. Instead, they answered the second-order questions. They ceded substantive decisions about religious liberties over to the states. And, as one might expect, there is evidence that some states implemented the traditionalist position (e.g., Massachusetts), while others embraced the voluntarist position (e.g., Virginia).[48] The framers offered no single or substantive theory for interpreting either the establishment clause or the free exercise clause.[49] And, by finding one in *Everson*, the court actually *repealed* the first amendment's religion clauses rather than to incorporate them. The court repealed them by fashioning a national, constitutional law, theory, and principle.[50]

Quite apart from an originalist approach to religious liberty, there are a number of judges and scholars who will insist that there must be a single principle of religious liberty. They will develop a theoretical assessment to discover it. Smith notes that the attempt to offer a theoretical approach to religious freedom is consistent with a judicial philosophy that sees law as a coherent whole, an integrated system, a body. It is, therefore, remarkably similar to those who develop elaborate theories of speech, equality, privacy, representation, and property (pp. 55–56).

The problem with the theoretical approach, briefly, is that it "founders on a basic theoretical conundrum."[51] The function of a theory of religious freedom is, argues Smith, to mediate among a variety of competing secular and religious positions, or to explain how government should umpire between these competing positions. To perform its function, however, the theory will inevitably prefer one of those positions at the expense of all others. "But a theory that privileges one of the competing positions and rejects others a priori," notes Smith, "is not truly a theory of religious freedom at all."[52] He elaborates upon the difficulty with preferred positions, argues against the possibility of fashioning a theory of neutrality between religious and secular concerns, and, finally, reveals how a theory that simply advocates a secular state fails to protect religious freedom.[53]

Finally, Smith reconsiders the "what to do?" question. He offers no "prescription for a new regime of religious freedom," but argues that his work does challenge two assumptions: first, that judicial review must be based upon something called "principle," and second, whether or not the courts "have a central role to play in the realization and protection of religious freedom."[54] He concludes by suggesting that "judicial intervention under the Constitution into matters of religious freedom is illegitimate and unjustified." He maintains that the myriad discussions about religious freedom will be more fruitful when scholars ease their fixation with judicial review and "relinquish their accompanying demand that the meaning of religious freedom be cabined within the narrow confines of a constitutional 'principle'."[55]

Like Choper, Professor Smith also acknowledges that his thesis is likely to be unpopular.[56] He will be challenged by scholars whose interpretation of the historical evidence at the time of the founding lead them to argue that the framers *did* indeed intend for a clear, single principle of religious freedom.[57] He will also receive criticism, generally, from those who are frightened by what his argument portends for the church-state debate, specifically, and for judicial power, generally. Perhaps ironically, although he rejects a comprehensive principle for interpreting the religion clauses, his observations about the futility of judicial review in this area might well suggest a more general approach to judicial authority (a theory of when *not* to exercise judicial power).

Undoubtedly, the criticism he is likely to receive most often, and most fervently, is that assuming the validity of his thesis, how *can* we talk about religious freedom? And what *should* we do to protect religious liberty? Is it acceptable, much less possible, to return to 1791, and therefore, to turn the whole question of defining individual liberties over to the states? And assuming that option is acceptable, what are the best of the many visions for religious liberty that they might choose? It still seems that *somebody* will be debating terms like "separation," "neutrality," "endorsement," "facial neutrality," "religious-based exemptions," and all the other jargon that permeates the ongoing discussion regarding how best to interpret the establishment clause and the free exercise clause.

Further, Professor Smith's argument against a principle predicated upon "neutrality" presumes that the legislatures and the courts maintain the two-step definition of neutrality discussed above. First, government must be neutral between competing religions, and then, secondly, government must be neutral between religion and nonreligion. His argument does not take out a neutrality principle where neutrality is defined to require that government must be neutral between the all-competing "religious" beliefs (one of which is what heretofore has been generally identified as "nonreligion").

So, Professor Choper and Professor Smith do contribute to the range of alternatives from which to interpret the first amendment's establishment clause. While both are irritated with the court's approach to the religious liberty clauses, Choper provides a full-fledged theory to undergird his specific principles for adjudicating the religion clauses. Smith takes a hammer to all such theories, and suggests that, rather than continuing to fashion a single principle upon which to interpret the religion clauses, the court should get out of the game. Professor Choper's approach, rather similar to Justice Kennedy's coercion test, would actually permit government to prefer, and even establish, religion. Professor Smith provides an alternative (of sorts) that is likely to be even more unacceptable to jurists and scholars.

From the court we have the choice of strict separation or softer separation (articulated in *Everson* and *Lemon*, and modified by O'Connor's endorsement test), preference (Kennedy's coercion test), and neutrality (Rehnquist's nonpreferentialism). From Choper and Smith, we can opt either for a comprehensive, exhaustive attempt to harmonize all the jurisprudence decided under the religion clauses, or we can hope that the court recognizes the failure inherent in seeking a single principle from which to interpret the religion clauses and, therefore, abandons them altogether to the states. In the next chapter, I will discuss which of these alternatives seems substantially more persuasive.

SEVEN

Beyond Incoherence:

Making Sense of the Church-State Debate

In the previous chapter, I reviewed some of the alternatives advanced by judges and scholars that are, admittedly, better than the court's approach to the establishment clause articulated in *Everson v Board of Education* (1947)[1] and *Lemon v Kurtzman* (1971).[2] Of the various options, one stands out as superior. In this chapter, I urge a serious reconsideration of Chief Justice William Rehnquist's nonpreferentialism (a version of which I will call "authentic neutrality"), and I discuss the advantages of this approach.[3]

There are two substantial benefits to an authentic neutrality.. First, it should harmonize the court's discordant jurisprudence—a jurisprudence doomed to incoherence from the outset by the way the court used the terms "separation" and "neutrality" back in *Everson*. The court's usage of separation and neutrality permits one of three possible interpretations. First, the court could have been offering the two terms as synonyms. That alternative is silly. Neither the commonly used definition, or a legal definition, of neutrality will permit such usage. Separation involves two or more persons who sever their existing relationship. Neutrality requires one be a third party to those in or out of a relationship.

Second, the court could have been isolating neutrality as a subcomponent of separation. This, too, is flawed because separation cannot coexist conceptually with neutrality when separation is the dominant concept. Neutrality cannot emerge from separation. If a nation X is neutral in its relationship with countries A and B, and country B is destroyed (or subsumed within country A), then X can no longer be neutral toward A, because neutrality, even following separation, requires there be a third party to whom X can be neutral. Similarly, the court cannot require government neutrality with religion. That would require the government to be both a third party and a participant to the same relationship simultaneously.

Third, the court could have been requiring both separation then neutrality—and leave neutrality, properly defined, as the dominant concept. This scenario presumes that government would separate from an established/quasi-established relationship. Then, following the separation, government would be free to be neutral between all competing religions. It is very similar to a nation engaged in apartheid first separating itself from the preferred/established race, and then finding itself free to be fair and neutral between all races and ethnic groups within the nation.

The beauty of embracing authentic neutrality is that both separation and accommodation can stem from "neutrality." Nation X can be neutral between countries A and B by cutting off benefits to both, or by offering them both weapons, food, or entrée into X's economic markets. Similarly, Congress and the states could, with equal constitutional legitimacy, embrace a policy of separation or accommodation depending upon the wishes of their people, the constraints upon their budgets, and the like. One caveat: if the state engages in either financial or ideological accommodation, it must be nonpreferential; it must be neutral in the formation and the application of public policy. If a particular policy proves coercive, oppressive, or partisan in either its formation or application, then it will not survive constitutional scrutiny. So, for example, vocal prayer in the public schools would probably not survive, whereas a moment of silent prayer and meditation most certainly would.

The second advantage emerging from authentic neutrality is that it keeps the church from the state and the state from the church without employing the "wall of separation" metaphor. As a result, America can begin the process of eradicating de facto separation. This will certainly be of extraordinary benefit to those Americans who want to exercise their religious liberty but find themselves at odds with teachers, employers, merchants, and others within the community.

Moreover, eradicating the perception that the Constitution requires separation should better protect religious expression in the marketplace of ideas. When Americans debate public policy, say, for instance, how to "ration" health care, religious voices will be welcome at the table. For example, does the state have to pay for heart surgery on an 87-year-old man in Wildwood Nursing home when, if the surgery is successful, it will mean that he might live three to six months on life support equipment in the hospital at an additional cost of $550,000 above the price tag for the surgery itself? The economist will offer his or her input. The medical community will talk about the limitations of the procedure. The social scientist might talk about public opinion. Additionally, the minister might enter into the discussion, with the understanding that his or her input will be valued to the degree that members of the community find it persuasive. The minister will not be eschewed from public debate because of the perception that to permit his or her participation would violate "the separation of church and state" and the secularist baggage that accompanies that expression.

THE ESTABLISHMENT CLAUSE AND "AUTHENTIC NEUTRALITY"

If one one gets beyond the camouflage, one will find that there is a fairly limited range of alternatives when it comes to interpreting the establishment clause.[4] One can champion the cause of *separation*—either strict separation or the softer kind traceable through from *Everson* to *Zorach v Clauson*[5] to *Abington Township v Schempp*[6] to *Lemon*. One might advocate government *preference* toward/*toleration* of religion in general, or even a particular expression of religious faith, as long as the state permits people to freely exercise their own respective faiths. Finally, one can read the establishment clause to require *neutrality* between government and the competing "religious" truth claims.

And, as I indicated above, I think one of these alternatives is superior and should be the bedrock for the court's interpretation of the establishment clause. Rehnquist's "nonpreferential accommodation," which is, again, synonymous with a common-sense understanding of neutrality, accomplishes several laudable goals. First, neutrality is the only alternative reading of the establishment clause that makes sense. I will demonstrate below that, in no small part, the court was doomed to incoherence from the time it introduced the wall of separation metaphor in *Everson*. By interpreting the Constitution's establishment clause to require neutrality, the court permits legislative flexibility. State and national legislators can pass legislation that either requires separation or accommodation, and still be consistent with the establishment clause's requirement of neutrality. Most important, it overcomes the consequences inherent within the "wall of separation" language proffered by the court.[7] I am not opposed to the idea that the establishment clause separates, in some form or fashion, government and religion, but the separation *doctrine* and the public perception that the establishment clause requires separation have dramatically outlived their usefulness.

The Supreme Court has defined the establishment clause to require separation of church and state (*Everson, McCollum*,[8] *Engel v Vitale*[9]). The court has also defined the establishment clause to require neutrality (*Everson, Zorach, Schempp, Lemon*). In the nearly fifty years since *Everson*, the court has softened and yet perpetuated the separation doctrine, embraced and elaborated upon its understanding of neutrality and, as a result, has created a theory of church-state relations that brings the two concepts together in one of three ways:

1. The court has defined separation *as* neutrality—so that they are synonyms and the terms can be used interchangeably.

2. The court has isolated neutrality as a subcomponent of separation.

3. The court has interpreted the establishment clause to require *both* separation and neutrality between church and state with neutrality emerging from separation.

Of the three interpretations, only the third is lucid. The others do not make sense. Unfortunately, the final interpretation does not jibe with most of the alternative approaches to the establishment clause (e.g., strict separation, the softer form of separation, *Lemon*'s neutrality, no endorsement, or noncoercion). It only squares with authentic neutrality.

One way to summarize the court's treatment of separation and neutrality is to argue they have been interpreted as synonyms. Thus, Justice Black, in *Everson*, intended to use the two words interchangeably in order to both create the separation doctrine and safeguard against hostility toward religion. If we were to diagram the *Everson* decision it might look something like this:

1. The establishment clause (EC) means strict separation (S) between government and religion. Thus the establishment clause is synonymous with separation.

2. Strict separation, however, often engenders hostility (H) between government and religion.

3. Therefore, the establishment clause also means there must be neutrality (N) between government and religion and nonreligion. Thus the establishment clause is synonymous with neutrality.

4. As a result, strict separation means, or is synonymous with, neutrality.

PUT IN THE FORM OF AN EQUATION IT WOULD READ:

Variables: Establishment Clause (EC)
             Is defined to mean (Means)
             Separation (S)
             Hostility (H)
             Neutrality (N)

Equation: EC means S, EC cannot tolerate H, therefore EC
             means N.
             Therefore EC means S, EC means N, therefore S
             means N.

It is a formula designed to produce chaos.

It is unlikely, however, that either Justice Black or the court intended to proffer this interpretation. Put very simply, it is a preposterous interpretation. Separation does not mean neutrality. Separation and neutrality cannot be used interchangeably.

Webster's Dictionary defines "separate" to mean "to withdraw or secede; to part, to come or draw apart or become disconnected." *Webster's* states that "separation implies the pulling apart of things previously united, joined, or assembled." The dictionary defines neutrality as "not taking part in either side in a dispute or quarrel, not aligning itself with either side in a power struggle."[10] *Black's Law Dictionary's* definition of "separation" comes from the law involving marriage and divorce. Separation means "a cessation of cohabitation of husband and wife by mutual agreement or . . . under decree of a court." The legal dictionary's definition for "neutrality" comes from international law and means "the state of a nation which takes no part between two or more nations at war."[11]

A single glance at the two sets of definitions should dissuade any serious attempt to use the terms interchangeably. Separation does not mean neutrality, and to define them as such is incoherent.

The two sets of definitions do, however, reveal something very intriguing about the two concepts—separation and neutrality. Separation means the breakup of two or more who are in a relationship. Separation *must* come from those within a closed set, such as a marriage, a covenant relationship, a club, or the members of a political organization. Their separation might be very bitter. It might be amiable. For obvious reasons, it cannot be "neutral."

Conceptually, neutrality need not be completely severed from separation. Neutrality, however, is but one possible relationship those previously outside the set might have with those who, from within the set, have separated. Those outside the set might be neutral to both parties. They might favor one party over the other. They might even merge with one of the parties who have separated and form a new set. To be neutral requires one to be a third party to a relationship. Neutrality refers to someone outside the closed set.

Consider several illustrations. A husband and wife might separate. They no longer share a relationship as partners. Their separation can be friendly. It can be hostile. It cannot, by definition, be neutral. Likewise, partners who separate in business can be friendly or hostile but not neutral. When the United States declared, and later enforced, its independence, we became separate from Great Britain. In the more than two hundred years since the separation, our relationship with Great Britain has often been hostile. It is often friendly. It is never neutral. In these instances of separation, there cannot be "neutrality" since the parties were participants in the original relationship.

The couple who separated might have a mutual friend, however. The friend *can*, conceivably, be neutral toward his or her two friends. He or she might be equally friendly toward them, or equally hostile, and can doubtless be neutral because he or she is a third party to the relationship. Further, the United States can, and has, remained neutral in squabbles between Great Britain and, say, Germany. Again, the difference is quite clear. The United States and the friend, in their respective examples, are third parties to an independent relationship.

As these examples illustrate, separation of church and state implies that these two institutions who had previously shared a relationship have, in effect, divorced; they have ceased sharing their previous commitment. Neutrality toward church and state, therefore, requires there be a third party who neither aligns with church nor with state. By definition, one cannot both be separate and neutral simultaneously.

Although one might embrace such an interpretation, it is unlikely the court intended to define separation of church and state to *mean* neutrality. Perhaps, however, one can rescue the court from its lack of clarity. Suppose, in *Everson*, the court had defined separation to *require* neutrality. The establishment clause requires separation of church and state. If anything can be used synonymously, it is "establishment clause" and "separation." But because of the potential of hostility to religion, however, neutrality is a necessary subcomponent of separation. Again, if we were to diagram the argument it might look something like this:

1. The establishment clause (EC) means strict separation (S) between government and religion. Thus the establishment clause is defined to mean separation (*Everson*).

2. Strict separation, however, often engenders hostility (H) between government and religion.

3. Therefore, the establishment clause, *requires* neutrality (N) between government and religion and nonreligion.

4. As a result, strict separation requires neutrality.

It is easy, however, to demonstrate that this explanation, too, is seriously flawed. Conceptually, separation cannot coexist with neutrality as long as separation is the dominant concept. To suggest otherwise engenders the same problems discussed above: definitional ambiguity and the failure to recognize the special nature of "neutrality."

PUT IN THE FORM OF AN EQUATION IT WOULD READ:

Variables: Establishment Clause (EC)
            Means (Means)
            Requires (Requires)
            Separation (S)
            Hostility (H)
            Neutrality (N)

Equation: EC means S, EC cannot tolerate H, therefore EC requires N. EC means S, EC requires N, therefore S requires N.

If a mother has two children, John and Mary, she has a relationship with each of them. The fair mother that she is, she tries to be neutral between her children. She does not favor one over the other when passing out household chores or when she hands out snacks and desserts. If John dies unexpectedly, then she has separated from her son. She certainly cannot be "neutral" toward her late son. Furthermore, it is no longer even possible for her to be neutral toward her son and Mary.

Likewise the court cannot, logically, expect the government to be neutral in its own relationship with religious institutions. That would require government to be both a participant in a relationship and a third party to the same relationship simultaneously. Each of the following statements describes a logically acceptable connection between government and religion:

> Government must be *separate* from religion.
> Government must be *hostile* toward religion.
> Government must be *benevolent* toward religion.

The following statement, however, describes a relationship that is folly:

> Government must be *neutral* toward religion.

The statement is incomplete. It demands we identify another party to whom government must be neutral—a party contending with religion. The following statements do make sense:

> Government must be neutral toward church *and those outside church.*
> Government must be neutral toward religion *and nonreligion.*
> Government must be neutral toward believers *and unbelievers.*

The court *can* dictate that government be neutral in its relationships with competing churches or in its relationship between religion and nonreligion. However, consistent with this analysis, the requirement of neutrality is not a subcomponent of separation. To require separation directly affects government in *its* own relationship with religion. Separation might be friendly or strict, but to be true to our definition, no *neutral* relationship can exist between church and state.

Separation, however, can be an acceptable subcomponent of neutrality. Helen is dating Bob and Joe—roommates who begin fighting over the rent. She tells them both she intends to remain neutral. As a neutral party she can continue to date both; she can offer to give each the money to pay the rent; or she can split up with both—refusing to see either man. The mother of Kevin and Kelly decides she will be neutral when arbitrating disputes between her children. Kevin and Kelly, expected to share the television set, come to their mother in an argument. Unable to tell who is at fault, she can let the two children fight it out, offer to give them both a television set, or she might walk away from the situation refusing to be arbiter and still be "neutral." Both Helen and the mother have several options open to them if they want to remain "neutral" in their respective situations. One of the options is separation. Another is accommodation. If separation is the objective, then it is illogical to speak of neutrality. If neutrality is the objective, then both separation *and* accommodation are legitimate responses.

Thus separation, like accommodation, is an acceptable subcomponent of neutrality. Separation can coexist with neutrality if neutrality is the dominant concept—neutrality requires separation.

At first glance, the first and second options do seem to place the court in a position of defending a logical inconsistency. The court cannot require government to be both separate from the church and neutral toward the church simultaneously. Why not? Neutrality requires a third party, outside the closed set of those in the original relationship, to deal with the separating parties. That is why the "wall of separation between church and state" is such a bad metaphor to describe a neutral relationship between government and the various religions in the United States.

The problem with evaluating the first and second interpretations, however, just might be in the assumption that the court's approach to the establishment clause is a *single-stage* process. As the illustrations offered above indicate, such an interpretation places the court in an impossible position. It is a root cause of the court's incoherence. If, however, one recognizes the court's interpretation of the establishment clause as a *two-stage* process, then the reasoning makes much more sense. The establishment clause requires both separation and neutrality with neutrality emerging from a condition of separation.

Suppose Helen and Bob marry. Helen, it turns out, is feuding with her sister Marie. Because of his relationship with Helen, Bob feels an obligation to side with his wife in her dispute with Marie. Helen is in a preferred relationship with Bob—one that makes it highly unlikely that he can endorse his sister-in-law. Likewise, the court can argue that "church" was in a preferred relationship with the state. Their relationship made it unlikely, despite constitutional assurances of religious liberty, that the government could support the position of those outside the church.

If Bob and Helen divorce, however, they have severed their preferred relationship. By separating from Helen, Bob is now free to be neutral in the dispute between Helen and Marie. In fact, in order to make sure that Bob does not act out any residual hostilities he might have toward Helen, the judge issuing the divorce decree might tell Bob that he must be neutral. Again, the court, not unlike a local judge in a divorce decree, declared a divorce, a separation, between the state and church. Church lost its preferred position with the state, and the state then became free to be neutral toward those outside the church. To guard against potential hostility toward church, the court declared that government must be neutral toward the contending parties.

In both instances, the illustration and the court's treatment of the establishment clause, *neutrality emerged from separation*. By severing a preferred relationship, both Bob and the government were free to elevate a party, previously in a subordinate position, to neutral status. For example, when a nation ends the practice of racial apartheid, and repudiates a doctrine of white supremacy, it is free to be neutral to all races by lifting up those previously at odds with the government into a position of neutrality.

This final interpretation explains how the court *could*, theoretically, mix separation and neutrality so freely in its establishment clause jurisprudence. The "wall of separation between church and state" admonishment makes sense if it is the first of a more comprehensive two-stage commandment—one that describes what should happen once church and state are separate.

Yet, although the court seemingly *must* have embraced this third interpretation, if its establishment clause jurisprudence is to make any sense, it did not do so. *First*, to defend this interpretation, the court would have had to prove that a church ever was in a *preferred* relationship with the national or state governments. That means, among other things, the court would have identified, specifically, the "church" or "religion" which enjoyed such a preferred relationship.[12] If there was no government preference shown toward the church, then the establishment clause requires the state to separate itself from an institution from which it is already separate. It would require there be a divorce when, in fact, there had been no marriage. A separation doctrine would, therefore, be redundant. There would be no need for government to be separate from the church—only to be neutral toward the church and those outside the church.

Second, if the court intended to proffer this interpretation, then why has it softened its definition of "separation"? The reason is that the justices recognized the unacceptable policy implications inherent in a position of strict separation and, therefore, have backed away from complete separation— *McCollum* or *Engel* separation—substituting in its place *Lemon* separation. However, the level of separation required by *Lemon* is doctrinally bankrupt. *Strict* separation between church and state, as the first of a two-stage process, was required for the court to be coherent. The court could have mandated complete separation of *church* and state and still have avoided the policy implications of strict separation, in its second step, by allowing for benevolent neutrality, even accommodation, between *religion* and state. The court cannot equivocate regarding "separation," however. The preferred relationship must be terminated in order to lift up the third party into a position of neutrality.

Why have the court's establishment clause decisions failed to persuade? Why do they resemble a fast-ball pitcher who cannot find the plate? One clear origin of the court's incoherent approach to the religion clauses, therefore, is its substitution of "separation" for "no law respecting an establishment." To avoid the policy implications of strict separation, the court has defined the establishment clause to require both separation and neutrality. As a result, it has created a theory of church-state relations that brings the two concepts together in one of three ways. Two interpretations are so illogical that it is impossible to believe the court could have seriously entertained them. The third interpretation makes better sense, but the court seriously damages the interpretation's applicability by softening the requirement of strict separation. Substituting "separation" for "no law respecting an establishment" doomed the court to incoherence.

It seems clear that the separation doctrine, whether the rigid brand offered in *Everson* or the softer alternative presented in *Lemon*, is unacceptable. It perpetuates the "naked public square" by helping to facilitate secularization, and it is damaging to individual religious liberty. Perhaps more amazing, the doctrine as articulated by the court does not even make sense because of its distorted usage of the terms separation and neutrality.

It might be okay to retain the "wall of separation" as a motto or a slogan—rather than a constitutional doctrine—if it proved not to be harmful, but the evidence in chapter 5 suggests that it might do more to damage religious liberties than to fortify them. A superior alternative is to embrace a more accurate definition of neutrality and, finally, go over the wall of separation. This approach would involve two distinct changes.

The Court Should Eliminate the Separation Doctrine

The "high wall of separation," the doctrinal position articulated by Justice Black in *Everson*, should be jettisoned for several reasons. First, as I suggested in chapter 5, strict separation is a practical impossibility. It is impossible for either the state or religion to meet the rigid standards of strict separation. The state would not want to be, and could not possibly be, completely separated from religion . Government would not be in a position to offer essential services to religious institutions, and it could not regulate individual or organizational activity performed in the name of religion that it finds undesirable. In addition to the problems faced by government, religious groups cannot instruct, nor should they instruct, their members to take no part in the political arena. Topics such as sexual morality, poverty, hunger, war and peace, economic empowerment, and administration of justice, to name a few, are issues with religious consequences as well as policy consequences. They are religious issues as well as political issues.[13]

If strict separation is a practical impossibility, then what purpose is served by embracing the doctrine? It certainly does not prevent the church from receiving millions of dollars in government support.[14] One might argue, correctly, that the doctrine conveys an important message to religion, to government, and to the people. Unfortunately, it is often the wrong message. The separation doctrine provides a doctrinal basis for unhealthy de facto separation—again, almost a motto, or battle cry, for those who support such a position. However, when in the eyes of its citizens a nation's relationship with religion can be summarized in five words, "separation of church and state," then that nation is bound to have instances where individuals are denied the right to freely exercise their religious beliefs, and religion is pushed further and further away from the public sphere.

Second, quite apart from its problems with workability, as a matter of constitutional law, the separation doctrine is a nightmare. For just that reason, although the court continues to cling to the separation doctrine (even if only indirectly), justices often measure the practical components of government programs that support religion with the neutrality yardstick formulated in *Lemon*. The court, however, cannot logically interpret the establishment clause to require both separation and neutrality unless neutrality emerges directly from disestablishing an institution that previously enjoyed a preferred relationship with the government. Otherwise the court is defining, simultaneously and erroneously, separation to mean neutrality.

Apart from the two-stage process that first, disestablishes a preferred religion, and second, elevates all other religions previously in a subordinate relationship with government to a position of neutrality, there is no way the separation doctrine can coexist with neutrality and not foster utter incoherence. Even for this two-stage interpretation to make sense, the court cannot equivocate as to the meaning of the establishment clause. It has to mean separation—or the end of preferred relations for at least one group or belief system. Thus, all the court has managed to do is to confuse the concepts of separation and neutrality, and needlessly engender opposition to religion, generally, when it was probably necessary only to disestablish the Christian church from its previously preferred relationship with the state.

Neutrality is a much more desirable alternative.[15] First, it maximizes the flexibility of the policymaking branches and although safeguarding the court's role in the interpretive process, takes the court largely out of the policymaking arena. The justices need no longer scrutinize programs using the three-part test almost like a judicial scalpel—dissecting legislative programs to see which parts are unconstitutional.

One unnecessary ramification of the separation doctrine and the three-part test is that these judicially created remedies give the justices policymaking authority on a case by case basis. Excessive policymaking by the court means either 1) the justices failed to define the establishment clause clearly and coherently—thus preventing the policymaking branches from identifying and acting upon a clear standard, 2) that the traditional policymaking branches have repeatedly ignored constitutional doctrine thereby requiring judicial intervention, or 3) that the court is unnecessarily encroaching into the traditional policymakers' domain. Those examples of judicial policymaking evident in the establishment clause cases are a serious indictment of the *Everson-Lemon* standard. Judicial activism need not license judicial policymaking.[16]

As the discussion above reveals, both separation and accommodation are acceptable subcomponents of neutrality. Two state legislatures might debate the merits of legislation providing government support for the homeless. One state legislature vows to reject any program supporting religion. The other creates objective standards to determine which groups shall receive government support. The second state decides that religious groups who meet the standards are eligible to receive aid. One state legislature favors separation. The other endorses accommodation. In both instances, the legislatures are quite neutral in their respective relationships with religion, and both options, if applied in a nondiscriminatory manner, would pass constitutional muster.

Instead of dissecting programs, or evaluating the psychological profiles of teachers in schools receiving aid, the court need only ask one simple question: Does the government support, or lack thereof, subjectively favor some religious groups over others? If not, then the policy is neutral and, therefore, constitutional. If hostility, or preferential treatment, is evident in a program's design or application, then the judicial branch must step in and strike down the unconstitutional policy. Strict neutrality provides the reasonable—or partial—level of separation necessary to protect religious groups, individuals, and the state.

Interestingly enough, if a legislative body were to apply this model, strict separation of state and religion and all of its deleterious consequences would still be an acceptable policy option—separation under the guise of *neutrality*. As I indicated through the example of government aid to the homeless, a state legislature, or Congress, could deal with religion by opting to separate from all religious organizations. As long as government was divorced from *all* religious groups, the neutrality doctrine would be satisfied. The decision to embrace total separation as a policy position, however, would not be made by the courts. It would be made by state legislatures and Congress. Further, separation would not be the standard by which the court determined all future church-state decisions. More important, citizens might begin associating the establishment clause with "neutrality" rather than "separation of church and state."

The Court Should Specify What it Means by "Neutrality"

Some time back, I watched the film *Apollo 13*. I happened to live in Florida during the first several Apollo launches, so I observed the actual launch from my backyard in 1970. The film reminded me of just how big and powerful was the rocket that thrust the command module and lunar excursion module into space. But once the multistage rocket had done its work, it was jettisoned. While the astronauts were not going to the moon without its initial launching power, it would have been counterproductive to keep it attached to the spacecraft once it had served its purpose.

The separation doctrine is much like the Saturn V. Americans would not enjoy religious liberty without the first big blast of disestablishment. But, once its purpose had been accomplished, it was time to jettison the doctrine and begin the process of defining and negotiating what the religious liberties clauses mean in a period of postreligious apartheid. Separation is the first stage to achieving religious liberty. Neutrality is the second stage. As I suggested above, it is not at all clear that the court ever understood the distinction between the "separation stage" and the "neutrality stage." As a result, it has not only confused what it means by separation. It also has offered an inferior grade of neutrality.

It would stand to reason that if the Christianity is the "church" in the wall of separation metaphor[17]—the entity that enjoyed a preferred relationship with the state—then the other parties would include non-Christian religious faiths, those who did not enjoy a preferred relationship with government, and that which is identified as "nonreligion." Thus, the situation before *Everson* would have looked something like:

Government is in a preferred relationship with:

The *Christian* Church.

Those in a subordinate position: Non-Christian faiths.
                                          Nonreligion.

The separation doctrine, properly interpreted, required government to sever its preferred relationship with Christianity and to elevate non-Christian faiths and nonreligion to an equal position with the government. The government, therefore, must be neutral. As I indicated above, neutrality might permit or forbid accommodation, but it would require the government to show no preference to Christian churches, non-Christian churches, or nonreligion. Such a relationship should have looked like:

Government is neutral in its treatment of:

Christian Churches.
Non-Christian faiths.
Nonreligion.

The problem came when the court departed from the narrow interpretation proffered in the *Everson* dicta, separation of church and state, and in subsequent cases, for example, *Zorach*, it substituted the term "religion" for "church." The court's treatment of church and religion is not unlike its treatment of separation and neutrality. It fosters definitional ambiguity.

Wait a minute! At first glance the court's substitution makes sense. After all, the religion clauses speak of "religion": Congress shall make no law respecting an establishment of *religion*. Congress shall not prohibit the free exercise of *religion*. But instead of using *church* exclusively in conjunction with the "separation stage," and *religion* in conjunction with the "neutrality stage," it mixed and meshed the two stages so that religion replaced church in the separation stage, and the separation stage became the model for neutrality. Properly articulated, the two-stage process would have looked like:

Properly defined:

Stage One:	Separation of state from church.
Stage Two:	Neutrality of state toward church and religion (persons outside the church) and nonreligion.

But by resubstituting religion back into the separation doctrine as it was articulated in *Everson*, the court changed the meaning of the doctrine. Instead of isolating and disestablishing the "church," meaning Christianity, the court lumped all religious faiths together, juxtaposed religion with nonreligion, and demanded that the government be neutral in its relationship between all religious faiths and nonreligion. Thus, it created a relationship that looks like:

Government is neutral in treatment of:	religion (Christian and non-its Christian faiths) nonreligion.

Then the court went too far. In the *Everson-Lemon* era of establishment clause jurisprudence, the court required government institutions contemplating support for religious groups to undergo a two-step approach. Government must first show that its policy does not favor any religion over the other competing religious truth claims. Having demonstrated that it is "neutral" between competing religions, government must then show that its actions do not favor "religion" over nonreligion. Government must show that its policy will not favor religious believers over nonbelievers.[18] Instead of separating the church from government, the *Everson-Lemon* doctrine needlessly separates the state from religion under the guise of neutrality.

This interpretation of separation and neutrality, church and religion, that culminates in the two-step process has, understandably, had some negative consequences. First, it has contributed to the general climate of establishment clause incoherence. The court breaks its own rules all the time, and it is not even very consistent about it at that. Sometimes it has permitted religious exemptions from general regulations, and it has upheld financial assistance to religious groups. Alternatively, sometimes it denies exemptions and financial assistance.[19]

Further, this two-step approach seems to suggest that, previously, *religion*, generally, enjoyed a preferred relationship with the state. Hence, to remedy the situation, the court disestablished religion from government and then elevated nonreligion to a position of neutrality. But this just is not so. While some religious faiths, namely Protestant Christianity, might well have been "established/quasi-established," other minority religious faiths were only, at best, *tolerated* by government. As I noted in chapter 1, often religious minorities were the target of discrimination by government. Yet the court's approach does not treat minority religions fairly. Minority religious faiths should have enjoyed the benefits of neutrality that followed from disestablishment, but the two-step approach simply lumps together all religious faiths—and pits them against "nonreligion." To safeguard nonreligion, the court treats minority faiths as if they, too, had benefited from a preferred relationship with government.

Most alarmingly, the two-step approach contributes greatly to the problem of secularization. As I argued in chapter 3, many of those who support secularization have religious/quasi-religious motives.[20] Thus, for the court to hold that the government must be neutral between religion and nonreligion, potentially gives nonreligion, or more accurately the religious secularists, a veto over anything touching religion. This could, if the court applied the two-step approach consistently, first, have the practical effect of elevating the high wall described in *Everson*, and, second, actually *establish/quasi-establish* nonreligion. Many a separationist claims that by providing, for instance, financial support to religion, even if the aid is dispensed generally to all groups, government "establishes" religion/church/belief over nonreligion/nonchurch/unbelief.[21] The argument can be reversed. For the court to deny support across the board to all religious faiths effectively "establishes," or makes the state an ally of, nonreligion.[22]

The church-state debate is, perhaps uniquely, one constitutional battle where a draw provides a solid victory for "nonreligious" religions. An illustration for this claim might be found in the biblical account, in 1 Kings 4, of King Solomon's wise adjudication between the two harlots claiming to be the mother of one living child. When Solomon threatened to cut the boy in half, giving a half to each mother, he quickly learned to whom the baby really belonged. The real mother begged Solomon to give the child to her adversary rather than to have him destroyed. The impostor could not care less. For this woman, motivated as much by jealousy of the real mother as her own craving for a baby, the king's pronouncement to destroy the child meant a significant victory for her.

In much the same way, the court decides between religion and nonreligion. Cutting off aid to religion is much like King Solomon's threat to halve the baby. It is only punitive for religion. For many who fall into the nonreligion category, this definition of separation and neutrality not only safeguards their liberties, but it actually assists them in fulfilling their agenda: to aggressively eliminate, or at least minimize, those religious beliefs they find to be dangerous superstition.

Thus, the nonreligious *religionists* win either way. They win if the court advocates strict separation of church and state, or more broadly, religion from government. Likewise, they win if government must be neutral, as it is currently defined, between religion and nonreligion.[23]

The neutrality doctrine could easily be rescued by simply requiring a one-step process. Government must prove that its actions do not prefer or discriminate against *any competing truth claim.* Employing the analysis offered above, nonreligion, for the purpose of interpreting the establishment clause, would be recognized not as a separate entity that has veto power even over any neutral government accommodation of religion, but, instead, as a competing religious truth claim.

Government "neutrality" is achievable through two judicially-crafted scenarios: the current judicial interpretation—*government must be neutral in its relationship between religion and nonreligion, church and nonchurch, belief and unbelief,* or an alternative version of neutrality that requires one step—*government must be neutral in its relationship between competing religions, churches, beliefs.* Interpretations of the "neutrality doctrine" below illustrates the two approaches.

Either interpretation might emanate reasonably from the first amendment's establishment clause. Both are divorced from the disastrous separation doctrine. Yet to be completely accurate, each interpretation would necessitate a subtle rewording of the establishment clause, *Congress shall make no law respecting an establishment of religion.* Each would take the constitutional provision in mutually exclusive directions.

The current judicial interpretation requires government neutrality between religion and nonreligion. By embracing this definition of neutrality, the establishment clause would better read *Congress shall make no law establishing religion.* Neither Congress nor the state governments have the authority to legislate concerning religion since aid to religion comes at the considerable expense of those who oppose religion. Any governmental aid therefore "establishes" religion over nonreligion.[24]

INTERPRETATIONS OF THE NEUTRALITY DOCTRINE

Two step approach:

GOVERNMENT = NEUTRAL	Religion
	Religion
	Religion
	Religion
	Religion

then, GOVERNMENT = NEUTRAL	Religion
	Nonreligion

One-step approach:

GOVERNMENT = NEUTRAL	Religion
	Religion
	Religion
	Religion
	Religion*

(*Formerly designated Nonreligion)

This research indicates, however, that the first scenario is not a preferable alternative. If our objective is to render a meaning to the establishment clause that eliminates the pitfalls inherent in the harsh language of *Everson* as well as the inherent ambiguity of *Lemon*, then this understanding of "neutrality" fails miserably.

First, it defines away important terms in the establishment clause ("respecting" and "an") and perpetuates the apparent conflict between the establishment clause and the free exercise clause. By disallowing funding to church groups or squelching religious practices, government appears to violate the free exercise clause. However, if the government becomes party to a religious practice, or extends financial aid to religion, it is an unconstitutional establishment of religion. Second, as I suggested above, the interpretation prefers nonreligion, nonchurch, and/or unbelief over religion by conferring to nonreligion absolute veto power over public support for the free exercise of religion. Unbelievers or adherents of minority beliefs have not only the freedom to refrain from activity they perceive to be religious, but also by invoking the establishment clause, can prevent the free exercise of believers.

As a result, this interpretation returns us back to square one. To secure "neutrality" the court must either require that the government separate from both religion and nonreligion, which restores *Everson*'s separation doctrine, or the court must give some general standards explaining why, though aid to religion is unconstitutional, it is going to permit some accommodation between church and state, which resurrects *Lemon*'s three-part test, or a functional equivalent. Either way the court perpetuates incoherence and engenders the consequences described in chapter 5.

The second scenario requires government to be neutral toward competing religions, churches, and beliefs. The establishment clause would then best read *Congress shall make no law establishing a religion.* The Constitution neither requires nor forbids government accommodation with religion. However, aid provided, either directly or indirectly, to religion by the government must be available to all religious groups without preference.

Unlike the first scenario, the second has tremendous potential. First, it eliminates the calamities of the *Everson-Lemon* standard. The standard is clear and consistent. Neutrality simply means neutrality. Religion, for the purposes of interpreting the establishment clause, includes the passionate appeals for secularization of the public square discussed in chapter 3. Further, the interpretation is significantly easier for the court to enforce without becoming entwined in the arguments and decisions better left to traditional policymakers. Legislation would have presumption unless it established or preferred one religious group over the others.

Second, it fosters harmony between the two religious clauses of the Constitution. For instance, government, restricted by the establishment clause, can make no law preferring one religion, church, or belief, nor can it, consistent with the free exercise clause, make laws circumscribing religious freedom. Thus, the court need not interpret the Bill of Rights as having created a hierarchy of religious freedoms—with the free exercise clause subordinate to the establishment clause.

Third, the standard adequately protects the nonreligious, nonchurched, and unbeliever by accurately characterizing them as proponents of a "religious" belief. By recognizing, for example Christianity, Islam, Judaism, Buddhism, *a*theism, and *h*umanism, all as religious beliefs, the Constitution offers both to groups and individuals sufficient protection. The free exercise clause protects their right to participate in or be free from participation in religious activities. The establishment clause requires complete neutrality between these diverse religions—none may be established over the others. This interpretation of the establishment clause, requiring nonpreferential neutrality, is clear, allows for good public policy, and substantially safeguards the rights of religious minorities.

APPLYING THE ALTERNATIVE APPROACH

After nearly seven chapters, I suspect I have now reached the point that most everybody is really interested in: the bottom line. What would "authentic neutrality" permit government, religious groups, and individuals to do under the establishment clause?

Currently, government support, or lack thereof, clusters into three large areas: government support given directly to individuals, government support given to religious institutions, and, finally, government support for religious activities (broadly defined). As I indicated in chapter 5, it is often very difficult to tell what level of support the court will tolerate under the *Lemon* test.

An interpretation of the establishment clause that required authentic neutrality would be fairly straightforward. If government chose to support religion generally, if must do so nonpreferentially. If government chose not to support religion, it, likewise, must do so without preference. If a government program, in its articulation or application, either coerces or fosters oppression of groups or individuals, then, since it cannot be *neutral*, government *cannot* support religion.[25]

As a result, most of the major programs where government has offered support directly to religious individuals would pass constitutional muster. Bus transportation to parochial schools,[26] textbook lending programs,[27] tax credits[28] or tax vouchers for expenses incurred in education,[29] aid to the blind used for expenses incurred in a religious college or university,[30] and use of government-paid interpreters to accompany deaf students in parochial schools,[31] are all constitutional providing the government disperses the support nonpreferentially. Since, with few exceptions, the court generally upholds support extended directly to individuals, the alternative approach does not represent much of a departure from the past precedent.

It is with respect to government support for institutions and for religious activities that one might start to see a greater departure from the court's current establishment clause jurisprudence. For example, the court's decisions regarding salary supplements offered to teachers in parochial schools,[32] educational equipment provided to parochial schools,[33] bus transportation for parochial school children for field trips and therapy for hearing-impaired students,[34] after school enrichment programs,[35] and remedial educational programs,[36] would likely be reversed. Alternatively, decisions that upheld support for parochial hospitals,[37] financial accommodation for parochial colleges,[38] diagnostic testing,[39] property tax breaks,[40] and the Adolescent Family Life Act,[41] would probably be preserved. Again, the court would look at legislation and regulations to see if they are provided without preference for particular beliefs, churches, or ideologies.

Undoubtedly the toughest decisions will come in the area of government accommodation for what I am terming "religious activities." Although my position regarding particular examples will undoubtedly change over time (in fact, it has already changed since the time I started looking seriously at church-state issues),[42] let me take stab at the some of the most provocative issues.

Under this approach, the court would likely uphold both off-campus and on-campus released time programs,[43] chaplaincy programs (whether legislative chaplains, military chaplains, or prison chaplains),[44] a moment of silence in public schools—even where a teacher clearly identifies prayer as an acceptable option during the period of silence,[45] most religious-based exemptions from general regulations,[46] and equal access by religious groups to public facilities.[47]

Furthermore, under some circumstances, the court could uphold the posting of the Ten Commandments in public school classrooms,[48] nativity scenes on public property,[49] prayer at graduation,[50] Sunday closing laws,[51] and the inclusion of "creation science" in high school biology classes.[52] Under different circumstances, however, the court would not permit these activities. If the Ten Commandments or the nativity scenes were used as vehicles for public officials, acting as agents of government, to endorse Judaism and/or Christianity, then they would not be neutral. Likewise, if Sunday closing laws were, arguably, a method of pressuring church attendance, then the court should find them coercive, oppressive, and, therefore, not neutral. Programs introducing creation science into high school biology classes would depend almost entirely upon whether creationists could make a case that theirs is good science.[53]

And, much to the chagrin of some patient readers, I would think that it would be almost impossible for state-sponsored vocal prayer in public schools to pass constitutional scrutiny. An official prayer, composed by a government organization, almost necessarily *must* promote some religious beliefs over others. A morning service in the public schools that asked for different students to voluntarily lead the class in prayer and that permitted them to pray in their own manner and to their own "god" appears to be neutral in its design. It is, however, probably not neutral in its application. In some communities one religion dominates all others making it less likely that children of other faiths would volunteer to pray, and more likely that either those who led the "funny" prayers—or who refused to participate at all—would be persecuted for their beliefs. Moreover, how would an *a*theist, or a *h*umanist, ever lead the class in "prayer"? A program of "prayer" would necessarily come at the expense of those holding these religious truth claims.

There are a great many writers who insist that America was, at the time of its founding, a Christian nation—a nation that embraced God and taught Judeo-Christian ethics. They argue that America must return to Christian foundations, and one important vehicle is the restoration of prayer to the public school.[54] Thus, they insist that the United States should *re*establish

Christianity while tolerating minority religious faiths. The argument is one
that deserves consideration, and given the consequences of four decades as a
"secular" state, it may even be valid. However, those who support reestablish-
ment will find no relief in this approach. It is designed to correct those unfortunate and unnecessary imbalances that result from unreasonable separation.
It is not intended to create new imbalances. To employ the government, in any
way, to purposefully return America to its Christian roots requires an *establishment* of religion that judges, employing this approach, would find unconstitutional.

What the alternative approach would do, however, is to "scale the wall
of separation between church and state." As a result, with the erosion of de
facto separation, religious individuals and groups can more freely exercise their
faith in school, on the job, and in the community—religion would no longer
be viewed as a "private" component of one's life unwelcome in the public
arena. Furthermore, eradicating the perception that the Constitution requires
separation should better protect religious expression in the marketplace of
ideas. As I suggested in the introduction to this chapter, when Americans
debate public policy, religious voices will be welcome at the table. By better
protecting religious liberties, and hopefully reversing some of the impact of
secularization, authentic neutrality is an alternative well worthy of serious
consideration.

The Question is *Not* Moot

In the last chapter, I introduced an alternative approach to the establishment clause that, although not wholly original, should serve to protect rights and liberties, and combat the effects of secularization. However, one might ask, "Aren't there other provisions in the Constitution that adequately ensure religious freedom? Hasn't the political and constitutional landscape changed rather dramatically in the past few years so as to make the issue moot? If you are really concerned with religious freedom, generally, and particularly, with religious *expression* in the public square, is it still necessary to completely rethink the way we interpret the first amendment's religion clauses?" These are pretty good questions. In fact, at first glance the questioner might appear to be right. For instance, the Constitution's *free exercise* clause is intended to secure religious freedom. Additionally, religious liberty received some statutory undergirding when the Religious Freedom Restoration Act (RFRA) became law in 1993.[1] Furthermore, in this decade the Christian Right has won a number of victories before the Supreme Court in cases where they have successfully pitted the free *speech* clause against the establishment clause to safeguard religious expression.[2] Finally, President Clinton issued a four-page directive, through the education department in July 1995, to the nation's school board superintendents designed to clarify students' religious liberties in public schools.[3]

In this conclusion, I will address these alternatives to a more complete reinterpretation of the establishment clause. I agree that their impact *should* make further interpretive activity unnecessary. They should make subsequent constitutional clarification moot, but they do not. The free exercise clause, as

interpreted by the court, offers no independent protection for religious liberties. Furthermore, RFRA, with its promises to religious practitioners, was shot
down by the court in its infancy.[4] The free speech strategy, and President
Clinton's directive are promising, but are inadequate to protect religious freedom. The best way to secure religious freedom is still to scale the wall of separation.

THE FREE EXERICISE CLAUSE FROM *REYNOLDS* TO *SMITH*: MUCH ADO ABOUT NOTHING?

I have noted previously that the first amendment has two separate clauses
intended to protect freedom of religion: The establishment clause (or, better,
the *no* establishment clause), and the free exercise clause. In this project, I have
devoted most of my attention to the former, regrettably, at the expense of a
more complete discussion of the latter. In that decision I am not unique. The
bulk of the attention given to the religious liberty clauses by jurists, scholars,
legislative leaders, and the public is reserved for the establishment clause.[5] The
two religious liberty clauses have their own personalities. The establishment
clause is unyielding. It marches forward. There can be no compromise. The
free exercise clause is very flexible. If necessary, it can become almost invisible.
Why is there more attention given to the establishment clause? Depending
upon the definition given to it, the establishment clause overshadows and
defines the parameters of the free exercise clause.[6]

It is easy, then, to dismiss the free exercise clause as a second-class citizen in the community of constitutional liberties. When the court hears a free
exercise case, it first balances the religious liberty claim against the restrictions
required by the criminal or civil law. More likely than not, the judgment of the
elected lawmakers will prevail.[7] Second, the court will test the liberty claim
against the establishment clause. Would the state effectuate an establishment
by satisfying a particular religious liberty claim? If so, then the free exercise
claim must take a back seat.[8]

Development of free exercise jurisprudence proceeded slowly. M.
Glenn Abernathy noted that religious minorities were too busy struggling for
their existence during the earlier periods of American history to put their
trust in the courts. Survival was their concern and as a result, religious
minorities accepted majority rules which simply pinched but did not destroy.
Once the major battles were won in the political arena—such as the freedom
to engage in public worship and freedom from taxes to support religion—the
time was ripe for settling the "secondary" issues of religious freedom through
litigation.[9]

Since the late nineteenth century, the Supreme Court has addressed cases respecting the free exercise of religion.[10] Although most attempts at categorization lead to overgeneralization, the case law might be broken down into several areas: the *Reynolds* "caveat," the *Sherbert-Yoder* "directive," and the return to *Reynolds*.

In the 1879 decision *Reynolds v United States*,[11] the court addressed the case of a man convicted of bigamy in the district court of Utah territory. He admitted to having entered a second marriage, thereby violating the revised statutes of the United States, but argued that, as a member of the Mormon Church, it was his religious *duty* to practice polygamy.[12] In his majority opinion, Chief Justice Waite carefully distinguished religious belief and opinions from religious practices. To disallow regulation of religious practice, noted Waite, would introduce a new element into the criminal law. Civil government could no longer interfere even to prevent a human sacrifice should the sacrifice be found a necessary part of religious worship.[13] "To permit this," argued Chief Justice Waite, "would be to make the professed doctrines of religious belief superior to the law of the land, and in effect to permit every citizen to become a law unto himself."[14]

Reynolds indicated the court's reluctance to protect an absolute right to engage in a course of action because one is compelled by religious duty. In *Cantwell v Connecticut*,[15] more than sixty years later, the court further distinguished between the free exercise of religion as belief and the free exercise of religion as action. The court held, "the Amendment embraces two concepts—freedom to believe and freedom to act. The first is absolute but, in the nature of things, the second cannot be. Conduct remains subject to regulation for the protection of society."[16] Thus, the court applied, although not without modification, the "valid regulation test" to the free exercise clause. Using this test, the court permitted the states to regulate antisocial conduct.[17] Government restrictions, when found reasonable by the courts, can be adopted to further the health, safety, morals, and convenience of the community, and they may be enforced against claims of religious liberty.[18]

The court warned in *Reynolds*, and reaffirmed in *Cantwell v Connecticut*, that while religious belief is beyond government intrusion, activity undertaken in the name of religion must occasionally countenance some restriction for the good of the larger community. If the state has a valid objective, like preventing suicide, stopping drug use, or ending polygamy, then it can enforce its criminal law even over free exercise claims.

Nearly ninety years after *Reynolds*, the court determined that the free exercise clause meant more than simply the right to believe.[19] At some level, albeit one difficult to discover, the clause requires government to act positively to remove barriers that might hinder one's religious practice. In the pivotal

1963 decision *Sherbert v Verner*,[20] the justices decided whether a state agency could deny unemployment compensation to those who refused, for religious reasons, any job requiring Saturday work.[21] The court held that denial of unemployment benefits to a Sabbatarian because of his or her refusal to work on Saturday constituted an abridgment of religious freedom.[22]

Law professor Stephen Pepper indicates that in *Sherbert*, the court "took the free exercise clause seriously" in many ways. First, the court protected religious activity beyond those associated with speech, press, and assembly—freedoms simultaneously protected by other components of the first amendment.[23] Second, the court recognized a new dimension to the free exercise clause. The court held that there were limits on the degree to which government can, through pervasive involvement in our lives, *indirectly* affect religious freedom. While withholding unemployment insurance did not *directly* force Sherbert to compromise her religious beliefs, the court noted that to "condition the availability of benefits upon this appellant's willingness to violate a cardinal principle of her religious faith effectively penalizes the free exercise of her constitutional liberties."[24] Third, the free exercise clause afforded "relatively absolute" protection—only extremely strong interests justify government restrictions on religious conduct. Finally, the burden of proof is upon government to demonstrate that strong interests exist, and how religious conduct harms them.[25]

In *Wisconsin v Yoder*,[26] the court ruled that a law compelling children to attend school until sixteen years of age severely threatened the survival of the Amish faith. In *Yoder*, the court balanced the very legitimate state interest in educating and protecting its children against the free exercise claims of the Amish community. The 1972 decision emphasized how vital it was that a religious issue, as opposed to a mode of living, was at stake. "Giving no weight to such secular considerations, however," Chief Justice Burger opined in *Yoder*, "we see that the record in this case abundantly supports the claim that the traditional way of life of the Amish is not merely a matter of personal preference, but one of deep religious conviction, shared by an organized group, and intimately related to daily living."[27]

Pepper argues that in *Yoder*, the court reaffirmed the elements of its holding in *Sherbert*. Moreover, he contends that the court reinforced the free exercise clause by adding a fifth significant test to *Sherbert*'s directives: the Court insisted the harm sustained by governmental interests "must be measured at the margin." The state must show a compelling reason to limit religious conduct and demonstrate that there is no less drastic means to reach its goal.[28] Thus *Yoder* gave rise to the "least drastic means" component of the balancing test. In *Sherbert v Verner*, and in *Wisconsin v Yoder*, the court held that the free exercise clause not only forbids legislation that would force one to violate one's religious beliefs but, at some level, it requires government to act positively to remove barriers that might hinder religious practice. *Sherbert* softened the consequences one might face for acting upon religious principles. Government cannot use public benefits to hold a religious practitioner hostage and exact conformity.

Sherbert served much like the court's equal protection jurisprudence to heighten scrutiny and to establish a two-tiered approach to examining legislation.[29] Just as with racially based legislation, where the government cannot simply provide a rational basis for a law (but must show a compelling reason if the legislation is to pass constitutional muster), the court held that there must be an overriding reason to restrict religious liberties.[30] In *Yoder*, despite the state's claim to a compelling governmental objective—educating fifteen- and sixteen-year-old children—the court found that exempting the Amish community proved no substantial threat to that objective.[31]

But since *Sherbert* and *Yoder*, the court has had, at best, a mixed record on free exercise claims. The court decided, in its 1982 decision *United States v Lee*,[32] that the Old Order Amish were not exempt from paying Social Security taxes although the court accepted their contention that "both payment and receipt of Social Security benefits is forbidden by the Amish faith."[33] The court held "the state may justify a limitation on religious liberty by showing that it is essential to accomplish an overriding governmental interest."[34]

Pepper indicates his concern that the *Lee* decision, along with *Bob Jones University v United States*[35] and *Goldman v Weinberger*,[36] seriously erode the *Sherbert-Yoder* doctrine. In these cases, Pepper argues, the court failed to apply each of the significant elements of the *Sherbert-Yoder* doctrine.[37] Similarly, the court departed from *Sherbert-Yoder* when it upheld the right of the government to build a road through burial and ceremonial grounds of a Native American tribe—although the road could have been built elsewhere[38]—and held that there is no constitutional right to religious tax exemptions.[39]

Pepper's concerns proved well-founded. Despite the guidelines articulated in *Yoder*, the court has dramatically reaffirmed its commitment to the *Reynolds* directive. The court held, in 1990, that *Yoder*'s compelling interest test would not apply to free exercise claims requesting exemption from neutral laws of general applicability.[40] In the 5-4 decision, *Employment Division v Smith*, the court reversed a verdict by the Oregon Supreme Court to allow unemployment compensation to two men, Alfred Smith and Galen Black, fired for ingesting peyote which act violated the state's controlled substance law.[41] Black and Smith were members of the Native American Church and ingested the peyote for sacramental purposes only. The Oregon Court reasoned that, following *Sherbert*, the men were entitled to unemployment compensation benefits.[42] Writing for the majority, Justice Scalia argued that:

> We have never held that an individual's religious beliefs excuse
> him from compliance with an otherwise valid law prohibiting con-
> duct that the State is free to regulate. On the contrary, the record
> of more than a century of our free exercise jurisprudence contra-
> dicts that proposition.[43]

Scalia went on to note:

> Subsequent decisions have consistently held that the right of free
> exercise does not relieve an individual of the obligation to comply
> with a `valid and neutral law of general applicability on the ground
> that the law proscribes (or prescribes) conduct that his religion
> prescribes (or proscribes).'[44]

Moreover, noted Scalia, there is no disharmony in the court's free exercise
jurisprudence. *Reynolds* is still good law. The only time the court held that an
individual's religious beliefs exempt him or her from a neutral, generally applicable law is when the free exercise claim is in conjunction with other constitutional protections.[45] Why does the court not simply use the compelling interest
test to overturn the Oregon Supreme Court and vitiate the unemployment benefit? Scalia maintains that with regard to race or free speech, exemptions are permitted to protect societal norms and aspirations. Accommodation is not offered
to protect abberant behavior. "What it would produce here—a private right to
ignore generally applicable laws," observes Scalia, "is a constitutional anomaly."[46]

There were scholars who were pleased with the court's post-*Yoder* treatment of the free exercise clause.[47] Others, however, regarded the "return to
Reynolds" with great alarm.[48]

The threat to religious liberties becomes even more pervasive when one
couples the court's interpretation of the free exercise clause in *Smith* with its
confused interpretation of the establishment clause that distorts the meaning
of the words "separation" and "neutrality."[49] The court's jurisprudence has created a mindset that the establishment clause requires strict separation of
church and state. This misperception by the American public about the
requirements of the establishment clause has obscured the vital role religion
plays in American public life. Additionally, it has cut deeply into the religious
rights of many American citizens.[50]

RFRA to the Rescue?

Congress, reacting to the *Smith* decision, intervened to protect religious liberty. On November 16, 1993, President Clinton signed the Religious Freedom
Restoration Act (RFRA). Specifically, RFRA dictates that government shall

not substantially burden a person's exercise of religion even if the burden
results from a rule of general applicability [unless the government demon-
strates] that application of the burden to the person (1) furthers a compelling
government interest; and (2) is the least restrictive means of furthering that
compelling government interest.[51]

It took three years from the time of its introduction in Congress for
RFRA to become law.[52] The delay was not because the bill was inherently
unpopular. A large coalition of highly divergent "liberal, conservative, and reli-
gious groups," including the ACLU, the National Council of Churches, the
American Jewish Congress, the National Conference of Catholic Bishops, the
Church of Jesus Christ of Latter Day Saints, the Southern Baptist
Convention, and the National Association of Evangelicals, were united in
support of the RFRA when it was signed into law.[53]

What exacerbated the delay was a fear that the language of RFRA
might render unconstitutional all restrictions on abortions—as violative of
free exercise rights—and that prisoners might make outrageous demands of
prison officials including special gourmet meals, and guns and knives for their
worship services.[54] This prompted a tentativeness in even those groups who
were otherwise predisposed to support this congressional effort to enact a
statutory version of the free exercise clause. Consequently, enough objections
were raised to slow its passage. Eventually, before passage of the bill, both of
these issues were resolved.[55]

Proponents of the RFRA argued that the great potential of the act is
that Congress has stepped forward, asserting its obligation to protect individual liberties, and declared that religious freedom is a substantive liberty—no
substantial burden should be placed upon one's religious freedom without a
compelling interest.[56] The effect of the RFRA, they claimed, is to reinstitute,
as a matter of statutory law, the tests articulated in *Sherbert* and *Yoder*.
Religious liberty is not simply a recapitulation of the freedom of speech.
Regulations that impact upon sincerely held religious beliefs must face a
heightened level of scrutiny by the judiciary—a strict level of scrutiny that
requires the state to show that there is a compelling interest in regulating religious belief. Further, it requires government to demonstrate its intention to
regulate religious people in order to prevent an actuality rather than a potential harm. Fears that motivate government regulation must be real and not
potential. Finally, the government must prove that there is no less drastic
means of accomplishing its goals.[57]

Supporters predicted that, as a result of the RFRA, religious groups and
individuals would enjoy a level of protection heretofore unexperienced in the
United States.[58] Professor Laycock argued that the RFRA is the best hope
America has to restore protection for religious liberty:

RFRA would solve the problem of perpetual religious conflict with interest groups and also the problem of religious minorities too small to be heard in the legislature. It would do so by creating an across-the-board right to argue for religious exemptions and make the government carry the burden of proof when it claims that it cannot afford to grant exemptions. RFRA has a chance to work because it is as universal as the Free Exercise Clause. It treats every religious faith and every government interest equally, granting neither special favors nor exceptions for any group. RFRA is America's only near-term hope to rise above the paralysis of interest group politics and restore protection for religious liberty.[59]

Likewise, there was a healthy skepticism about RFRA. Some doubted that RFRA would provide some balance in cases pitting the free exercise clause against the establishment clause or just how extensively RFRA could shield free exercise claims from the will of the majority as articulated through the criminal law. They identified several pitfalls that were likely to arise in the application and interpretation of RFRA that would dramatically undercut its effectiveness.[60] First, they argued, RFRA subjects religious religious liberties to the predilections of political majorities. One promise of RFRA is that it offers protection to religious minorities in America—the Native American Church, the Hare Krishnas, Jehovah's Witnesses, Mormons, Muslims, Buddhists, are a few that come to mind—that are not provided for under the free exercise clause after *Smith*.[61] In reality, however, by protecting religious freedom through statutory law, rather than constitutional law, it is still very much subject to the whims of the majority. Congress may amend RFRA to forbid the religious practices of "unpopular" or minority religious groups. They could place particular religious acts out from under the protection of RFRA.[62] The protection religious people can hope to receive from the act might depend upon the level of toleration exhibited by members of Congress and their constituents. This might be more comforting than looking to foster and maintain a majority on the Supreme Court, but it is probably not much more so—and not always the case.

Second, the judiciary could effectively undermine the legislation. Perhaps the most serious threat to the RFRA is that the court could subvert the legislation simply by defining what constitutes a "compelling interest" very broadly. Thus, when a religious liberty claim is juxtaposed against a state law, and the regulation is deemed "compelling," the liberty claim will be unsuccessful.[63]

Third, despite the promises RFRA does not restore the *Sherbert-Yoder* directive. Unlike the rule articulated in *Sherbert*, RFRA requires that the government place a "substantial" burden on the religious group or individual to inaugurate its protections.[64] In *Sherbert*, the court held that pressure from the state, even if it is indirect or incidental, is constitutionally unacceptable.[65] The primary difference between the two tests is the trigger necessary to engender the protection of the free exercise clause, as interpreted in *Sherbert*, and the safeguards listed in RFRA.[66] John Whitehead and Alexis Crow argue that there is no jurisprudential determination of what a "substantial" burden will be. They note:

> It was relatively easy to find 'a' burden under *Sherbert*, especially since the Supreme Court held that even an 'incidental' burden meets the threshold test. But under RFRA, there is not way to predict whether the Court would find a . . . 'substantial' burden . . . This means that RFRA has not accomplished a full return to *Sherbert*.[67]

Fourth, RFRA fights only half the battle. The establishment clause is still controlling. As I argued above, the two largest legal obstacles to the free exercise clause are its fragility when pitted against either the criminal law or the court's confused interpretation of the establishment clause. RFRA, as a legislative effort to overturn *Smith*, reckons with the former—religious liberty claims that cut against the criminal law. Section 7 of RFRA reads, in part, "nothing in this Act shall be construed to affect, interpret, or in any way address that portion of the First Amendment prohibiting laws respecting the establishment of religion."[68] In other words, RFRA specifically codifies the limits placed upon free exercise by the court through its interpretation of the establishment clause. Whitehead and Crow argue that those hostile to religion could use "the Supreme Court's most important conceptual tool for limiting the free exercise of religion: psychological coercion under the Establishment Clause," as articulated in *Lee v Weisman*,[69] as a "free exercise" claim against government practices that have previously only been challenged under the establishment clause.[70] And, in *Board of Education of Kiryas Joel v Grumet*,[71] the court upheld the establishment clause over the free exercise concerns of the Orthodox Jews. Justice Souter held that religious communities can pursue their own concerns free from government interference. Further, they can insist that government accommodate those interests by removing special burdens to free exercise. However, he noted, the law creating the school district went well beyond these principles, and, thus, violated the establishment clause.[72]

Whether RFRA would have fulfilled its promises or been largely ineffective is no longer relevant. In the 1997 decision *Boerne v Flores* the Supreme Court struck down RFRA. The case involved a Catholic church, in Boerne, Texas, that wanted to expand its building to accommodate the needs of a

growing congregation. The Boerne City Council passed an ordinance autho-
rizing its historic landmark commission to prepare a preservation plan. Based
upon the plan, the church was denied a building permit to expand. The church
challenged the city's decision in light of RFRA—government cannot interfere
with religion unless there is a compelling interest.[73]

Instead of limiting its analysis to whether Boerne could show a compelling interest in preserving the existing church building, the court took on
RFRA directly. Justice Kennedy argued that Congress passed RFRA in direct
response to the *Smith* decision under the guise of protecting the fourteenth
amendment. However, he noted that any such legislation must be remedial or
preventative in nature. Section five of the fourteenth amendment was never
designed to permit Congress to *amplify* or *redefine* constitutional rights.[74] The
effect of *Boerne* is that there is no longer even a statutory shield against *Smith*.

Kennedy's analysis is akin to Justice Robert Jackson's concurring opinion in *Youngstown Sheet & Tube Co. v. Sawyer*.[75] Jackson set up a standard for
reviewing presidential action. He suggested that when the president's policy
has congressional approval, then it is presumed to be constitutional. When
Congres is silent, then the court must offer greater scrutiny to the presidential action. When the president is at odds with Congress, then his or her
action is presumed to be unconstitutional.[76] Kennedy's applies the standard to
disputes between Congress and the court. If Congress is consistent with the
court's constitutional interpretation, then the legislation is likely to be valid. If
Congress speaks without the court, then the justices must look carefully. If
Congress acts in opposition to the court, then it is strongly presumed that its
action is constitutionally infirm.[77]

THE "FREE SPEECH STRATEGY" FOR SECURING RELIGIOUS LIBERTIES

Since efforts to protect religious liberty through the free exercise clause are
inadequate, and Congress' attempt to give some statutory muscle to the free
exercise clause was aborted by the court, perhaps one might look to other sec-
tions in the Bill of Rights to secure religious liberty. Is it possible to do an end-
run around the free exercise clause?

If one looks at a series of cases involving Jehovah's Witnesses in the
1940s, one will find that the Witnesses often prospered before the court when
they would blur the line differentiating the freedom of religion from the freedom of speech.[78] The Witnesses were reacting to the *Reynolds* decision—the
court's first, and arguably most restrictive interpretation, of the free exercise
clause. Their persistent efforts to defend free exercise, or at least a combina-
tion of free exercise and free speech, dramatically expanded their religious lib-

erty—even if it came at the expense of a robust interpretation of the free exercise clause.[79] The right to believe includes the right to speak, and the right to
speak can, generally, only be limited if there is a clear and present danger.

Nearly fifty years after the Jehovah's Witnesses, the so-called Christian
Right is using a similar strategy effectively to protect religious liberty. As I
argued in the first chapter, these evangelical groups have used the media to
educate their members.[80] They have mobilized and become more active in the
political arena.[81] Moreover, they have developed legal organizations designed
to protect religious liberty claims in the courts.[82]

Professor Hubert Morken revealed some preliminary results of his study
of seven different evangelical "law firms": the Christian Legal Society, and its
legal arm the Center for Law and Religious Freedom, the Christian Law
Association, the Home School Legal Defense Association, the National Legal
Foundation (NLF), Christian Advocates Serving Evangelism (CASE), the
American Center for Law and Justice (ACLJ), and the American Family
Association Law Center.[83] Two of the more important organizations were
both started by religious broadcaster-political activist, Pat Robertson. The
National Legal Foundation was Robertson's first attempt to defend religious
liberties through an extensive, sustained, and organized pool of litigation. The
National Legal Foundation is no longer associated with Robertson, but it has
a 17,000-member donor base, an annual budget of about $350,000, a large
group of affiliate attorneys across the country, and a thorough "brief bank" of
relevant first amendment cases available to local attorneys.[84] The American
Center for Law and Justice is Robertson's latest effort to protect "pro-liberty,
pro-life, and pro-family causes."[85] The ACLJ has a growing mailing list
exceeding 110,000 names and takes in over $2,000,000 annually. The organi-
zation is housed in Virginia Beach, Virginia, and works closely with the law
school at Regent University. There are branch offices in Washington, D.C.,
Atlanta, and Louisville, and the ACLJ eventually intends to have offices
throughout the country. There are 75 affiliate attorneys, and the ACLJ plans
to build an extensive attorney network, create a publication ("Law and
Justice"), and hold conferences on constitutional rights and liberties at least
twice a year.[86] Commenting upon the ACLJ, Barry Steinhardt, associate direc
tor of the ACLU, notes, "It's a part of a growing movement within the religious right to press their agenda. It's a sign that they've become increasingly
sophisticated."[87]

Not only are the Christian law firms becoming increasingly sophisticated in their structure and organization, they are also often successful. The
ACLJ receives some 150 requests per week from people seeking their help in
first amendment cases. Roy Rivenburg, writing in December 1992, observed,
"To date, the two-year-old center hasn't lost a case."[88] He notes, "the group's

success has sent chills through entities like the American Civil Liberties Union."[89] Furthermore, they have been victorious at the highest appellate level. *Westside Community Schools v Mergens*,[90] in which the court upheld the equal access act permitting religious clubs to meet in public schools, "was a NLF case from start to finish."[91] And the ACLJ prevailed twice in cases before the Supreme Court in 1993. In *Bray v Alexandria Women's Health Clinic*,[92] the court refused to extend the application of the civil rights act of 1871, better known as the Ku Klux Klan act, to enjoin antiabortion protesters from blockading abortion clinics.[93] In *Lamb's Chapel v Center Moriches Free Union School District*,[94] the court held that a community cannot deny access to public school facilities to a church group that wanted to use them after hours—assuming the community makes the facilities available to other, nonreligious groups as well.

One advantage available to the ACLJ is that its lead counsel, Jay Sekulow, is an experienced and respected first amendment attorney who has argued nearly a dozen cases before the United States Supreme Court representing CASE, the NLF, the organization "Jews for Jesus," Concerned Women For America, Free Speech Advocates, Operation Rescue, and also the ACLJ.[95]

It appears that one "strategy" that has contributed to Sekulow's success, and the organizations he represents, including the ACJL, is to litigate on the basis of freedom of expression rather than more traditional religious liberty claims. Other Christian organizations tend to focus upon the latter.[96] Defending the decision to found the organization (CASE), Sekulow articulates his approach:

> We deal with problems concerning access to parks, school cam-
> puses at every level, malls, street corners and, of course, airports. .
> CASE was started because I saw a gap. There were already aggres-
> sive, effective Christian organizations that specialized in litigating
> religious freedom issues—The National Legal Foundation and the
> Rutherford Institute, for example—but I saw a growing need to
> challenge the state's infringement upon the right of Christians to
> proclaim the gospel.[97]

Similarly, Keith Fournier, director of the ACLJ, posits that an "odd sort of irony" has emerged. Those who backed civil rights and peace demonstrations in the 1960s now work to enjoin the speech of religious and prolife groups in the 1990s.[98] Fournier insists that students used to be told "you don't leave your (free speech) rights behind at the school door." Now they are notified that the rules are different if the speech involves religion. "Our position is simple," argues Fournier, "Speech is speech . . . . The content shouldn't matter."[99] The strategy is remarkably similar to that implemented by Jehovah's Witnesses more than a half-century ago. The Witnesses were faced with an interpretation of the free exercise clause that made it likely the courts would rank the government over their religious liberty claim. Likewise, contemporary believers must buck an interpretation of the establishment clause, and, following *Smith*, the free exercise clause, that often cripples their religious liberty argument. Though they faced different constitutional barriers, the solution was essentially the same: to link the religious liberty claim to the right of free expression. It is almost as if the ACLJ has conceded that the free exercise clause was largely subsumed within the protections afforded by the free speech clause—and is determined to pit the free speech claim against the establishment clause claim whenever possible.

In *Mergens*, the majority held that the equal access act[100] (EAA) was intended to protect certain types of speech that might be excluded from what is otherwise a limited open forum. Since the liberty at stake was the students' freedom of expression, and not free exercise of religion, the court determined that there must be a compelling reason to squelch the speech. Justice O'Connor, writing for the majority, postulated that the risk of an establishment of religion might provide a compelling reason.[101] Thus, the court pitted the free speech clause against the establishment clause.

Justice O'Connor applied her own "endorsement" test.[102] She decided that the EAA did not constitute an endorsement of religion. For the school district to maintain an open forum and to permit noncurriculum related groups to meet on campus after school, and then to restrict access to religious groups, would demonstrate hostility toward religion.[103] Even if one applied the infamous *Lemon* test, she argued, the EAA, and the existence of the Bible club on the campus did not have the primary effect of advancing religion.[104]

The effectiveness of the strategy is evident when one reads the concurring opinion of Justice Marshall and Justice Brennan. Marshall and Brennan, along with Justice Stevens, were the three members of the court deciding *Mergens* who were most likely to sacrifice a free exercise claim to their rigid defense of the establishment clause—despite whatever test was employed to balance the competing concerns. Leonard Levy notes:

> No matter what test has been employed by the present members
> of the Court, Justices William J. Brennan, Thurgood Marshall,
> and John Paul Stevens will probably find a violation of the estab-
> lishment clause.[105]

In *Mergens*, however, Marshall and Brennan embraced O'Connor's endorsement test and acknowledged, even though it was a close call, and that they were, indeed, bothered by the court's definition of a noncurriculum related group, the risk of an establishment was not compelling enough to override the right to free expression:

> In addition, to the extent that Congress intended the Act to track this Court's free speech jurisprudence, as the dissent argues, the majority's construction is faithful to our commitment to nondiscriminatory access to open fora in public schools . . . . When a school allows student-initiated clubs not directly tied to the school's curriculum to use school facilities, it has "created a forum generally open to student groups" and is therefore constitutionally prohibited from enforcing a "content-based exclusion" of other student speech. In this respect, the Act as construed by the majority simply codifies in statute what is already constitutionally mandated: schools may not discriminate among student-initiated groups that seek access to school facilities for expressive purposes not directly related to the school's curriculum.[106]

In *Lamb's Chapel*, the court held that the decision whether or not to open access to public school facilities belonged to the school district.[107] They made these facilities available to "social, civic, and recreational" groups, and excluded "using the facilities for religious purposes."[108] The sole reason for rejecting the church's petition to use a school auditorium—to show a Christian-based film series promoting family values by Dr. James Dobson—was, argued Justice White in the majority opinion, because it dealt with a subject from a religious standpoint.[109] Consistent with White's analysis, it is acceptable for a school district to say to off-campus groups:

> *All religious worship is unacceptable on public school grounds.*

That is content-neutral. It is not permissible to say:

> *Family values speeches are apropos.*
> *Health lectures are welcome.*
> *Debates addressing the question of reproductive choice are acceptable.*
> *"How to Get Good Grades" seminars are appreciated.*

but then exclude these, or other sorts of topics, if they are taught from a religious perspective.[110]

The court followed its reasoning in *Mergens*: 1) the free speech claim must prevail unless there is a compelling interest, 2) a risk of an establishment of religion might provide the state with a compelling interest, and 3) after applying either the *Lemon* test or the endorsement test, there is not a sufficient fear of an establishment.[111]

Understandably, the district tried to scuttle the free speech argument by advancing precisely the two kinds of arguments used historically, and effectively, to block free exercise claims. In addition to the appeal to the establishment clause, the district also made an appeal to their police power and their fear that, should they permit the church to show the film series, it would lead to threats of public unrest and even violence.[112] Had the church opted to present a traditional free exercise argument, and had either of these arguments been launched against them, one might hypothesize that the church would have almost surely lost its case. Since the establishment and police powers arguments were used to defeat a free speech claim, however, Lamb's Chapel proved victorious.

Armed with the court's decisions in *Mergens* and *Lamb's Chapel*, the ACLJ took offensive steps to protect the free *speech* rights of religious believers. For example, in December 1993, less than a month *after* President Clinton signed the RFRA, Sekulow sent an informational letter to 14,766 school superintendents across the United States addressing the questions of students' rights to participate in Christmas observances in public schools, the inclusion of Christmas carols and other "religious" expression in holiday programs, and even the legitimacy of retaining the "Christmas vacation" (as opposed to renaming it "winter vacation"). Similar letters were sent in the spring, explaining the ACLJ's position regarding student-initiated graduation prayer.[113] Only a few months later, the ACLJ initiated a nationwide legal campaign against school districts that bar students from forming Bible clubs. In an attempt to force school districts to comply with *Mergens*, the ACLJ has filed eighty-five lawsuits in twenty-eight states. Sekulow also petitioned the justice department to start actively enforcing the EAA. "Students here in Virginia and elsewhere," notes Sekulow, "are not going to be denied their rights simply because they choose to speak out on religion."[114]

In June 1995, the court decided the case *Rosenberger v Rector*—a Virginia case involving the University of Virginia's policy of refusing student activities monies for religious activities.[115] *Wide Awake*, a student-run magazine at the university, was denied student-activity money because it publishes articles from a Christian perspective. The university argued that the principles of separation of church and state included in the establishment clause prohibited it from subsidizing the magazine.[116] Law professor Michael McConnell, representing *Wide Awake* editor Ronald Rosenberger, responded that for the university to single out the magazine was inequitable and had violated their freedom of *speech* simply because of the religious nature of the speech.[117] McConnell's analysis prevailed; once again the free speech strategy was used successfully to bolster freedom of religion.

Therefore, despite the passage of RFRA, the free speech strategy for securing free exercise rights is both viable and effective. Several successful "law firms" representing the so-called Christian Right are still counting on the strategy as a forceful tool for securing their religious liberty.

There is one serious drawback to the free speech strategy, however. Certainly Jehovah's Witnesses' vigorous commitment to litigation hastened the introduction of what law professor Mark Tushnet calls the "reduction principle."[118] The reduction principle strips from religious belief anything that would distinguish it from other types of belief. The rituals of religious belief are treated like symbolic speech and tested by standards developed in symbolic speech cases.[119] Further, the reduction principle applies similar rules to actions motivated by religious beliefs that govern in cases where speech is suppressed because of its effect on governmental interests.[120]

Tushnet argues that one decision in particular illustrates the reduction principle: *Widmar v Vincent* (1981).[121] In *Widmar*, nestled between the Jehovah's Witnesses cases, and the cases brought by the Christian Right in the 1990s, the court considered a decision by the University of Missouri at Kansas City to exclude a religious group from meeting on campus. The exclusion was based upon a regulation adopted by the university's board that forbade the use of the school's building or grounds "for the purposes of religious worship or religious teaching."[122] The court held that the establishment clause does not prohibit an "equal access" policy in which on-campus facilities are open to groups and speakers of all kinds. Further, by opening the campus up to more than 100 student groups, the university had created a "public forum."[123] Thus, the regulation prohibiting religious expression constituted a content-based discrimination against religious speech that violated the free speech clause of the first amendment.[124] The majority granted that the university, as an institution of the state, could limit the freedom of expression if there were a compelling interest, and evidence that the state had established religion might constitute a compelling interest.[125] However, after applying the "*Lemon* test," the court found that there was indeed no establishment.[126]

Professor Tushnet maintains that the decision in *Widmar* both documents the existence of, and potential consequences inherent as a result of the reduction principle:

> The reduction principle may have reached its fullest flower in *Widmar v. Vincent*, in which, in a case crying out for free exercise treatment, the Court adopted a free-expression analysis instead. There the University of Missouri denied a group of students permission to conduct its prayer meetings in University buildings even though the buildings were available to nonreligious organizations for their meetings. A free exercise analysis would treat this as a simple case of discrimination against religion. The Court's free speech analysis treated it as a content-based restriction on speech, which could be justified by a compelling state interest. Religion entered the Court's analysis by the back door, as the Court rejected the University's claim that it had a compelling interest in avoid-

ing the appearance of an establishment of religion. As William Marshall has said, "Because few activities are more profoundly religious than prayer, Widmar suggests that there is no core religious activity exclusively protected by the free exercise clause."[127]

Incredibly, in *Widmar* the court treats "worship" as a type or subcategory of "speech." Therefore, it is unacceptable, without a compelling interest, to limit "speech," one type of which is "worship."[128]

Only former Justice White, in dissent, fought for the integrity of the free exercise clause. He contended that speech and worship were separate liberties with their own, separate sources of constitutional protection.[129] Although he conceded that "religious speech designed to win religious converts" was protected by the free speech clause, he insisted that there is a difference between this sort of speech and "religious worship by persons already converted."[130] In this instance, argued White, the religious group wanted to meet on campus to worship. Though the state *can* protect these distinctly religious activities, it is not obliged to do so.[131]

Thus, although evangelicals have used the free speech clause to successful carve out space for religious groups over the traditional government claims to police power, and the fear that protecting religious liberty might constitute an establishment of religion, they have contributed to the fortification of the reduction principle. Their willingness to cash in on the court's liberality with respect to free speech, while allowing the free exercise clause to remain in a weakened, atrophied state, may be prudent in the short term. I am not sure how wise it will prove to be in the long run.

A PRESIDENTIAL BODYGUARD FOR RELIGIOUS LIBERTY?

Proponents of religious freedom recently found an ally in President Bill Clinton. In a speech at James Madison High School in Vienna, Virginia, the president, a Southern Baptist from Arkansas, argued against secularizing the public square, in favor of public expression of religious faith (even in public schools which, he noted, were never intended to be "religion-free zones"), and offered a directive, through the department of education, to the fifteen thousand public school superintendents across the United States.[132]

In the four-page directive, the president affirmed students' rights to hold religious discussions, to take classes about comparative religions, to pass out religious literature if other groups are allowed to pass out nonschool related materials, to wear religious clothing, and to get released time for religious instruction.[133] Specifically, the directive highlights the following activities as permissible in public schools, or barred because of the establishment clause:

examples of activities permitted:
students praying alone or in after-school groups
students discussing or advocating religion
teaching about religion and its importance on society
making religious remarks in the course of classroom discussion, or in
      written assignments
equal access for religious clubs.

examples of activities barred from public schools:
requiring students to participate in religious activities like prayer or
      Bible reading
requiring a moment of silence for meditation or prayer
government funding of secular or religious education at parochial
      schools
school sponsored prayer at graduation ceremonies
teachers advocating religious doctrines
observing holidays as religious events[134]

The president said that the directive was necessary because students'
religious rights have been abridged in public schools. Although he believed
such incidents were rare, he conceded that damage done to the free exercise
rights of public school students necessitated some clarity:

> Students can pray privately and individually whenever they want.
> They can say grace to themselves before lunch. There are times
> when they can pray out loud together. Student religious clubs in
> high schools can and should be treated just like any other extracur-
> ricular clubs. They can advertise their meetings, meet on school
> grounds, use school facilities, just as other clubs can. When stu-
> dents can choose to read a book to themselves, they have every
> right to read the Bible or any other religious text they want.
> Teachers can and certainly should teach about religion and the
> contributions it has made to our history, our values, our knowl-
> edge, to our music and our art in our country and around the world
> and to the development of the kind of people we are.[135]

Clinton stressed that the rights he outlined are already protected under
the first amendment, and he cautioned against the oft-repeated efforts to alter
the Constitution in order to clarify religious freedom. "The Constitution protected the free exercise of religion, but prohibited the establishment of religion," the president noted. "It's a careful balance. It's uniquely American. It's
the genius of the first Amendment."[136]

ASSESSMENT?

As I have suggested from the outset, my concern primarily is that religious people are afforded basic liberties, and that religious expression might have an opportunity to flourish in the marketplace of ideas. Therefore, even though I presented a more sweeping reform in the previous chapter, one that asks the court and the elected policymakers to rethink what kind of relationship we want to have between church and state, my concern is not that religious groups become partners with the state in a whole range of social policies. Some cooperation, particularly in the areas of social welfare, caring for children and the elderly, food distribution, education, hospital care, and the like, not only seems somewhat inevitable but also very prudent. However, these areas of accommodation are far less important to me than are securing basic liberties and protecting religious expression from ever-increasing secularization.

Therefore, although I am deeply disappointed with the court's emasculation of the free exercise clause in *Smith* and its constitutional power-play at the expense of religious liberty in *Boerne*, I am somewhat torn by the impact of the rather revolutionary changes in the political landscape that I discussed in this chapter: the development of the free speech strategy for securing religious liberties and President Clinton's defense of basic religious liberty and religious expression. On the one hand, they have modest potential for securing religious freedom. On the other hand, the impact that the free speech strategy might have upon the free exercise clause and the extraordinary volatility of support from the political branches—particularly from the president—for religious freedom still leave me convinced that the surest way to protect religious freedom is through a comprehensive reinterpretation of the establishment clause still commonly interpreted as requiring a "wall of separation."

For the court to articulate a coherent alternative approach to the establishment clause, the justices must do some serious balancing. Quite obviously, separating church from state, at least at a partial level, is necessary to protect church, state, and individual citizens. Strict separation, however, should be dismissed as a failed experiment. As I have indicated in previous chapters, it continues to rear its ugly head from time to time, and Justice Black's famous dicta in *Everson* still overshadow the public debate. Strict separation is impossible to implement, and even if it were possible, it engenders unacceptable consequences. Too, the court should jettison the "softer separation" that it has camouflaged as "neutrality." It is no wonder the public continues to embrace the strict separation doctrine. At least it is readily understandable unlike the complicated formula devised in *Lemon*. The separation doctrine, now fifty years old, has outlived whatever usefulness it might have originally offered.

A successful alternative would, therefore, contain two provisions. First, it would catapult us "over the wall." It would formally put an end to the separation doctrine. Even though a partial level of separation *is* imperative to secure religious liberty, the phrase "separation of church and state" has come to be associated with total separation. It is much better for the court to speak of the establishment clause as requiring neutrality—the authentic neutrality proposed in the previous chapter. Rather than the complicated formula advanced in *Lemon*, which is, when applied on a case-by-case basis, intolerably contradictory, the court should eliminate the second two-step process (requiring government neutrality between all religions and then neutrality between religion and nonreligion), define "nonreligion" as a competing religious truth claim, and require government to be neutral among all religious groups. The alternative model proposed here would permit a significant level of government support for religion but would strike down those programs that are not neutral in either their design or application.

Quite obviously, presenting a different definition of neutrality is a substantial departure from the court's fifty-year-old approach to interpreting the establishment clause: separation of church and state. Given, however, the results of both strict and softer separation—incoherence, controversy, and the damage done to individual liberties—perhaps the alternative endorsed here is really not much of a gamble at all. Despite the seemingly successful strategy of protecting religious liberty via the free speech clause, and a president who appears bent on endorsing religious expression in the public square, the establishment clause nightmare continues to preserve a risk to freedom that is simply unacceptable.

Notes

✤

Introduction

1. See the discussion about America's "civil religion"—one component is the requirement that presidents ask God to bless us at every opportunity—in Stephen Carter, The Culture of Disbelief (1993) 51-52; Kenneth Wald, *Religion and Politics* (1987), 48–55; Robert Booth Fowler & Allen Hertzke, *Religion and Politics in America* (1995), 243–245. For a more extensive treatment of what Fowler and Hertzke call "the civil religion thesis," see Robert Bellah et al., *Habits of the Heart* (1985); Sanford Kessler, *Tocqueville's Civil Religion* (1994); Martin Marty, *Religion and Republic* (1987); Merle H. Weiner, "Civilizing the Next Generation: A Response to Civility: Manners, Morals, and the Etiquette of Democracy by Stephen L. Carter," 42 *How. L.J.* 241 (1999).

2. Wald, xi.

3. The book that probably best brings these two debates together is Stephen Carter's influential treatise, *The Culture of Disbelief* (1993). Professor Carter devotes the entirety of Section II of the book to "The Subject of the First Amendment." *Over the Wall* expands upon Professor Carter's argument respecting the "trivialization" of religious expression, and in it I offer a substantially more complete departure from *Lemon v Kurtzman*, 403 U.S. 602 (1971) as a means of addressing the establishment clause. Of course Carter's book is not the first attempt to free religious expression and exercise from the shackles placed upon it by a rigid interpretation of the establishment clause. See Richard John Neuhaus, *The Naked Public Square* (1984); Garry Wills, *Under God* (1990); Michael Perry, *Love and Power* (1991). When I read Mark Dewolfe Howe's, *The Garden and the Wilderness* (1965), I discovered that the issues raised were similar to those discussed by authors in the 1980s and 1990s, and that his solution was very much like the one I present in chapter 7. Two important works, written subsequently to Carter's treatise, touch upon many of the same subjects and often with even greater sophistication: Frederick Mark Gedicks, *The Rhetoric of Church & State* (1995) and Ronald Thiemann, *Religion in Public Life* (1996).

149

4. With a picture of a triumphant Pat Robertson on its cover, *U.S News and World Report* (April 24, 1995) states: "For God's Sake: Religious Conservatives Think Their Time Has Come." More recently, the same magazine (August 12, 1996) 8, reported that Christian Coalition was under investigation by the Federal Election Commission for allegedly contributing "over $1.4 million to GOP candidates seeking federal office." Further, the FEC went ahead with a lawsuit against the Christian Coalition for "violating election laws that bar corporations from working to elect candidates."

5. 330 U.S. 1 (1947).

CHAPTER ONE

1. See Richard John Neuhaus, *The Naked Public Square* (1984); James Davidson Hunter and Os Guiness (ed.), *Articles of Faith, Articles of Peace* (1990); Michael Perry, *Love and Power* (1991); Stephen Carter, *The Culture of Disbelief* (1993); Frederick Mark Gedicks, *The Rhetoric of Church and State* (1995); Ronald Thiemann, *Religion in Public Life* (1996); Steven Smith, "The Rise and Fall of Religious Freedom in Constitutional Discourse," 140 *U. Pa. L. Rev.* 149 (1991); David Smolin, "Regulating Religious and Cultural Conflict in Postmodern America: A Response to Professor Perry," 76 *Iowa L. Rev.* 1067 (1991); Michael McConnell, "'God is Dead and We Have Killed Him!': Freedom of Religion in the Post-Modern Age," 1993 *B.Y.U. L. Rev.* 163 (1993).

2. Who do I mean when I refer to *evangelicals*? See Robert Booth Fowler and Allen Hertzke, *Religion and Politics in America* (1995) 14. "The branch of Protestantism that teaches traditional tenets of Christian faith and stresses the adult conversion experience and aggressive evangelizing (seeking converts)." Why *evangelical* Christians? Because their burgeoning political activism helps to shape public attitudes about religion and politics. See chapter 6 in Fowler and Hertzke; Clyde Wilcox, *Onward Christian Soldiers*? (1996). When Americans react to excesses of religion and politics, it is generally directed at groups like the Christian Coalition and other leaders within the so-called Christian Right.

3. Judith Baer, in "Reading the Fourteenth Amendment: Inevitability of Noninterpretivism," *Politics and the Constitution* (1990) 69, notes that even those constitutional interpreters who support original intent reach different conclusions. Lief Carter argues, "Even those who profess strict fidelity to the past often arrive at contradictory conclusions. Raoul Berger, Charles Fairman, and William Crosskey all sought truth from the details of the historical records, but they came to very different legal conclusions." See Lief Carter, *Contemporary Constitutional Lawmaking* (1985) 53. I have done an empirical analysis of Baer's and Carter's practical critique of historical analysis (or of an original intent-based judicial philosophy). What I discovered is that their criticism is largely valid. Different scholars, with different political positions, will look at the same historical evidence and reach markedly different conclusions. See

Frank Guliuzza, "The Practical Perils of an Original Intent-Based Judicial Philosophy: Originalism and the Church State Test Case," 42 *Drake L. Rev.* 343 (1993).

4. See Loren Beth, *The American Theory of Church and State* (1958) 123–24; Max Sevelle and Darold Wax, *A History of Colonial America* (1973) 168–69; John Mecklin, *The Story of American Dissent* (1970) 3; John Noonan, *The Believers and The Powers that are* (1987) xiv. Additionally, see William Lee Miller, *The First Liberty* (1988); Mark Noll, *A History of Christianity in the United States and Canada* (1992); Donald Swanson, "Religion in the Public Schools," 59 *Nebraska L. Rev.* 428 (1980); Peter Marshall and David Manuel, *The Light and The Glory* (1977); Anson Stoke's exhaustive classic, *Church and State in the United States* (1950).

5. Beth, 36.

6. Swanson, 428.

7. Sevelle and Wax, 168–69. Beth, 36, offers an example of the Congregationalists' usage of their civil power to support their religious claims. One of their early documents record:

> If therefore Heretikes be manifestly knowne and publikely hurt-
> full, they are to be restrained of the Magistrate by publike power.
> And, if they be manifestly blasphemous, and partenacious, and
> stubborne in those blasphemes, may suffer capitall punishment.

8. Alvin Johnson and Frank Yost, *Separation of Church and State in the United States* (1948) 1. For a more thorough discussion of Roger Williams' enormous impact on religion and politics in America, see Noll, 58–60; Mecklin 82–115; John Murrin, "Religion and Politics in America from the First Settlements to the Civil War," in Noll, *Religion and American Politics* (1990) hereafter Noll, "Religion" 19. Timothy Hall, Separating Church and State (1998). In *The Garden and The Wilderness* (1965), Mark DeWolfe Howe contrasts Roger Williams fear that the state would corrupt church, and, therefore his case for separation, with Thomas Jefferson's concern that church might damage the secular state. Further, see Gregory Sisk, "Stating the Obvious: Protecting Religion for Religion's Sake," 47 Drake L. Rev. 45 (1998).

9. Noll, 26–29; Johnson and Yost, 3; Savelle and Wax, 198–99.

10. Noll, 65–68; Johnson and Yost, 3.

11. Leo Pfeffer, *God, Caesar, and the Constitution* (1975) 358.

12. Leonard Levy, *The Establishment Clause* (1986) 53–60, summarizes the struggle for religious liberty in Virginia.

13. U.S. Const. amend. 1. It is quite impossible to study the two clauses in isolation. A strict interpretation of the free exercise clause will necessarily bring it into conflict with the right of the states and national government to formulate their own criminal law; it will also bring the two religious clauses into conflict. There are occasions when, if government is to accommodate one's right to "free exercise," it will collide with the definition the court has given to the requirement that there be no state

"establishment." This point is not lost on those who teach constitutional law. See Alpheus T. Mason and D. Grier Stephenson, *American Constitutional Law* (1993) 478; Ralph Rossum and G. Alan Tarr, *American Constitutional Law* (1987) 395; David O'Brien, *Constitutional Law and Politics: Civil Rights and Civil Liberties* (1989) 635; William Lockhart, Yale Kamisar, Jesse Choper, and Steven Shiffrin, *Constitutional Law* (1986) who note, 1027, that:

> It is difficult to explore either clause in isolation from the other. The extent to which the clauses interact may be illustrated by the matter of public financial aid to parochial schools, the subject of a number of cases that follow: On the one hand, does such aid violate the establishment clause? On the other hand, does a state's failure to provide such aid violate the free exercise clause? Another example of the potential conflict between the two clauses . . . is whether, on the one hand, a state's exemption of church buildings from property taxes contravenes the establishment clause or whether, on the other hand, a state's taxing these buildings contravenes the free exercise clause.

14. The following is a very partial list of the recent articles and books addressing the establishment clause debate: Robert Alley, *James Madison on Religious Liberty* (1985); Gerard Bradley, *Church-State Relationships in America* (1987); Jesse Choper, *Securing Religious Liberty* (1995); Robert Cord, *Separation of Church and State* (1982); Thomas Curry, *The First Freedoms* (1986); Derek Davis, *Original Intent* (1991); Donald Drakeman, *Church-State Constitutional Issues*, (1991); Daniel Dreisbach, *Real Threats and Mere Shadows* (1987); Leonard Levy, *The Establishment Clause* (1986); Leo Pfeffer, *Religion, State, and the Burger Court* (1985); Steven Smith, *Foreordained Failure* (1995); Winnefred Sullivan, *Paying the Words Extra* (1994); Stephen Feldman, *Please Don't Wish Me a Merry Christmas* (1997). Harold Berman, "Religion and Law: The First Amendment in Historical Perspective," 35 *Emory L.J.* 777 (1986); Gerard Bradley, "No Religious Test Clause and the Constitution of Religious Liberty," 37 *Case W. L. Rev.* 674 (1987); Gordon Butler, "Cometh the Revolution: The Case for Overruling McCollum v. Board of Education," 99 *Dickinson L. Rev.* 843 (1995); Jesse Choper, "Separation of Church and State: 'New' Directions by the 'New' Supreme Court," 34 J. *Church and State* 363 (1992); Carl Esbeck, "A Restatement of the Supreme Court's Law of Religious Freedom: Coherence, Conflict, or Chaos," 70 *Notre Dame L. Rev.* 581 (1995); Steven Gey, "Why is Religion Special? Reconsidering the Accommodation of Religion Under the Religion Clauses of the First Amendment," 52 *U. Pitt. L. Rev.* 75 (1990); Gary Glenn, "Forgotten Purposes of the First Amendment Religion Clauses," 47 *Rev. Pol.* 340 (1987); Richard Hoskins, "The Original Separation of Church and State in America," 2 *J. L. and Religion* 221 (1984); Stanley Ingber, "Religion or Ideology: A Needed Clarification of the Religion Clauses," 41 *Stan. L. Rev.* 233 (1989); Kurt Lash, "The Second Adoption of the Establishment Clause: The Rise of the Nonestablishment Principle," 27 *Ariz. St. L. J.* 1085 (1995); Rosalie Berger Levinson, "Separation of Church and State: And the Wall Came

Tumbling Down," 18 *Val. L. Rev.* 707 (1984); Douglas Laycock, "'Nonpreferential' Aid to Religion: A False Claim About Original Intent," 27 *Wm. and Mary L. Rev.* 875 (1986); Laycock, "'Noncoercive' Support for Religion: Another False Claim About the Establishment Clause," 26 *Val. L. Rev.* (1991); William Marshall, "The Concept of Offensiveness in Establishment Clause and Free Exercise Clause Jurisprudence," 66 *Ind. L. J.* 351 (1990); Marshall, "We Know It When We See It: The Supreme Court and Establishment," 59 *S. Cal. L. Rev.* 495 (1986); Michael McConnell, "Religious Freedom at a Crossroads," 59 *U. Chi. L. Rev.* 115 (1992); McConnell, "Coercion: The Lost Element of Establishment," 27 *Wm. and Mary L. Rev.* 933 (1986); Thomas McCoy and Gary Kurtz, "A Unifying Theory for the Religion Clauses of the First Amendment," 39 *Vand. L. Rev.* 249 (1986); McCoy, "A Coherent Methodology for First Amendment Speech and Religion Clauses," 48 *Vand. L. Rev.* 1335 (1995); Dallin Oaks, "Separation and Accommodation, and the Future of Church and State," 35 *Depaul L. Rev.* 1 (1985); Rodney Smith, "Establishment Clause Analysis: A Liberty Maximizing Proposal," 4 *Notre Dame J. L., Ethics, Pub. Pol'y* 463 (1990); Matthew Steffey, "The Establishment Clause and the Lessons of Context," 26 *Rutgers L. J.* 775 (1995); Kathleen Sullivan, "Religion and Liberal Democracy," 59 *U. Chi. L. Rev.* 195 (1992); John Witte, "The Essential Rights and Liberties of Religion in the American Constitutional Experiment," 71 *Notre Dame L. Rev.* 371 (1996); Kurt Lash, "Should We Amend the Religion Clauses of the United States Constitution? The Status of Constitutional Religious Liberty at the End of the Millennium," 32 *Loy. L.A. L. Rev.* 1 (1998); Kent Greenawalt, "Should the Religion Clauses of the Constitution be Amended?," 32 *Loy. L.A. L. Rev.* 9 (1998); Kurt Lash, "Power and the Subject of Religion," 59 *Ohio St. L.J. 1069* (1998); Richard Ansson, Jr., "Drawing Lines in the Shifting Sand: Where Should the Establishment Wall Stand?" 8 *Temple Pol. & Civ. Rts. L. Rev.* 1 (1998). Lucy Salsbury Payne, in "Uncovering the First Amendment: A Research Guide to the Religion Clauses," 4 *Notre Dame J. L., Ethics, Pub. Pol'y* 825 (1990), offers an extensive annotated bibliography—really a comprehensive research guide—for those interested in studying the establishment clause and free exercise clause.

15. See the extensive discussion of the court's vexatious establishment clause jurisrprudence in chapter 5.

16. Which interpretation did the framers really support? See the positions offered by Levy, 83–84, and Douglas Laycock, "'Nonpreferential' Aid to Religion: A False Claim About Original Intent," 27 *Wm. and Mary L. Rev.* 875 (1986) 881–85, compared with those presented by Bradley, 93–97, and Dreisbach, 65–66. Each carefully scrutinizes the historical evidence. Levy and Laycock embrace the broader interpretation of the establishment clause. Bradley and Dreisbach argue for the more narrow. After analyzing their respective arguments, I concluded that, while they "present a fairly consistent account of what occurred in the First Congress during the Summer of 1789," several areas of disagreement exist, including:

1) What was the role of James Madison in the process?

2) What are the ramifications of the House debates?

3) What conclusions can be drawn from the senate's handling of the establishment clause?

4) Did the Conference Committee construct a broad version of the establishment clause?

5) What of the actions taken by the first Congress simultaneously with the crafting of the establishment clause?

See Guliuzza, 363, 366–79. The historical debate over the establishment clause is not new. Justice Hugo Black initiated the debate in *Everson*, with his interpretation of the history of the first amendment, and historical analysis certainly was present in the early cluster of establishment clauses cases, *McCollum v Board*, 333 U.S. 203 (1948), *Zorach v Clauson*, 343 U.S. 306 (1952), *Engel v Vitale*, 370 U.S. 421 (1962), and *Abington Township v Schempp*, 374 U.S. 203 (1963). Likewise, Chief Justice Burger employed historical analysis in *Marsh v Chambers*, 463 U.S. 783 (1983), and *Lynch v Donnelly*, 465 U.S. 668 (1984). The most complete rejection of Justice Black's historical argument in Everson is found in Justice Rehnquist's dissenting opinion in *Wallace v Jaffree*, 472 U.S. 38 (1985). In addition to Levy and Laycock, those who would argue that the framers of the establishment clause wanted a stricter separation of church and state would include: Alley; Curry; Davis; Oaks; James Wood (ed.) *Religion and the State* (1985); and, most especially, Leo Pfeffer. See Pfeffer's, *Church, State, and Freedom* (1967); *Religious Freedom* (1977). Those who would join with Bradley and Dreisbach, and argue that the framers intended a more narrow reading of the establishment clause, include: Cord; Berman; Glenn; McConnell; Chester Antieau, Arthur Downey, and Edward Roberts, *Freedom from Federal Establishment* (1964); Michael Malbin, *Religion and Politics* (1978).

17. See *Cantwell v Connecticut*, 310 U.S. 296 (1940) and *Everson v Board of Education*, 330 U.S. 1 (1947).

18. Levy, 38. Harold Berman, in *Faith and Order* (1993) 211–13, provides evidence of establishments, in the various states until well into the nineteenth century. Professor Steven Smith, 122–27 argues that the framers intended for the establishment clause to restrict national power with respect to religion, and they permitted states to flesh out religious issues for themselves. Consequently, he is opposed to the court's efforts to discover a single, national meaning for the religion clauses.

19. Levy, 93–99; Laycock, 916–918, 923.

20. See Dreisbach, 66–68; Bradley, 97–104.

21. Laycock, 918–19. See Ruth Bloch, "Religion and Ideological Change in the American Revolution," in Noll, "Religion" 57.

22. Dreisbach, 66–68.

23. See Alexis de Tocqueville, *Democracy in America* (1835); Sanford Kessler, *Tocqueville's Civil Religion* (1994).

24. See *Church of Holy Trinity v U.S.*, 143 U.S. 457, 471 (1892), and note Justice William O. Douglas's relatively recent admonishment that American institutions presuppose the existence of a "Supreme Being" in *Zorach v Clauson*, 343 U.S. 306 (1952).

25. See Bruce Ackerman, *We the People* (1991).

26. Kenneth Wald, *Religion and Politics in the United States* (1987). In addition, see Robert Bellah (et al.) *Habits of the Heart* (1985); Bellah and Phillip Hammond, *Varieties of Civil Religion* (1980); Russell Richey and Donald Jones (eds.) *American Civil Religion* (1974); Martin Marty, "The Sacred and the Secular in American History," in M.L. Bradbury and James Gilbert (eds.), *Transforming Faith: The Sacred and Secular in Modern American History* (1989).

27. See Noll, 304, and Martin Marty, in *Religion and Republic* (1987), 115, discusses the social gospel movement and indicates that it drew negative reactions from more than just fundamentalists. For instance, Reinhold Niebuhr, certainly no biblical fundamentalist, was also an outspoken critic of the movement.

28. George Marsden, "The Religious Right: A Historical Overview," in Michael Cromartie (ed.) *No Longer Exiles* (1993) 1–16. Further, see Robert Handy, "Protestant Theological Tensions and Political Styles in the Progressive Period, in Noll, "Religion" 282; Robert Wuthnow and Matthew Lawson, "Sources of Christian Fundamentalism in the United States," in Martin Marty and Scott Appleby (eds.) *Accounting for Fundamentalisms*, Vol. 4 (1994); Paul Carter, *The Twenties in America* (1968) 80–81, Michael Lienesch, "Mobilizing against Modernity: The World's Christian Fundamentals Association and the Fundamentalist Movement" Address at the 1995 Annual Meeting of the American Political Science Association. Admittedly, this characterization, while essentially accurate, is far too sweeping. There certainly were fundamentalists who participated in the social gospel movement and who were political progressives.

29. See Stephen Carter, *The Culture of Disbelief* (1993) at 112. See William Martin, *With God on our Side* (1996) at 12.

30. See Noll, 282, and Grant Wacker, "Response (to Marsden)," in Cromartie, 17.

31. Noll, 382, notes that World War I served to mobilize fundamentalists. The despair expressed by many intellectuals after the war gave conservative Christians a window of opportunity to exercise intellectual and cultural leadership in the United States. See Mecklin, 220, and Edward Larson, *Trial and Error* (1985) 41.

32. An abbreviated reference to *Tennessee v John Thomas Scopes* (1925). Larson argues, 41, that, although conservative Christians were poised to step into the intellectual and cultural void left after World War I, their first concerted effort was an attack upon Darwinism. See Noll, 430; Marty, 24; Martin, 15; Paul Carter, 78; Paul Carter, *Another Part of the Twenties* (1977) hereafter Carter, "Another Part"; and Ray Ginger's, *Six Days or Forever?* (1958).

33. Alan Hertzke, *Echoes of Discontent* (1993) 48. However, Professor David Weeks, in "The Moral Basis of Evangelical Political Involvement," address at the 1995 Annual Meeting of the American Political Science Association, examines the moral arguments proffered by evangelicals to justify political participation. He indicates that they were first formulated in the 1940s and 50s. The phenomenon I am describing, the flight from grassroots politics, seems not to be limited to white, conservative evangelicals. Fowler and Hertzke note, 155:

To be sure, there has been a long tradition of teaching by the African-American church regarding a just and equitable society. Thre were also many ways in which the black church before the 1960s sought power in society—often working   quietly behind the scenes. Nonetheless there was broad agreement that the public arena was a dangerous place and one to be avoided.

34. See Noll, 445 and Robert Wuthnow, "The Future of the Religious Right," in Cromartie, 38.

35. See Stephen Carter, 56–66; Martin, 192–94.

36. Stephen Carter, 264.

37. See Francis Schaeffer, *The Great Evangelical Disaster* (1984). Again, evangelicals are not the only religious people active in politics. Mainline Protestants, Catholics, Jews, African American believers, and others, actively participate in politics with a multitude of approaches and strategies. See Wald; Fowler, and Hertzke; Kessler at chapters 5–9; Lyman Kellstedt and Mark Noll, "Religion, Voting for President, and Party Identification," in Noll, "Religion" 355.

38. Several of the authors I have cited above, including Cromartie, Hertzke, and Wald, discuss the rise of political activism among conservative evangelicals, and the linkage between their theological conservativism and political conservativism. As one who is both a minister, and who has been somewhat politically active, I have noticed the tendency to mesh what might be called "citizenship responsibilities" with a believer's "Christian responsibilities." I do not regard this linkage as *necessarily* invalid or as *necessarily* a bad thing. It can go too far. I remember attending a party county convention as a delegate. I was more than a little uneasy when our congressman commended us for "doing the Lord's work." I do not think he was offering a careful, theological justification for Christian citizenship. He was not arguing that God ordained three institutions—the church, the family, and the government—to nurture and develop fallen persons. He was not arguing that, consistent with our responsibility to support the latter of these institutions, it is good that God's people be involved with government. Rather, he seemed to be offering a partisan political statement: "God's on our side. Therefore, to be active in the politics of the party means you are doing God's will!"

39. Lyman Kellstedt, "Religion, the Neglected Variable: An Agenda for Future Research on Religion and Political Behavior," in David Leege and Lyman Kellstedt, *Rediscovering the Religious Factor in American Politics* (1993), 288. Corwin Smidt, in his article "Evangelical Voting Patterns: 1976–1988," in Cromartie, 94, looks empirically at the impact of Carter's candidacy on evangelicals in the 1976 election.

40. See Martin, 191–220, for an explanation as to why evangelicals turned from supporting President Carter toward Ronald Reagan during the 1980 campaign. For an analysis of what might be termed "the first wave" of contemporary evangelical political activism (e.g., from 1980 to 1988), see David Wells and John Woodbridge, *The Evangelicals* (1985); Douglas Frank, *Less than Conquerors* (1986); Robert Liebman and

Robert Wuthnow (eds.), *The New Christian Right* (1983); David Bromley and Anson Shupe (eds.), *New Christian Politics* (1984).

41. Ted Jelen and Clyde Wilcox, "Preaching to the Converted: The Causes and Consequences of Viewing Religious Television," in Leege and Kellstedt, 255.

42. Hertzke, 19. Hubert Morken, in Pat Robertson, *Where He Stands* (1988), outlined Robertson's position on the issues that arose during the 1988 campaign.

43. Wacker, 19, argues that "while most politically conservative evangelicals today are aligned with the Republican Party, the Republican Party hardly is aligned with the Evangelical Right. . . . the high command of the Republican Party has shown itself stubbornly uninterested in the fundamental concerns of the Evangelical Right." Contrast that position with the evidence presented by Richard Berke in "Religious Right Gains Influence and Spreads Discord in G.O.P.," *N.Y Times* (June 3, 1994) A1. Berke writes that:

> Christians who cleave to a strict interpretation of the Bible have effectively taken over the Republican Party in Texas, Virginia, Oregon, Iowa, Washington, and South Carolina, and have made significant advances in several states including Florida, New York, California, and Louisiana.

Berke notes that the rise of evangelical Christians as a force in the Republican Party coincides with and has grown substantially since Pat Robertson's candidacy for president. He observes that religious conservatives push the party to adopt more conservative platforms, they are getting elected to local offices, and they "are beginning to have an influence on higher offices." See Berke, "As Christians Pull the G.O.P to the Right, Its Leaders Argue Over Holding the Center," *N.Y. Times* (June 27, 1994) A12. An issue of *U.S. News and World Report* (April 24, 1995) discussed the increasing impact of religious conservatives. With a picture of Robertson on the cover, it states: "For God's Sake: Religious Conservatives Think Their Time Has Come." I would call attention to the conversation between conservative Christian leaders in *Christianity Today* (Septemebr 6, 1999). Some of those featured in the cover story question the ongoing impact of the Christian Right in electoral politics. Perhaps more important, the various leaders debate whether Christians even *should* continue in the effort to advance their concerns and solutions through the political process.

44. See Laurence Barrett, "Fighting for God and the Right Wing," *Time* (September 13, 1993) 58.

45. Roy Rivenburg, "Litigating for a 'Godly Heritage,'" *Los Angeles Times* (December 30, 1992) E1; Tim Stafford, "Move Over ACLU," *Christianity Today* (October 25, 1993) 20–24; and Morken, "The Evangelical Legal Response to the ACLU: Religion, Politics, and the First Amendment," presented at the 1992 Annual Meeting of the American Political Science Association, Chicago (September 3–6, 1992). I also discussed the important role played by the National Legal Foundation,

and the American Center for Law and Justice, in two recent Supreme Court decisions, *Westside Community Schools v Mergens*, 496 U.S. 226 (1990) and *Lamb's Chapel v Center Moriches School District*, 113 S.Ct. 2141 (1993). See Guliuzza, "'Tis a Lesson You Should Heed. Try, Try, Again. If at First You Don't Succeed . . .': The Christian Right's 'Free Speech Strategy' for Securing 'Free Exercise' of Religion," Address at the 1994 Annual Meeting of the American Political Science Association, New York (September 1–4, 1994). For a thoroughly pejorative look at Robertson's political and legal activism, see Robert Boston, *The Most Dangerous Man in America?* (1996).

46. Oliver Thomas, "Comments on the Papers by Milner Ball and Frederick Geddicks," 4 *Notre Dame J. L. Ethics and Public Policy* 451 (1990) 453. Theodore Blumoff, in 20 *Cap. U. L. Rev.* 159 (1991) 186, agrees. To those who claim that religion has lost its clout in the public arena, Blumoff responds:

> It is as if they had missed the last three decades: the Moral Majority, the Reverends Billy Graham, Martin Luther King, Jesse Jackson, Jerry Falwell, Theodore Hesbergh, and others—all have taken their turns in the political limelight.

See also Kessler, 11; Christopher Mooney, *Public Virtue* (1986) 18. Peter Benson and Dorothy Williams, in *Religion on Capitol Hill* (1982), discuss the pervasiveness of religion in politics.

47. See Bellah; Kessler; Marty (chapters 3 and 4); Wald, 48; Yehudah Mirsky, "Civil Religion and The Establishment Clause," 95 *Yale L. J.* 1237 (1986).

48. Stephen Carter, 44–45. Kessler, 12–13 offers evidence that supports a secularization thesis.

49. And, perhaps, that is what really counts. Thomas Dye and Harmon Zeigler, in their prominent textbook in American Politics, *The Irony of Democracy* (1993) v, argue that America is governed by elites. They claim that "only a tiny handful of people make decisions that shape the lives of all of us . . . we have little direct influence over these decisions."

50. See the references to these earlier works in Perry, 146 n. 6, and Richard John Neuhaus, *The Naked Public Square* (1984) 84. Marty, 63, discusses why Niebuhr, Murray, and others were concerned about the growing minimalization of religious influence present in American public life.

51. Mark Tushnet, "The Constitution of Religion," 50 *Rev. Pol.* 628 (1988).

52. Harold Berman, "Religion and the Law"; Berman, *Faith and Order* (1993).

53. Robert Bellah, "Cultural Pluralism and Religious Particularism," in Henry Clark (ed.) *Freedom of Religion in America* (1982) 35.

54. A. James Reichley, *Religion in American Public Life* (1985).

55. Paul Vitz, *Censorship: Evidence of Bias in our Children's Textbooks* (1986).

56. James Davidson Hunter and Os Guiness, *Articles of Faith, Articles of Peace* (1990).

57. Frederick Mark Gedicks, *The Rhetoric of Church and State* (1995).

58. Ronald Thiemann, *Religion in Public Life* (1996).

59. Franklin Gamwell, *The Meaning of Religious Freedom* (1994).

CHAPTER TWO

1. Thomas Dye and Harmon Zeigler, in their American politics textbook, *The Irony of Democracy* (1993), v, argue that America is governed by elites. They claim that "only a tiny handful of people make decisions that shape the lives of all of us . . . we have little direct influence over these decisions." C. Wright Mills, *The Power Elite* (1956), isolated three institutions—major corporations, political executives, and the military—and argued that individuals within emerge to form a "power elite." Today, however, when one discusses "elites," the conversation is not limited to economic, political, or military elites. Dye and Zeigler, 139–163, include the media in their cornucopia of elites. See also Robert Lichter, Stanley Rothman, Linda Lichter, *The Media Elite* (1986). The growing awareness that the public has reached the same conclusion has received a good deal of recent attention. See, Stephen Budiansky, "The Media's Message," *U.S New and World Report*, Jan. 9, 1995, 45. Moreover, in addition to the media elite, one might also discuss an academic (or educational) elite. Michael Barone, in "Needed: A Rendezvous With History," 34, distinguishes between the economic elite and the cultural and educational elite. Sanford Kessler, in *Tocqueville's Civil Religion* (1994), discusses the "forces which shape American values—the universities, the media, and the arts." Too, Dean Kelley, counselor for the National Council of Churches, in his praise of Professor Stephen Carter's book, *The Culture of Disbelief* (1993), discusses the "intellectual elite." These are the folks with whom I am concerned in this chapter.

2. Peter Berger, "Afterword," in James Davidson Hunter and Os Guiness (eds.), *Articles of Faith, Articles of Peace* (1990), 120. See Michael Dorf, "God and Man in the Yale Dormitories," 84 Va. L. Rev. 843 (1998); Timothy Fort, "Religion in the Workplace: Mediating Religion's Good, Bad, and Ugly Naturally," 12 ND J.L. Ethics & Pub. Pol'y 121 (1998). The journal *Academe*, published by the AAUP, devoted its November/December 1996 (vol. 82) issue to the way religion is treated in the academy. I will refer to several of those articles in this chapter. The lead article, by church historian Martin Marty, 14, reveals that "You *Get* to Teach and Study Religion"—his case for including religion in colleges and universities.

3. Richard Neuhaus, in *The Naked Public Square* (1984), 140, notes the difference between the level of expertise intellectuals have with respect to Plato and Aristotle, and their lack of hegemony over biblical knowledge: "The exegesis of Aristotle and Plato is reserved for the academy, whereas the exegesis of the Bible is a mass industry employing millions of professional and part-time believers." Neuhaus suggests, therefore, intellectuals have a vested interest in trumpeting classical religion and dismissing biblical religion. That makes sense to me. My concern is with those intellectuals who, when dismissing religion, pontificate as if they are experts in the subject.

4. Michael Perry, *Love and Power* (1991), 67.

5. And Stephen Carter, in *The Culture of Disbelief* (1993) 13, suggests, "The consistent message of modern American society is that whenever the demand of one's religion conflict with what one has to do to get ahead, one is expected to ignore the religious demands and act . . . well . . . *rationally.*"

6. Id., 14–15.

7. Kenneth Wald, *Religion and Politics* (1987) 4. The impact of the Enlightenment upon American public life, including American religious life, is discussed in Martin Marty, *Religion and Republic* (1987) 42, 49–50, 130, 271; Kessler, 10, 91; Mark Dewolfe Howe, *The Garden and the Wilderness* (1965) 2; Harold Berman, *Faith and Order* (1993) 215.

8. Id. Kessler, 5, argues that there is a very real "culture war" between the modernists and religious believers. They have different views of morality, and proffer different visions for America's future. The war, he notes, "is currently being fought on many fronts—the family, the churches, the schools and universities, the law, electoral politics, and, most important, the court of public opinion." For one to convert the crowd, it is certainly helpful to persuade the messenger, and Kessler notes, 184, the messengers are typically those in the universities, the media, and the arts. Further, if one wants to sway particularly a religious audience, it helps to convert religious leaders. Kessler argues, 172–184, that, to a greater or lesser extent, mainline Protestants, Catholics, and even evangelical Christians, have capitulated to modernism.

9. See Gedicks definition of postmodern, 9–10. Too, see Michael McConnell, "'God is Dead and We Have Killed Him!': Freedom of Religion in the Post-modern Age," 1993 *B.Y.U. L. Rev. 163 (1993)*.

10. Langdon Gilkey, a theologian from the University of Chicago who testified *against* the Arkansas law designed to give equal time to creation science, *McClean v Arkansas*, 529 F. Supp. 1255 (*E.D. Ark.* 1982), noted subsequently, that:

> Many scientists share with the fundamentalists the confused notion that so-called religious knowledge and scientific knowledge exist on the same level and that, as science advances, scientific knowledge simply replaces and dissolves religious myth. . . One encounters this view of science as dissolving religious truth in the writings of Julian Huxley, Gaylord Simpson, Jacob Bronowski, and Carl Sagan.

See Edward Larson, in *Trial and Error* (1985) 128.

11. See Robert Wuthnow, *Meaning and Moral Order* (1987).

12. See Wuthnow, 265–298, Ralph Burhoe (ed.), *Science and Human Values in the 21st Century* (1962); Stanley Jaki, *The Road of Science and The Ways to God* (1988).

13. See, for example, Colin Campbell, *The Case for Christianity* (1981); Josh McDowell and Don Stewart, *Understanding Secular Religions* (1982).

14. I first heard this argument advanced by Professor Graham Walker in a conversation we had at the University of Notre Dame in the late 1980s. I agree with Professor Gedicks, 11, who argues that religious communitarian discourse presupposes a faith that is based, primarily, upon tradition and authority, but, even if secondarily, employs reason to "articulate and defend these values and practices." See Kent Greenawalt, *Private Consciences and Public Reasons* (1995) 85; Suzanna Sherry, "Religion and the Public Square: Making Democracy Safe for Religious Minorities," 47 DePaul L. Rev. 499 (1998); Linda McClain, "Toleration, Autonomy, and Governmental Promotion of Good Lives: Beyond 'Empty' Toleration as Respect," 59 Ohio St. L.J. 19 (1998).

15. See Bruce Lincoln, Discourse and the Construction of Society (1989); Robert Segal, *Joseph Campbell: An Introduction* (1987); Joseph Campbell, *The Power of Myth* (1988).

16. McConnell, 164, suggests that the postmodernists are pretty tolerant of, even if condescending toward, religious believers:

> And in like manner, the post-modern world is willing to leave the believer in peace. Religious belief, we realize, is precious to those who have it, and it would be pointless and mean to interfere with it.

17. Id. See also Belden Lane, "The *Power of Myth*: Lessons From Joseph Campbell," *The Christian Century* (1989) 652; and Joseph Byrnes, *The Psychology of Religion* (1984).

18. There is a very close parallel in constitutional theory. In his provocative book, *An Introduction to Constitutional Interpretation* (1991), Professor Lief Carter argues that modern science, modern religion, and modern philosophy (what I am calling "postmodern") have liberated us from domination by both religious authority and scientific tyranny (the claim that if science says something, it must be true). In so doing, we are left with the realization that nothing is fully and finally true. Rather, all arguments, claims, legislation, judicial edicts, and the like, must be placed into the context of the communication expressed within the communities of their respective authors. They are not to be evaluated based upon their truth, legitimacy, or even their qualitative merit per se. Instead, we should determine whether or not they are "good" based upon whether they are coherent, honest, and further the narrative that undergirds their respective communities. My concern is that I do not think Professor Carter overcomes the problem of appealing to authority—of determining in very subjective terms what is really good versus bad, better versus worse. It seems that by embracing the "postmoderns" (science, theology, and philosophy), and simultaneously clinging to an aspirational society (the notion that we eventually triumph over our sinful behavior—his "story for the community"), Carter's approach does not fully abandon the more authoritative ways of knowing and communicating that he rejects.

19. While there are multiple usages for the terms "premodern," "modern," and "postmodern," there are some scholars who maintain that *all* Christian theology is premodern. Although they do not make the claim that Christianity equals bad faith, they

do argue that its premodern status justifies its exclusion from serious study at our universities. See Isaac Kramnick and R. Laurence Moore, "The Godless University," 82 *Academe* 18 (1996) 22.

20. The distinction between "good" versus "bad" religion is illustrated in the Academy Award winning film, *Dead Men Walking*. There is a pivotal exchange between the central character, a nun, ministering at a state prison to a death-row inmate, and her supervising priest about what should be her purpose in sharing the love of Christ. Note the difference between the two views of Jesus presented by the priest and nun. The priest's Jesus came to earth because God will eventually judge sin. His Jesus focus is "other worldly." His Jesus died to redeem lost souls. Her Jesus came to comfort and bless. Her Jesus is "this worldly." Her Jesus came to provide and fortify the self-esteem of prostitutes and tax collectors. While I happen to embrace *both* representations of Jesus' ministry, clearly the filmmakers were able to choose between the two. Sister Jean was the heroine. The priest was constantly in the way. He was a potential threat to her objectives. Thus, her Jesus is consistent with "good" religion. His Jesus exemplified "bad" religion.

21. Stephen Carter, 7. Carter, id., goes on to relate a story about a network news program that distinguished between churches as places of worship, and churches doing things that are far more meaningful. It is also worth noting his discussion of the Maria Von Trapp story, as related in the film, *The Sound of Music*, and how it might fare with therapists Stephen Arterburn and Jack Felton, authors of the book *Toxic Faith: Understanding and Overcoming Religious Addiction* (1991). In their work, Arterburn and Felton determine that some religious faiths are dysfunctional and others are not. Not only do academics and other cultural elites differentiate between progressive and regressive faiths, their distinction between various religious leaders is even more pronounced. Consider, for example, how the media treated the Rev. Jerry Falwell and, twenty years earlier, the Rev. Martin Luther King Jr. See Stephen Carter, 59.

22. Although evidence of prejudice toward Jewish students is quite obviously discernable within the academic community, Carter, 12-13, suggests that it is often indicative of the more general bigotry toward religious devotion. He recounts the public exchange between Berkeley sociologist Harry Edwards and Harvard law professor Alan Dershowitz over Edward's decision to schedule an examination on Yom Kippur. Dershowitz argued that such behavior is evidence that "Jewish students are second-class citizens in Professor Edwards's classes." Carter, id., suggests that Dershowitz has, indeed, identified the right crime even if he has the wrong villain. Dershowitz, notes Carter, has tapped into more than a prejudice against Jewish students. He has illustrated the prejudice against religious devotion—"a prejudice that masquerades as 'neutrality.'"

23. Berger, 119. Professor William Scott Green, in "Religion within the Limits," 82 *Academe* 24 (1996), notes, 26:

> Consequently, tolerance—both intellectual and social—has become an urgent and primary academic virtue, and the contem-

porary academy claims to be one of society's basic training grounds for it. But even academic tolerance has its limits, and religion surely marks one of them.

See George Marsden, *The Soul of the American University* (1994).

24. See the editorial, "LDS Church Speaks; Legislature Will Listen," *Ogden Standard Examiner* (June 9, 1996) 20A. The LDS population across the state of Utah is well over 70 percent, and the percentage of Mormons in the state legislature is substantially higher.

25. The charges of anti-Mormon bigotry at the University of Utah continue. See "U of U Leader Tries to Dispel Anti-LDS 'Myths'", *Ogden Standard Examiner* (October 28, 1995) 1A, and Paul Rolly and Joann Jacobsen-Wells, "Church and State?", *Salt Lake Tribune* (October 23, 1995) D2.

26. See D. Kurapka, "Hate Story," *New Republic* (May 30, 1988) 19, and Bill Turque, "Playing a Different Tune," *Newsweek* (June 28, 1993) 30.

27. See Eloise Salholtz, "Acting Up to Fight AIDS," *Newsweek* (June 6, 1988) 42, John Leo, "Here Come the Wild Creatures," *U.S. News and World Report* (October 19, 1992), 27, and Leo, "The Politics of Intimidation," *U.S. News and World Report* (April 6, 1992), 24.

28. Note the impact when power is coupled with bigotry. In *Beyond the Burning Cross* (1994), Edward Cleary examines how racial prejudice plus power translates in violence. In *With Justice for Some* (1995), George Fletcher argues that power can be exercised against the powerless effectively even if it is not imminently violent.

29. In September, 1991, ABC television, on its news magazine, *Prime Time Live*, did an investigation into on-going racism in America. They put two men in St. Louis. The only significant (identifiable) difference between the two men was that one was white and the other man was black. The segment revealed just how bigotry could be coupled with power, and how this worked to the detriment of the African American gentleman: when he was looking for housing, purchasing goods, and on the job market.

30. And it is not limited to the academy—that is where I can speak with some confidence. But surely this tendency to couple antireligious bigotry with an exercise in power cuts across the other traditional and cultural elites. Stephen Carter, 7, relates a story very similar to the one involving my friend.

31. Id., 57. Professor Carter discusses survey data that suggest the underrepresentation of those who are devoutly religious on college campuses. This underrepresentation of those who are devout is likely to continue into the future. Kramnick and Moore, 21, speculate as to the impact one's faith might have on his or her job security:

> The claim by a biologist that Darwinian science leaves no room for God is not a cause for scandal in the modern university, whereas the claim by a professor of English that students ought to believe what the Bible says *would be a good reason to deny tenure.* Without

a doubt, we live in an intellectual world where committed theism, but not atheism, is presumed to get in the way of learning (emphasis added).

32. Kessler, 10, notes that:

> The scholarly dispute over the nature, strength, and direction of American religion today is generally known as the secularization debate. Peter L. Berger defines secularization as the "process by which sectors of society and culture are removed from the domination of religious institutions and symbols."

Paul Weber, in *Equal Separation* (1990) 4, links the secularization debate with the constitutional arguments employed when interpreting the first amendment's establishment clause. One type of separation (of church and state) is, argues Weber, "transvaluing separation," and he suggests that it has a devoted following in the United States. Transvaluing separation:

> holds that one objective of government is to secularize the political culture of the nation, that is, to reject as politically illegitimate the use of all religious symbols, or the appeal to religious values, motivations, or policy objectives in the political arena.

33. Leo Pfeffer, "The 'Religion' of Secular Humanism," 29 *J. Church and State* 495, 504 (1987).

34. Gedicks, 27, notes:

> secular individualist discourse locates the boundary between public and private life in a different conceptual place than does religious communitarian discourse, thereby excluding religion from public life as more properly a matter of private, individual devotion.

35. Stanley Hauerwas, *A Community of Character* (1981), 79.

36. Perry, 4.

37. Stephen Carter, 25. See *Robert Bellah* (et al.) *Habits of the Heart* (1985) 223.

38. Note Professor Gedicks' distinction, however, between *institutional* separation and *political* or *cultural* separation. To be a secular nation requires the former. See Gedicks, 11.

39. Wald, 36–47, discusses that the linkage between religious belief and political involvement in America precedes the Revolution. The intrusion of religious ideas and solutions was acceptable to religious people. It was, likewise, acceptable to those in political power. It was acceptable, Wald argues, because it was impossible to separate the two. Wald observes that imprint of religion generally, Protestant Christianity particularly, is pervasive: the imprint of the Bible's teachings is evident on thousands of

founding documents authored between 1760 and 1805. Three Christian doctrines particularly influenced the American's political mindset—covenant theology, original sin, and the idea that Americans were a special (a chosen) people. Harold Berman, in "Religious Freedom and the Challenge of the Modern State," in James Davison Hunter and Os Guiness (eds.), *Articles of Faith, Articles of Peace* (1990) 41, supports Wald's contention that at the time of the founding, there was substantial interaction between church and government. Berman argues that, for the framers, this was not a constitutional problem. The framers understood that what they were doing was substantially different from the formal establishments found in Europe. For an alternative perspective on how the framers perceived the linkage between church and state, see Leonard Levy, *The Establishment Clause* (1986), and Douglas Laycock, "'Nonpreferential' Aid to Religion: A False Claim About Original Intent," 27 *Wm. and Mary L. Rev.* 875 (1986).

40. Berman, 43. See Gedicks, 82.

41. Id., 47. See Nathan Hatch, in "The Democratization of Christianity and the Character of American Politics," Mark Noll (ed.), *Religion and American Politics* (1990) 93.

42. Although I make the argument with some caution, Richard John Neuhaus, note 1, 155, boldly asserts that there is a concerted effort to empower the state at the expense of religion. He notes that there is a "philosophical and legal effort to isolate and exclude the religious dimension of culture." It is interesting to look at Professor Stephen Carter's treatment of Neuhaus 51–52. Carter argues that Neuhaus "tells us that in America, the public square has become openly hostile toward religion." He claims that, rather than open hostility, religion is treated more as a hobby. Even Neuhaus, 25, dismisses the argument proffered by the so-called Religious Right that there is a conspiracy by atheists and secular humanists to take over America. Both agree, notes Carter, 51, "the rules of our public square exist on uneasy terms with religion." I am mindful of the discussion I had recently with Professor Kyle Pasewark. Pasewark contends that academic, cultural, and media elites are increasingly receptive to religious-based argument. He observes that the attitude of these elites is more like, "Okay, we're listening. What do you have to say?" Pasewark is concerned that, all too often, people of faith have little to contribute to the discussion. I am still skeptical about how welcome religious-based expression might be within the marketplace. I am persuaded by Professor Pasewark, however, that those who would advance a faith-based argument in, say, the political market place ought to be more sure that they have something to contribute than they are to be perpetually worried about whether the argument will be received.

43. Richard John Neuhaus' characterization. See Neuhaus, 160.

44. See McConnell, 165.

45. Berman, 48–49.

46. Id., 49.

47. Id., 50. Professor Gedicks argues, 43, that:

the privatization of religion by secular individualist discourse is an act of power that can plausibly be defended as religiously neutral only if religion is presented as a "naturally" private activity, excluded from public life like all value preferences. Within religious communitarian discourse, by contrast, where religion has important public dimensions, privatization constitutes bald—and unwise—religious persecution.

48. Id.

49. Neuhaus, 155, links the two phenomena: the effort to extinguish religious voices from the public square and the strategy to exalt the state:

> Our problems, then, stem in large part from the philosophical and legal effort to isolate and exclude the religious dimension of culture. Instead of the three great powers of Burckhardt, we now have two great powers of state and culture. But of the two only the state can, in his words, "lay claim to compulsive authority." . . . But, from the viewpoint of those who desire a nearly unitary social order, the most problematic "loose cannon" on the deck is religion. That is because, of all the institutions in society, only religion can invoke against the state a transcendent authority and have its invocation seconded by "the people" to whom a democratic state is presumably accountable. For the state to be secured from such challenge, religion must be redefined as a private, emphatically not public, phenomenon. In addition, because truly value-less existence is impossible for persons or societies, the state must displace religion as the generator and bearer of values. Therefore it must screen out of public discourse and decision-making those values too closely associated with religion, lest public recognition be given to a source of moral authority other than the state itself. To put it differently: in the eyes of the state the dangerous child today is not the child who points out that the emperor has no clothes but the child who sees that the emperor's garments of moral authority have been stolen from the religion he has sent into exile from the public square.

See Gedicks, 12.

50. Not surprisingly, religious individuals and groups are relying upon the free speech clause as a means of protecting their free exercise rights. See Frank Guliuzza, "'Tis a Lesson You Should Heed. Try, Try, Again. If at First You Don't Succeed . . .': The Christian Right's 'Free Speech Strategy' For Securing 'Free Exercise' of Religion," address at the 1994 annual meeting of the American Political Science Association.

51. Oliver Thomas, "Comments on the Papers by Milner Ball and Frederick Geddicks," 4 *Notre Dame J. L. Ethics and Public Policy* 451 (1990).

52. Stephen Carter argues, 54, that there is quite a difference between a public square that is formally open to religion and one that welcome religious expression.

53. See Professor Carter argument, id., 52. For an alternative perspective, see Michael Kinsley, "Martyr Complex," *New Republic* (September 13, 1993) 4; Theodore Blumoff, "The New Religionists' Newest Social Gospel: On the Rhetoric and Reality of Religion's 'Marginalization' in Public Life," 51 *U. Miami L. Rev.* 1 (1996).

54. Id., 52–53.

55. Neuhaus, 148–149.

56. Carter, 227. See also Stephen Carter, "The Constitution and the Religious University," 47 DePaul L. Rev. 479 (1998); Stephen Carter, *Civility* (1998).

57. In an interview with *Playboy* magazine, Dr. King identifies precisely what motivated his political activism. King expressed his disappointment at white ministers in the south for failing to stand up for a cause that was so clearly just. The interviewer from *Playboy* asked: "Their stated reason for refusing to help was that it was not the proper role of the church to 'intervene in secular affairs.' Do you disagree with this view?" Dr. King responded:

> Most emphatically. The essence of the Epistles of Paul is that Christians should *rejoice* at being deemed worthy to suffer for what they believe. The projection of a social gospel, in my opinion, is the true witness of a Christian life. This is the meaning of the true *ekklesia*—the inner, spiritual church. The church once changed society. It was then a thermostat of society. But today, I feel that too much of the church is merely a thermometer, which measures rather than molds public opinion.

See James Melvin Washington (ed.), *A Testament of Hope* (1986) 345. The same kind of argument is advanced in Francis Schaeffer's *The Great Evangelical Disaster* (1984). Schaeffer calls evangelical Christians to political actions in, for instance, the fight for the unborn, as a way of living out their faith.

CHAPTER THREE

1. See, for example, chapter 1, 24–25, footnotes 51–59.

2. See, for example, Oliver Thomas, "Comments on Papers by Milner Ball and Frederick Gedicks," 4 *Notre Dame J. L. Ethics and Pub. Pol'y* 451 (1990); Abner Greene, "The Irreducible Constitution," 7 *J. Contemp. Legal Issues* 293 (1996); Theodore Blumoff, "The New Religionists' Newest Social Gospel: On the Rhetoric and Reality of Religion's 'Marginalization' in Public Life," 51 *U. Miami L. Rev.* 1 (1996); Laurence Bennett, "Fighting for God and the Right Wing," *Time*, Sept. 13, 1993, 58; Richard Berke, "Religious Right Gains Influence and Spreads Discord in G.O.P.," *N.Y. Times*, June 3, 1994, A1; and Berke, "As Christians Pull the G.O.P. to the Right, Its Leaders

Argue Over Holding the Center," *N.Y. Times*, June 27, 1994, A12; Clyde Wilcox, *Onward Christian Soldiers?* (1996); Robert Boston, *The Most Dangerous Man in America?* (1996). Alternatively, others note the influence of the clergy on the civil rights movement—an important legislative item for the Democratic Party during the 1960s. See Stephen Carter, *The Culture of Disbelief* (1993), 227. Kathleen Sullivan, in "Religion and Liberal Democracy," *The Bill of Rights in the Modern State* (eds.) Geoffrey Stone, Richard Epstein, and Cass Sunstein (1992), 195–96 argues:

> To begin with, I find any picture of rampant secularization diffi-
> cult to square with numerous indicators of religion's lively role in
> contemporary American social and political life. To name but a
> few examples, powerful Roman Catholic Archbishops such as
> John Cardinal O'Connor in New York and Bernard Cardinal Law
> in Boston exercise substantial political power from the pulpit—
> they control large constituencies and influence government poli-
> cies on abortion, AIDS education and prevention, charitable ser-
> vices, and gay rights. Evangelical Protestant ministers such as the
> Reverend Jerry Falwell and Reverend Donald Wildmon likewise
> play an active role in politics, having abandoned earlier fundamen-
> talist approaches favoring retreat from the fallen world rather than
> engagement with it. Masters of direct mail campaigns experienced
> at monitoring and boycotting commercial media for "anti-
> Christian" or "anti-family" themes, Falwell and Wildmon recently
> mobilized a series of highly effective campaigns against publicly
> subsidized art they deemed blasphemy or filth. Roman Catholic
> clerical opposition to a public television documentary about gay
> protestors at St. Patrick's Cathedral led the Public Broadcasting
> System to pressure its member stations to take it off the air. And
> religious convictions and institutions have played a pivotal role in
> nation-wide political activism against abortion.

3. See the conference sponsored by the Rainbow Coalition analyzing the 1994 congressional elections, televised on C-SPAN, January 6, 1995.

4. Leo Pfeffer, "The 'Religion' of Secular Humanism," 29 *J. Church and State* 495, 504 (1987).

5. Id.

6. Note the treatment of science and the scientific method offered in Robert Wuthnow, *Meaning and Moral Order* (1987), and Stanley Jaki, *The Road of Science and the Ways to God* (1978).

7. Note that I am differentiating this kind of religious argument from an argu- ment for strict separation of church and state made by those within the more tradi- tional "religious" communities. It is not just the Madeline Murray O'Haires who advo- cate separation. Many religious people argue that separation is necessary to protect religious faith. See James Wood and Derek Davis, *The Role of Government in*

Monitoring and Regulating Religion in Public Life (1993), Paul Weber, *Equal Separation* (1990)—particularly the article by James Dunn, "Neutrality and the Establishment Clause," 55. A conservative evangelical may advocate separation to protect others of like mind from the pressure of the state. Note the distinction between Roger Williams' case for separation (to protect *church* from *state*) and Thomas Jefferson's motivation for separation (to protect *state* from *church*). I will take up the constitutional question of separation later in this chapter, and later in the book. However, what I am discussing here is not separation to *protect* religious people. I am talking about secularizing the public arena in order to *silence* religious people, and how this motivation becomes, in a sense, a kind of religious mission. I am also distinguishing between religious belief and "church." One might not generally call a sustained effort to undermine God a "church" per se—not unless the effort had the characteristics of a "church." Note the definitions of "church" and "sect" in Barbara Hargrove, *The Sociology of Religion* (1979), 3–14 and Michael Hill, *A Sociology of Religion* (1973), 41–43. Hill, 44–69 provides a review of the prominent definitions of "church" in the academic literature. I think the distinction I am making between church and religion is even evident when contrasting their respective dictionary definitions. *Webster's Dictionary* defines *church*, when used as a noun, to mean "a building for public worship, especially Christian worship; the clergy or officialdom of a religious body; a body or organization of religious believers as (a) whole body of Christians, (b) the denomination, (c) congregation, a public divine worship; the clerical profession." I would argue that one who is committed to extricating God from the public arena is exercising his or her religious beliefs. *Webster's* defines *religion* as "the service and worship of God or the supernatural; commitment to religious faith or observance; . . . a personal set or institutionalized set of religious attitudes, beliefs, and practices; scrupulous conformity; *a cause, principle, or system of beliefs held to with ardor and faith."* *Religious* means "relating to or manifesting faithful devotion to an acknowledged *ultimate reality* or deity; of, relating to, or devoted to religious beliefs or observances; *scrupulously and conscientiously faithful; fervent, zealous."* It appear that, on one hand, religion refers to a system of beliefs—and practice of those beliefs. On the other hand, church refers to the institution or organization of people who share religious beliefs and put them into practice.

8. John Swomley, *Religious Liberty and the Secular State* (1987) 125.

9. Id., 118. Note how Swomley's limited definition of humanism reveals his intense desire for secularization. Swomley's definition is hardly exhaustive. He is talking about a specific strain, or type, or subgroup of humanism. He is talking about "secular" humanism. Richard John Neuhaus, in *The Naked Public Square* (1984), 24, argues that "there is a venerable tradition of humanism, also called Christian humanism that is not secularistic."

10. Note that I am not arguing that there is a formal religion, secular humanism, that is responsible for widespread secularization. I am talking about secularized humanism. The distinction seems to be important to some folks. In a footnote to his opinion in *Torcaso v Watkins*, 367 U.S. 488 (1961) Justice Black, 492–93, penned the oft cited assertion, "Among *religions* in this country which do not teach what would

generally be considered a belief in the existence of God are Buddhism, Taoism, Ethical Culture, *Secular Humanism*, and others." Typically, the claim that there are "religious" people bent on driving God out of the public square, usually identified as "secular humanists," is associated with the so-called Christian Right. However, the fear that America might well establish secularism, or secular humanism, as a national religion is not first associated with the moral majority in the 1980s. In 1948, a prominent Catholic scholar, John Courtney Murray, in "Law or Prepossessions," 14 *L. and Contemp. Prob.* 23 (1948) advanced the argument in response to the Supreme Court's decisions, *Everson v Board*, 330 U.S 1 (1947), and *McCollum v Board*, 333 U.S. 203 (1948). In 1963, Justice Potter Stewart also proclaimed that the court had established secularism when he dissented in *Abington Township v Schempp*, 373 U.S. 203 (1963). Secularists, like Pfeffer, a powerful champion for the cause of church-state separation, often reverse the presumption implied by Black's quotation—that secular humanism is a religious faith—by citing the decision and arguing that, since Justice Black said secular humanism is a religion, it is up to critics to prove it exists. "Show us a Secular Humanist," they demand. Pfeffer, 504, argued impressively that if secular humanism is a religion, then it is a funny kind of religion. It has no credo other than humanism. It has no great founder or leader. It has no prayers, no sermons, no rituals, no priesthoods, or no symbols. Marriage ceremonies performed by secular humanists are not likely to be recognized by the state. "Most important," Pfeffer noted that: "The recently published *Encyclopedia of Religion* has no reference to secular humanism. It is difficult to attribute the status of a religion to persons who are not recognized as such in undoubtedly the foremost authoritative encyclopedia of religion, particularly if it is claimed that they existed as long ago as 1961 when *Torcaso* was decided." Professor Swomley, 118, makes the same argument. He calls secular humanism "a slogan without precise definition." Pfeffer and Swomley have convinced me. There is no "First Church of the Secular Humanist." There are only "secularists" and secularized "humanists." I think the distinction is simply a matter of semantics. Formal or not, their arguments are religious or quasi-religious claims.

11. See Max Weber, *The Sociology of Religion* (1922—English trans. 1963), John Noss, *Man's Religions* (1974), and J. Alan Winter, *Continuities in the Sociology of Religion* (1977).

12. *Humanist Manifestos I and II* (New York: Prometheus Books, 1973).

13. *Humanist Manifesto I*, preface.

14. Id.

15. *Humanist Manifesto I*, 8.

16. *Humanist Manifesto II*, 13.

17. *Humanist Manifesto I*, preface.

18. See James Davison Hunter, "Religious Freedom and the Challenge of Modern Pluralism," in James Davison Hunter and Os Guiness (eds.), *Articles of Faith, Articles of Peace* (1990) 63–64.

19. Francis Schaeffer, *A Christian Manifesto*, (1981), published in *The Complete Works of Francis Schaeffer*, Vol. 5 (1982) 427. Judge Brevard Hand, in *Smith v Board of School Commissioners of Mobile County*, 655 F. Supp. 939 (S.D. Ala. 1987), rev'd. 827 F.2d 684 (11th Cir. 1987), banned 44 textbooks from Alabama public schools because they allegedly advance the religion of Secular Humanism. His decision, which was reversed by the Eleventh Circuit Court of Appeals, spells out his reasons for ruling secular humanism to be a religion.

20. Schaeffer, 425.

21. Id.

22. John Dewey, *A Common Faith* (1934), 84. See historians Martin Marty, *Religion and Republic* (1987), 62–63; Paul Carter, *Revolt against Destiny* (1989), 179. Marty and Carter discuss Dewey's fervent efforts to shut down religion. I would suggest that Dewey was on a *religious* mission to marginalize religion. In fact, Marty likened Dewey's work to an effort to establish religion.

23. *Humanist Manifesto II*, 19. See Swomley, 11, 87.

24. Paul Blanshard, "Three Cheers for Our Secular State," *The Humanist* (March/April, 1976), 17.

25. John Dunphy, "A Religion for a New Age," *The Humanist* (January/February, 1983), 26. Emphasis added. Why the unabashed hostility? Frederick Mark Gedicks argues, in *The Rhetoric of Church and State* (1995), 12, that is because secularists consider religion to be an antirational, regressive, antisocial force responsible for "social division, violence, and anarchy."

26. McHenry, 186fn. 86, lists several groups, the American Humanist Association, the Council for Democratic and Secular Humanism, the Ethical and Cultural Fellowship, American Rationalist Association, and Unitarian Universalist, who might make up this humanist "movement" or "religion." McHenry does, however, indicate that these groups do not share a full set of common beliefs. As such, it would be unfair to pull statements from Group A and assume that they are shared by Group B, Group C, etc. That is why I have, generally, confined my remarks to information about the American Humanist Association.

27. Francis Schaeffer, *The Great Evangelical Disaster* (1984), 35–36.

28. Id.

29. See, for example, this discussion in *Zorach v Clauson*, 343 U.S. 306 (1952).

30. Stanley Ingber, "Religion or Ideology: A Needed Clarification of the Religion Clauses," 41 *Stan. L. Rev.* 233 (1989) 310, distinguishes between an "irreligious" ideology, one which is opposed or hostile to religion, and a "nonreligious" ideology, for which the existence or nonexistence of religion is irrelevant. The group to whom Schaeffer refers would be apologists for an "irreligious" ideology. I will explain below why I think this ideology should be characterized as a *religious* claim.

31. Swomley, 121. Emphasis added.

32. Marty, 77, does point out that, for most people, every important issue does not become, simultaneously, a religious issue.

33. See Paul Tillich, *Systematic Theology*, Vol. 2 (1957) 9. Also consider *John A. T. Robinson, Honest to God* (1963).

34. See J. Morris Clark, "Guidelines for the Free Exercise Clause," 83 *Harv. L. Rev.* 327 (1969).

35. 380 U.S. 163 (1965).

36. This was precisely the argument advanced by those parents who claimed that their children's textbooks, selected and issued by their school boards, teach a "religion," a secular humanism. See *Mozert v Hawkins*, 827 F.2d 1058 (6th Cir. 1987), and *Smith v Board of School Commissioners*, 827 F.2d 684 (11th Cir. 1987).

37. James McBride, "Paul Tillich and the Supreme Court: Tillich's 'Ultimate Concern' as a Standard in Judicial Interpretation," 30 *J. of Church and State* 245 (1988).

38. Id., 269.

39. Id., 270.

40. Id., 270–71. Perhaps McBride is representing the distinction between Tillich's personal belief, as a cristocentric theologian—that "ultimate concern" is best expressed through the cross—and Tillich's argument, as a commentator on religion—that one's own ultimate concern, even if it is deficient, is that which is ultimately important to him or her. See the discussion of Tillich in Kyle Pasewark, *A Theology of Power* (1993).

41. In order to permit what Professor Ingber is calling "ideology" to be taught freely in the classroom, without the stigma of religion attached, McBride narrowly constructs a definition of the set "religion." Everything outside of this narrow set is something other than religion. McBride's solution would so greatly restrict what could be defined as "religion," for the purpose of determining constitutional protection, that there would be virtually no safeguard for the free exercise of religion for minority religious faiths. Decisions like *Seeger, Torcaso, U.S. v Ballard*, 322 U.S 78 (1944), *Sherbert v Verner*, 374 U.S. 398 (1963), and *Wisconsin v Yoder*, 406 U.S. 205 (1972), might well be rendered toothless should the court embrace McBride's proposal. It could have the effect of eliminating religious-based exemptions. However, with regard to the results he might attain, McBride is on solid ground. See *Employment Division v Smith*, 494 U.S. 872 (1990), where the court indicated that the compelling interest test would not apply to free exercise claims seeking exemption from neutral laws of general applicability. Also see the debate in the literature regarding religious-based exceptions including: Ellis West, "The Case Against a Right to Religious-Based Exemptions," 4 *Notre Dame J. L. Ethics, Pub. Pol'y* 591 (1990), Gerard Bradley, "Commentary on West and Garvey," id., 639, William Marshall, "The Case Against the Constitutionality of Compelled Free Exercise Exemptions," 40 *Case Western Reserve Law Review* 357 (1990), Michael McConnell, "The Origins and Historical Understanding of Free Exercise of Religion," *Harvard Law Review* (1990) 103:1410, Scott Williams, "Religious Exemptions and the Limits of Neutrality," 74 *Tex. L. Rev.* 119 (1995), and

David Steinberg, "Rejecting the Case Against the Free Exercise Exemptions and the Limits of Neutrality," 75 *B.U. L. Rev.* 241 (1995).

42. Swomley, 121–22.

43. Neuhaus, 24.

44. Id.

45. Id.

46. Id.

47. Hunter, 56.

48. Id., 57. See Martin Marty, 5; William Marty, "To Favor Neither Religion Nor Nonreligion: Schools in a Pluralist Society," in Weber 95; Leo Pfeffer, "Issues That Divide: The Triumph of Secular Humanism," 19 *J. Church and State* 203 (1977).

49. Pfeffer, 504.

50. I want to, again, distinguish between *religious motives* for secularism and those traditionally thought to be *religious persons* advocating secularization. For example, Baptists have traditionally championed the cause of church-state separation. These are, no doubt, religious people advocating secularization, but one should look at their motivation. They want to be free to practice their faith without government intrusion. Hence, they support separation. Their motivation is *liberty*—a *secular* motive. Religious liberty is extremely important. It helps Baptists to evangelize—something they believe is a commandment from Christ—and to allow others to freely come to the savior without pressure from an established faith. But, for the most part, religious liberty is *not* an essential element of a Baptist's faith. With or without the religious freedom that we are afforded as Americans, the truth, as Baptists understand it, remains the same. Their mission remains the same. This situation differs substantially from that which motivates the Humanist/humanist. The Humanist/humanist wants to shut down religious expression because he or she believes that this kind of expression *cuts against the truth*. Secularization is not something that helps them to undertake their mission more effectively. Secularization is their mission. Thus, theirs is, even if it seems somewhat paradoxical, a *religious* motivation.

51. See, for example, Bruce Ackerman, *Social Justice in the Liberal State* (1980); Kent Greenawalt's, *Religious Conviction and Personal Choice* (1988) and *Private Consciences and Public Reasons* (1995) hereafter "Public Reasons"; Steven Holmes, "Gag Rules or the Politics of Omission," in Jon Elster and Rune Slagstad, eds., *Constitutionalism and Democracy* (1988); Judith Shklar, *Ordinary Voices* (1984); Thomas Nagel, "Moral Conflict and Political Legitimacy," 16 *Philo. and Pub. Affairs* 215 (1987); Kathleen Sullivan, supra, note 3.

52. See, for example, John Rawls's, *A Theory of Justice* (1971) and *Political Liberalism* (1993); Ronald Dworkin, *A Matter of Principle* (1985). Two recent works, authored by religion scholars, also attempt to categorize the arguments of those whom I would identify as having a "secular" motivation. Professor Frank Gamwell, in *The Meaning of Religious Freedom* (1995) identifies three predominant positions in the lit-

erature: the Privatist view, the Partisan view, and the Pluralist view. Dean Ronald Thiemann, in *Religion in Public Life* (1996), looks at, by and large, the same literature and sorts participants into those advocating two very different kinds of liberalism: political liberalism and philosophical or comprehensive liberalism.

53. Jay Shafritz, *The Dorsey Dictionary of American Government and Politics* (1988) 325. I will elaborate upon the definition of "contemporary" liberalism, particularly in the context of maximizing rights and liberties, below.

54. See Frederick Mark Gedicks, *The Rhetoric of Church and State* (1995). Professor Gedicks summarizes some of the premises inherent within classical liberalism:

> In the Lockean tradition of natural rights, citizens are thought to have inalienable rights against government that are held independently of the government's existence. This necessitates the conceptual division of human life into mutually exclusive public and private spheres. Under such a political regime, the reach of permissible government action (public life) depends on the boundaries of the inviolable sphere of individual rights (private life).

55. Id. It is *not* my contention that every proponent of liberalism embraces *each* of these premises. Proponents of classical liberalism cut across the political spectrum.

56. Steven Holmes, "Gag Rules or the Politics of Omission," in Jon Elster and Rune Slagstad, eds., *Constitutionalism and Democracy* (1988), 20–21.

57. Bruce Ackerman, *Social Justice in the Liberal State* (1980).

58. Id., 17–18.

59. Kent Greenawalt, *Religious Conviction and Personal Choice* (1988) 7. Greenawalt's definition of liberalism, 26, includes the following premises, "indirect democratic governance, extensive individual liberty, separation of governmental and religious institutions, nonsponsorship of religion by government, and secular purposes for laws." Additionally, see Kathleen Sullivan's argument for a "secular public moral order"—one which, by the way, she believes may "well function as a belief system with substantive content . . .," 198–99. I will discuss Professor Sullivan's argument at greater length in chapter 4. See also philosopher Robert Audi's case for secularism in "The Place of Religious Argument in a Free and Democratic Society," 30 *San Diego L. Rev.* 677 (1993).

60. Holmes, 45.

61. Greenawalt, 7.

62. Id.

63. Id, 27.

64. Id., 217.

65. Id., 216–17.

66. Id., 228.

67. Greenawalt, "Public Reasons," 7.

68. An argument put to me in a discussion with Professor Kyle Pasewark. Pasewark's position, that one's political activism (or lack thereof) should simply be an extension of one's core beliefs is articulated in Kyle Pasewark and Garrett Paul, *The Emphatic Christian Center* (1999). See Stephen Carter, *Civility* (1998); Merle Weiner, "'Civilizing' the Next Generation: A Response to Civility: Manners, Morals, and the Etiquette of Democracy by Stephen L. Carter," 42 How. L.J. 241 (1999).

69. Perry, 10. Also, see Gedicks, 30–31.

70. Id.

71. Id., 20.

72. Id., 19.

73. Ackerman, 22.

74. Perry, 9. See Gamwell's presentation, and critique, of the pluralist position, 97–115, and Thiemann's critique of philosophical or comprehensive liberalism, 95–113.

75. Shafritz, 407.

76. Perry, 8.

77. See Carl Esbeck, "Pluralism Without a Center," *Liberty* (May/June, 1995) 20.

78. Neuhaus, 146. Professor Esbeck, 20–21, disagrees. He maintains that pluralism is not synonymous with relativism. Too, he argues that pluralism simply provides a level playing field where one can win or lose based upon the strength of his or her argument.

79. Robert Bellah, in "Cultural Pluralism and Religious Particularism," in Henry Clark, ed., *Freedom of Religion in America* (1982) 35, identifies two threats to a national consensus. The first attack comes from cultural particularism, or the understanding of America to be a nation blessed with a unique national environment and spiritual energies, most often characterized by Christian groups who opt for a particularly Protestant version of the American consensus—one shorn of rationalistic and deistic overtones—and who generally reject ecumenism. The second, and more serious attack comes from radical utilitarian individualism—very similar to what I am describing as an oft used contemporary definition for pluralism. Bellah suggests that it is radical utilitarian individualism, premised upon cultural relativism—leaving moral truth to be discovered by the individual—which has become the new American consensus. Radical utilitarianism is making a claim among younger, better educated, and more well-to-do Americans. Additionally, see Bellah's argument in Robert Bellah, Richard Madsen, William Sullivan, Ann Swindler, and Steven Tipton, *Habits of the Heart* (1985) 225. See also Gerald Bradley, "Dogmatomachy—A "Privatization" Theory of the Religion Clause Cases," 30 *St. Louis L. Rev. 275* (1986); James Hitchcock, "Church, State, and Moral Values: The Limits of American Pluralism," 44 *L. and Contemp. Soc.* 3 (1981); Daniel McGarry, "The Unconstitutionality of Exclusive Government Support for Entirely Secularistic Education," 28 *Catholic Lawyer* 1 (1983); John Courtney Murray,

"Law or Prepossessions," 14 *L. and Contemp. Prob.* 23 (1948); Wilbur Katz, "Freedom of Religion and State Neutrality," 20 *U. Chi. L. Rev.* 426 (1953); Robert Drinan, in "State and Federal Aid to Parochial Schools," 7 *J. Church and State* 67 (1965).

80. Carter, 33.

81. Id.

82. Id.

83. Id., 33–34.

84. Even Michael Perry, 100, who champions the right of religious people to participate in the political arena, links "fallibilism" and "pluralism" together. "Two attitudes essential to the practice of ecumenical political dialogue," Perry claims, "are fallibilism and pluralism." By linking the two concepts together, Perry actually limits those religious folk who should participate in political discussion. This was a major weakness in his argument, and he has moved to be even more inclusive of religious-based expression. See Michael Perry, "Religion, Morality, and Political Choice: Further Thoughts and Second Thoughts on *Love and Power*," 30 *San Diego L. Rev.* 703 (1993); Michael Perry, *Religion in Politics* (1997); David Smollin, "Regulating Religious and Cultural Conflict in Postmodern America: A Response to Professor Perry," 76 *Iowa L. Rev.* (1991).

85. A term I am borrowing from Professor Gedicks. Gedicks, 10, defines progressivists as:

> liberals with a "libertarian social agenda" whose first instinct is not to reaffirm traditional Judeo-Christian beliefs, but rather to reinterpret them "according to the prevailing assumptions of contemporary life" relying for moral authority on the "self grounded rational discourse" of "Enlightenment rationalism."

86. Henry Abraham and Barbara Perry, *Freedom and the Court* (1994) 10.

87. Id.

88. Id., 11.

89. Michael Sandel, "Freedom of Conscience or Freedom of Choice?" in Hunter and Guiness, 75. The quotation comes from Ronald Dworkin's "Liberalism," in Stuart Hampshire, ed., *Public and Private Morality* (1978).

90. The arguments advanced forcefully by Professors Rawls and Dworkin, supra, note 51. See the lengthy critiques of John Rawls' *A Theory of Justice* in Gamwell, 50–75, and of Dworkin and Rawls in Thiemann, 74–90. According to Thiemann, the objective of the political liberals, such as Dworkin and Rawls, is to secure a secular, pluralistic society. Professor Dworkin argues, for example, that liberalism requires the state to be neutral with regard to questions of the good life. Too, the judiciary is acting properly when courts prioritize right over good. Rawls, in his 1993 work *Political Liberalism*, contends that there should be freestanding moral/political conceptions for

the basic structure of society. Like Dworkin, Rawl's state would prioritize right over good. Rawls seeks to achieve public consensus. Thus, public reasons, which he contrasts with comprehensive reasons (including religious belief), are to be the standard for nearly all civic discourse—with very few exceptions. Within the realm of public life, fundamental principles of democracy should take precedence over comprehensive schemes. These principles require using "public reasons" when debating fundamental matters. One distinction, perhaps, between Rawl's case for secular political expression, and Greenawalt's is that the classical (philosophical) liberals insist that, while personal religious convictions are (may be) important, but they cannot be rationally or publicly assessed. Thus, Thiemann notes, the philosophical liberals *primary* concern with religion is one of the "publicity" of ideas conveyed in the public square.

91. Id. See Michael Perry's discussion, 24–27, of John Rawl's conception of human good that aims to achieve a "rights-prior-to-Good" (RpG) justification of his principles of justice.

92. See Peter Augustine Lawler, *Under God with Liberty* (1994). Lawler, chapters 1 and 2, links "contemporary liberalism" and "humanism" together. If his argument is valid, then he has observed a bridging of the gap between the religious and political motives for secularization.

93. Sandel, 74.

94. Carter, 3. Of course Carter's own criticisms of the Christian Right are leveled because he does not like their politics. He is highly critical of their policy preferences. "What was wrong with the 1992 Republican Convention," argues Professor Carter, 239, "was not the effort to link the name of God to secular ends. What was wrong was the choice of secular ends to which the name of God was linked." What distinguishes Carter from other scholars is that his target is the particular policy options, and not the "God-talk" (49–50) used to justify them. See Blumoff, 6.

95. Id., 58.

96. 410 U.S. 113 (1973).

97. Carter, 58.

98. Id. Carter maintains that since liberals for the last 25–30 years have distanced themselves from religious rhetoric, it leaves political observers with "the eerie sense that the right was asserting ownership in God."

99. Id., 64.

100. Id., 19.

101. Id., 3.

102. One option is to simply allow everyone entry into the public square armed with whatever rhetorical arrows they wish to place in their quivers and limited only by their ability or inability to persuade. I am squarely with law professor Sanford Levinson, who argues in "Religious Language and the Public Square," 105 *Harv. L. Rev.* 2061 (1992) at 2077:

Why doesn't liberal democracy give everyone an equal right, without engaging in any version of epistemic abstinence, to make his or her own arguments, subject, obviously, to the prerogative of listeners to reject the arguments should they be unpersuasive (which will be the case, almost by definition, with arguments that are not widely accessible or are otherwise marginal)?

Note the rebuttal to Professor Levinson offered by Abner Greene in "The Political Balance of the Religion Clauses," 102 *Yale L. J. 1611* (1993), 1623.

103. Carter, 264–65.

104. Carter includes a cornucopia of examples in his first several chapters, 3–66. See Frank Guliuzza, "The Supreme Court, the Establishment Clause, and Incoherence," in Luis Lugo (ed.), *Religion, Public Life, and the American Polity* (1994), 132–36. I continue this discussion in greater detail in chapter 5.

105. Tim Stafford, "Move Over, ACLU," *Christianity Today* (October 25, 1993), 20–24.

106. Political preachers are "spiritual leaders who try to explain to their flocks what God wants them to do in the political world." Id., 68–70.

107. Carter, 35–43. I return to, and elaborate upon, this argument—that believers should serve as critics of culture—in chapter 5. I would concede that the most important work in which religious people engage is most often outside of the secular-political arena. I am sensitive to the argument that, first and foremost, the church "should be the church" and that its principal function is to worship, to disciple, to evangelize, and to love. I am not convinced, however, that the prophetic role of religion—to serve as an outside critic of government and culture—is at odds with its principal function.

108. Of course, some would define "fervent extremists" pretty broadly. Sociologist Arthur Jipson, who studies white supremacy sects, urges scholars to recognize the linkage between white supremacists, the "Constitutionalist" and "Patriot Militia" movements—groups that have attracted serious attention from the FBI—and conservative Christians. See "Humanities Scholars Meet in Duluth," *Research Review* (June, 1995), 8–9. When I spoke with Professor Jipson privately, and asked him if he meant to include the so-called Christian right in this list (folk like Pat Robertson), he made it very clear that he had. Fortunately, Jipson seems to be a friend of the first amendment. Imagine, however, what one who shares Jipson's beliefs about conservative Christians, but who does not share his passion for free speech, might do to religious-based dialogue if suddenly given power to make public policy. It is more than a little frightening when one listens to those who think they can silence argument by dismissing it as extremist. During the 1996 presidential campaign "extremism" took it on the chin. It seems that if one wanted to discredit his or her opponent's position, the strategy of choice was to identify it as "extremist." It is worth comparing the pejorative outlook toward extremism evident the 1996 campaign to Martin Luther King's understanding of extremism. As a self-identified extremist, King noted in "Letter from Birmingham City Jail":

But I have tried to say that this normal and healthy discontent can be channelized through the creative outlet of nonviolent direct action. Now this approach is being dismissed as extremist. I must admit that I was initially disappointed in being so categorized. But as I continued to think about the matter I gradually gained a bit of satisfaction from being considered an extremist. Was not Jesus an extremist in love—"Love your enemies, bless them that curse you, pray for them that despitefully use you." Was not Amos an extremist for justice—"Let justice roll down like waters and righteousness like a mighty stream." Was not Paul an extremist for the gospel of Jesus Christ—"I bear in my body the marks of the Lord Jesus." Was not Martin Luther an extremist—"Here I stand; I can do none other so help me God." Was not John Bunyan an extremist— "I will stay in jail to the end of my days before I make a butchery of my conscience." Was not Abraham Lincoln an extremist— "This nation cannot survive half slave and half free." Was not Thomas Jefferson an extremist—"We hold these truths to be self evident, that all men are created equal." So the question is not whether we will be extremist but what kind of extremist will we be. Will we be extremists for hate or will we be extremists for love? Will we be extremists for the preservation of injustice—or will we be extremists for the cause of justice? In that dramatic scene on Calvary's hill, three men were crucified for the same crime—the crime of extremism. Two were extremists for immorality, and thusly fell below their environment. The other, Jesus Christ, was an extremist for love, truth and goodness, and thereby rose above his environment. So, after all, maybe the South, the nation and the world are in dire need of creative extremists.

See James Washington (ed), *A Testament of Hope: the Essential Writings of Martin Luther King, Jr.* (1986), 297–98.

109. A more recognized typology is provided in H. Richard Niebuhr's time-honored work, *Christ and Culture* (1956). Niebuhr examines five possible relationships that the Christian community might have with the world: Christ against culture, the Christ of culture, Christ above culture, Christ and culture in paradox, and Christ the transformer of culture.

Chapter Four

1. See Mark Dewolfe Howe, *Garden in the Wilderness* (1965). Howe, 2, observes that the linkage predates the founding. It is consistent with Jefferson's interpretation of religious establishment (or, rather, nonestablishment). As I indicated in the previous chapter, I am well aware that those who advocate separating

church and state to achieve *secularization* are but a subset of those who contend for *separation*. There are many *religious* separationists whose chief conern is with the impact of an oppressive government—especially one that is allied with a hegemonic church.

2. John Swomley, *Religious Liberty and the Secular State* (1987).

3. Id., 7.

4. Id.

5. Id., 14.

6. Robert Audi, "The Place of Religious Argument," 30 *San Diego L. Rev.* 677 (1993); Robert Audi and Nicholas Wolterstorff, *Religion in the Public Square* (1996).

7. Id., 691.

8. Id.

9. Id.

10. Id. See Professor Kent Greenawalt's treatment of Audi's argument in *Private Consciences and Public Reasons* (1995) 64. Professor Audi's case for separating religion from secular political debate is advanced in Robert Audi and Nicholas Wolterstorff, *Religion in the Public Square* (1997).

11. Kathleen Sullivan, "Religion and Liberal Democracy," in Geoffrey Stone, Richard Epstein, and Cass Sunstein (eds.), *The Bill of Rights in the Modern State* (1992), 198.

12. Id., 197.

13. Id., 198.

14. 333 U.S 203 (1948).

15. 492 U.S. 490 (1989).

16. *McCollum*, 216–17.

17. Id., 231.

18. Id., 217, 231. Frankfurter notes further, 232, "We renew our conviction that 'we have staked the very existence of our country on the faith that complete separation of church and state is best for the state and best for religion.'" *Everson*. If nowhere else, in the relation between church and state, "good fences make good neighbors."

19. Frankfurter's position in *McCollum* provides evidence for what Professor Howe, 109–18, suggested was a clearly secular mindset on the court. See Frederick Mark Gedicks, *The Rhetoric of Church and State* (1995). Gedicks, 52, argues that the court's separation decisions are consistent with the "secular individualist thesis."

20. 472 U.S 38 (1985).

21. 482 U.S. 578 (1987).

22. *Webster*, 490.

23. Id., 566.

24. See Bernard Nathanson's film, *The Silent Scream* (1984).

25. Identifying a secular purpose (mission, objective) is a task that might not be that hard to accomplish. See Carl Esbeck, "The Lemon Test: Should it be Retained, Reformulated or Rejected?", 4 *Notre Dame J. L. Ethics and Pub. Pol'y* 513 (1990), 515–21.

26. See Ronald Thiemann, *Religion in Public Life* (1996). Dean Thiemann notes, 75, that "The defenders of political liberalism are virtually unanimous in their staunch advocacy of the 'wall of separation' between church and state.'"

27. Gedicks, 117.

28. See Chief Justice Burger's discussion of "benevolent neutrality" in *Walz v Tax Commission*, 397 U.S. 664, 669 (1970).

29. See A. E. Dick Howard, "The Supreme Court and the Establishment of Religion," in Robert Alley (ed.), *James Madison on Religious Liberty* (1985); David Leitch, in "The Myth of Religious Neutrality by Separation in Education," 71 *Virg. L. Rev.* 625 (1925); David Felsen, in "Developments in Approaches to Establishment Clause Analysis: Consistency for the Future," 38 *Am. U. L. R.* 395 (1989); Douglas Laycock, "Formal, Substantive, and Disaggregated Neutrality Toward Religion, 39 *De Paul L. Rev.* 993 (1990); Gedicks, 81; Thiemann, 42–64.

30. 330 U.S. 1 (1947).

31. 403 U.S. 602 (1971).

32. *Everson*, 18.

33. Id., 17–18.

34. Id.

35. Id.

36. *Everson* was a 5-4 decision. Justice Rutledge authored a dissenting opinion that is far less ambiguous. Rutledge argued for a very consistent separationist position. He did not view the New Jersey program as part of the general government services to be afforded to religious groups. Rather, he felt New Jersey used its taxing power to furnish support for religion. And, he held, this sort of taxing power was a threat to strict separation:

> Hence, today, apart from efforts to inject religious training or exercise and sectarian issues into the public schools, the only serious surviving threat to maintaining that complete and permanent separation of religion and civil power which the first amendment commands is through the use of taxing power to support religion, religious establishments, or establishments having a religious foundation whatever their form or special religious function.

37. *Everson*, 18.

38. Id., 211.

39. Id.

40. Id. He does not explain why it is not "hostility." Rather, he almost waves off the charge by, in effect, saying "It's not hostility. Hostility would be wrong." Black notes, "A manifestation of such hostility would be at war with our national tradition as embodied in the first amendment's guarantee of the free exercise of religion."

41. Id., 232. Justice Frankfurter, in his concurring opinion, agreed with Black's separationist argument:

> We renew our conviction that 'we have staked the very existence of our country on the faith that complete separation between state and religion is best for the state and best for religion.' Everson v Board of Education. If nowhere else, in the relation between Church and State, good fences make good neighbors.

42. 343 U.S. 306 (1952).

43. See, for example, Edward Corwin, "The Supreme Court as National School Board," 14 *L. and Contemp. Prob. 3* (1949), and John Courtney Murray, "Law and Prepossession," id., 23.

44. *Zorach*, 311. Note that in *McCollum* the court held neutrality of this sort was not sufficient to satisfy the separation requirement.

45. Id., 312.

46. Id., 314.

47. Id., 313–14.

48. Ibid., 315. Emphasis added.

49. See Justice Douglas' dissent in *Walz*, 700.

50. 370 U.S 421 (1962).

51. 374 U.S. 203 (1963).

52. *Engel*, 425.

53. Id., 434–35.

54. *Schempp*, 222.

55. Id.

56. Id., 225–26. Emphasis added.

57. Id., 295.

58. Id., 299. Some of Justice Brennan's argument illustrates the reasoning discussed in the introduction. Why is providing a public building to a congregation for worship services *not* an unconstitutional advancement of religion? Why can government pay for religious services for soldiers and prisoners and not for students who are compelled, by law, to attend school five days a week? If government is not *required* to provide chaplains or draft exemptions—in other words if it can refuse to do so—why is that *not* "official hostility" toward religion by Brennan's own definition? It seems that

several of the justices are unwilling to address these potential inconsistencies.

59. See note 30. Howard identifies a transition in the court's establishment clause requirements from separation to accommodation; Leitch offers three distinct phases of establishment clause interpretation by the court: separation (*Everson*), accommodation (*Lemon*), and pluralistic integration (*Widmar v Vincent*, 450 U.S. 909 [1981]). Felsen lists three doctrinal positions—strict separation, accommodation, and pluralism—"which encourages government's equal treatment of all religions." These are all approaches, he argues, aimed at producing "neutrality." Laycock also reads the court's decisions as requiring and fleshing out the definition of "neutrality." Gedicks, 81, uses the term "secular neutrality" for that which I maintain is simply a different, albeit less rigid, definition of separation. Dean Ronald Thiemann notes, 42–43, that the court embraced the separation thesis, and it is the separation thesis that dominates our understanding of the establishment clause. Thiemann later observes, 56, that "during the past four decades, the notion of 'government neutrality' has attained doctrinal status equal to the separation principle itself. Why? Because they are, in fact, the same doctrine. See Paul Weber, *Equal Separation* (1990). Professor Weber, 2–5, accurately treats all the more recognized categories of establishment clause jurisprudence, e.g., separation, neutrality, accommodation, and the like, as divergent meanings of the term separation. He offers five distinct meanings: structural separation, absolute separation, transvaluing separation, supportive separation, and equal separation.

60. *Schempp*, 222.

61. 473 U.S. 373 (1985). One might argue convincingly that even though "strict separation" can never be a reality, the doctrine is operative well after Justice Brennan left the court. Consider the court's favorable treatment of the *Everson* decision and the concept of "separation" in *Lee v Weisman*, 505 U.S. 577 (1992).

62. 392 U.S. 236 (1968).

63. Id., 242.

64. Walz, 669.

65. Id.

66. Id., 676. He went on to say:

> Separation in this context cannot mean absence of all contact; the complexities of modern life inevitably produce some contact and the fire and police protection received by houses of worship are within a State's boundaries, along with many other exempt organizations.

67. *Lemon*, 614.

68. Leonard Levy, in *The Establishment Clause* (1986), 177, agrees that it is impossible to fully extricate government from religion. In fact, argues Levy, it is probably counterproductive to try:

> Those who profess to be broad separationists ought to understand

that popular government will continue to aid religion and show
respect for it, and that not every accommodation with religion,
deriving from incidental assistance, is necessarily unconstitutional.
. . . Even if they profoundly believe that a practice is unconstitutional, wisdom sometimes dictates against pressing a suit. Trying
to insure that the wall of separation is really impregnable might be
futile and dangerously counterproductive. Indeed, the cracks in the
wall might be more numerous than at present without seriously
harming it or the values that it protects.

Levy cautions strict separationists not to lose sight of their greater goals in order to
fight what are essentially rhetorical battles. The late Leo Pfeffer, in *Religion, State,
and The Burger Court* (1985), indicated that he, Pfeffer, always wanted to fight them.
"I constantly defend," Pfeffer remarked, x, "a position called absolutist or extremist or
unrealistic or uncompromising." What of Levy's appeal to the separationists that they
pick their battles carefully? Pfeffer acknowledged that complete separation of church
and state is an impossibility, but that did not diminish his pursuit of that objective:

Those defending the strict separationist interpretation of the first
amendment's establishment clause recognize that absolute separation of church and state is not possible, but what does that prove?
Does the reality that no person is immortal mean that medical and
pharmaceutical professions should be abolished? Realistic separationists recognize that the absolute separation of church and state
cannot be achieved, else what's a secularist heaven for?
Nevertheless, that is the direction they would have constitutional
law relating to the Religion Clauses take, fully aware that perfec-
tion will never be attained.

69. See Plato's "Statesman," in *The Collected Dialogues of Plato* 1018 (eds.
Hamilton and Cairns, 1971).

70. 413 U.S. 756 (1973).

71. Id.

72. Id.

73. Id., 761.

74. See Gedicks, 117–21; Greenawalt, 4.

75. Michael McConnell, "Religious Freedom at a Crossroads," in *The Bill of
Rights in the Modern State*, (eds.) Geoffrey Stone, Richard Epstein, and Cass Sunstein
(1993), 120.

76. Audi, 678.

77. McConnell, 123.

78. Stephen Carter, *The Culture of Disbelief* (1993), 122–23.

79. Id. Professor Gedicks maintains:

The answer that secular individualism can give—that religion is a regressive, antisocial force that should be strictly confined to private life and subordinate to secular goals in order to preserve rationality and order in public life—is unacceptable and unpersuasive to most religious Americans.

CHAPTER FIVE

1. 403 U.S. 602 (1971).

2. Recent works include Paul Weber, *Equal Separation* (1990); Derek Davis, *Original Intent* (1991); Donald Drakeman, *Church-State Constitutional Issues* (1991); Terry Eastland, ed., *Religious Liberty in the Supreme Court* (1993); Stephen Carter, *The Culture of Disbelief* (1993); Steven Smith, *Foreordained Failure* (1995); Jesse Choper, *Securing Religious Liberty* (1995); Frederick Mark Gedicks, *The Rhetoric of Church and State* (1995); Ronald Thiemann, *Religion in Public Life* (1996).

3. See Carter, 110.

4. 330 U.S. 1 (1947).

5. *Lemon*, 618–19.

6. Id., 619.

7. *Wolman v Walter*, 433 U.S. 229 (1977), 241–48.

8. Id., 244.

9. 473 U.S. 373 (1985).

10. 473 U.S. 402 (1985).

11. Fortunately, the court recently overruled portions of *Aguilar v Felton* and *Grand Rapids v Ball* in *Agostini v Felton*, US SupCt. nos. 96-552 and 96-553 (6/23/97).

12. 465 U.S. 668 (1984).

13. *Lynch*, 678–85.

14. 492 U.S. 573 (1989).

15. Id., 578.

16. Id. Professor Gedicks, 77, argues that, although these cases are often understood as victories for those who advocate accommodation of religion, they simply strip religious symbols of their religious meanings. They "strive to empty them of their spiritual content and replace it with secular meaning."

17. *Lee v Weisman*, 2683.

18. 487 U.S. 589 (1988).

19. See *Wallace v Jaffree*, 472 U.S. 38 (1985) 110.

20. 42 U.S.C. ss 300z to 300z-10 (1988) (legislation that supplied grants to religious groups and other organizations providing counseling on teenage sexuality).

21. *Bowen*, 603–17.

22. Of course this particular example might say more about Chief Justice Rehnquist's character, or his leadership style on the court, than it does about the court's establishment clause jurisprudence. I have addressed these issues elsewhere. See Guliuzza, "Protecting Judicial Leadership: Did Rehnquist Prefer to Switch Than Fight?," 29 *Willamette L. Rev.* 151 (1993). The point is that Rehnquist had plenty of options available to him because the church-state jurisprudence is so confusing.

23. *Wolman*, 252–54.

24. 392 U.S. 236 (1968).

25. *Meek v Pittenger*, 421 U.S. 349 (1975).

26. See *Wallace v Jaffree*, 472 U.S. 38 (1972), 110.

27. *Wolman*, 241–48.

28. *Engel v Vitale*, 370 U.S. 421 (1962) and *Abington Township v Schempp*, 374 U.S. 203 (1963).

29. *Lee v Weisman*, 112 S.Ct. 2649 (1992).

30. The court's holding in the *Jaffree* decision.

31. *Marsh v Chambers*, 463 U.S. 783 (1983).

32. *Westside Community Board of Education v Mergens*, 496 U.S. 226 (1990).

33. *Grand Rapids School District v Ball*, 473 U.S. 373 (1985), and *Aguilar v Felton*, 473 U.S. 402 (1985).

34. *Bowen v Kendrick*, 487 U.S. 589 (1988).

35. See Norman Redlich, "Separation of Church and State," 60 *Notre Dame L. Rev.* 1094 (1985), and Gedicks, 118.

36. Stephen Pepper, "The Conundrum of the Free Exercise Clause—Some Reflections on Recent Cases," 9 *N. Ky. L. Rev.* 303 (1982).

37. Mark Tushnet, *Red, White, and Blue* (1988), 247.

38. Leonard Levy, *The Establishment Clause* (1986), 140.

39. Gerard Bradley, *Church-State Relationships in America* (1987) xiii. See Gedicks, 1–2.

40. Francis Lee, *Wall of Controversy* (1986), 6. Gedicks, 122, concludes:

> While constitutional doctrine might succeed if it lacks either coherence or popular support, it is destined to fail it if lacks both, which is the current dubious state of religion clause jurisprudence. Secular individualist discourse cannot plausibly account for religion clause doctrine, and, while it is the discourse within which most cultural elites make their intellectual home, its assumptions are rejected by large number of Americans—too many for even a fully coherent secular individualist doctrine to entertain hope of

success. As a result, religion clause doctrine in the 1990s stands in the same position as economic due process stood in the 1930s—a failed jurisprudence ripe for dismantling.

41. Carter, 109.

42. Id., note 105.

43. M. Glenn Abernathy, *Civil Liberties under the Constitution* (1968), 249.

44. Gerard Bradley, "Church Autonomy in the Constitutional Order: The End of Church and State," 49 *Louisiana L. Rev.* 1057 (1989). Emphasis added.

45. 98 U.S. 145 (1879).

46. 374 U.S. 398 (1963).

47. Id.

48. Id.

49. Carter, 184. See Gedicks, 58–59.

50. Paul Vitz, *Censorship: Evidence of Bias in our Children's Textbooks* (1986) 15–16.

51. Charles Colson, *Kingdoms in Conflict* (1987). For a summary of Vitz's study, see Vitz, "A Study of Religion and Traditional Values in Public School Textbooks," R.J. Neuhaus (ed.), *Democracy and the Renewal of Public Education* (1987) 116–40; Douglas Bandow, *Beyond Good Intentions* (1988) 24; William Marty, "To Favor Neither Religion Nor Nonreligion: Schools in a Pluralist Society," in Weber, 98. Patricia Lines, in "Three Criteria for Constitutional Interpretation: Predictability, Flexibility, and Intelligibility," 4 *Notre Dame J. L. and Pub. Pol'y* 549 (1990) 553–54, provides many examples that support Vitz's study: book editors who delete the words God, Bible, Jews from stories, high school classes in comparative religion that are abruptly canceled, school libraries that refuse donated books that have religious content—or even, on some occasions, take a position that is associated with a religious point of view. Lines notes:

> Publishers of public school texts routinely censor religious references from classic works. . . . For example, a story by Nobel laureate Isaac Bashevis Singer, "Zlateh the Goat," tells of a boy, lost in a blizzard, who prays "to God" for himself and his goat, lost with him. In an edited version appearing in the Macmillan grade 6 reader, *Catch the Wind*, the boy prays, but the phrase "to God" is deleted. When the boy is rescued, Singer's sentence, "Thank God that in the hay it was not cold," is changed to "Thank Goodness."

52. Loren Beth, *The American Theory of Church and State* (1958), 123–24.

53. Id.

54. Id., 126.

55. Id.

56. Id., 126, 133–35.

57. Id., 133–35.

58. Id., 134.

59. See the discussion in chapter 3. Bruce Ackerman, *Social Justice in the Liberal State* (1980); Kent Greenawalt, *Religious Conviction and Personal Choice* (1988); Kathleen Sullivan, "Religion and Liberal Democracy," 59 *U. Chi. L. Rev.* 195 (1992); Stephen Holmes, "Gag Rules or the Politics of Omission," in Jon Elster and Rune Slagstad (eds.) *Constitutionalism and Democracy* (1988) 19; Robert Audi, "The Place of Religious Argument in a Free Society," 30 *San Diego L. Rev.* 677 (1993).

60. Id., 143.

61. Id., 135.

62. Robert Bellah, "Cultural Pluralism and Religious Particularism," in Henry Clark (ed.), *Freedom of Religion in America* (1982), 35.

63. A. James Reichley, *Religion in American Public Life* (1985) 376.

64. Tushnet, 270.

65. Carter, 35.

66. R.J. Neuhaus, *The Naked Public Square* (1984) 86.

67. Id.

68. Id.

69. Id.

70. There are several others who maintain that religious people should offer the prophetic critique to culture. See John Wilson, "Religion, Government, and Power in the New American Nation," in Mark Noll, *Religion and American Politics* (1990), 89; Nathan Hatch, "The Democratization of Christianity and the Character of American Politics," in Noll, 92; Stephen Monsma, "The Neutrality Principle and a Pluralist Concept of Accommodation," in Weber, 84–90; Sanford Kessler, *Tocqueville's Civil Religion* (1994).

71. Tushnet, 257–64.

72. Id., 264.

73. Id., 272.

74. Neuhaus, 25.

75. Id.

76. "Federal Employees Punished For Religious Harassment," *Church and State* (May 1988) 112.

77. Sociologist Arthur Jipson, who studies white supremacy sects, urges scholars to recognize the linkage between white supremacists, the "Constitutionalist" and "Patriot Militia movements—groups that have attracted serious attention from the FBI, and conservative Christians. See "Humanities Scholars Meet in Duluth," *Research Review* (June 1995) 8–9. I would argue that is more important to understand the often

very different motives behind these groups rather than lumping them all together. Moreover, I do not think there is any linkage between conservative Christians, generally, and those white supremacists who use religious language and symbols. But the fact that the racists use such language, and that they are willing to oppress and kill in the name of Christ (albeit their own warped understanding thereof), means that religious persecution will remain an ongoing problem.

78. "Jewish Family Targeted For Intolerance After Football Player Flap," *Church and State* (January 1988) 14, and "Prayer Before Football Calms Crowd," id., 135. In March 1988, the U.S. District Court held that Crestview's public invocations are responsible "at least in part, for the clearly secular purpose of lowering the emotional state of the crowd, solemnizing public occasions and encouraging the recognition of what is worthy of appreciation." The court noted that the prayers "also satisfy the religious desires of the public" and denied that the thirty-five-year old practice "coerces adherence to the religious beliefs it embodies or produces religious intolerance." See *Berlin v Okaloosa County School District* (1988) cited in id.

79. Rob Boston, "Whose Kids Are They, Anyway?," id., 127. Boston included several examples: public elementary school teachers who reportedly read their Bible, told Bible stories, and often led prayers in their classrooms, a principal who allegedly pressured a science teacher to downplay evolution and push creationism and read the Bible to students in school.

80. See *Brandenburg v Ohio*, 395 U.S. 444 (1969).

81. In Frank Guliuzza, "'Tis a Lesson You Should Heed. Try, Try, Again. If At First You Don't Succeed': The Christian Right's 'Free Speech Strategy' For Securing 'Free Exercise' of Religion," Address at the 1994 Annual Meeting of the American Political Science Association, New York, NY, September 2, 1994, I examined the successful strategy of pitting the establishment clause against the *free speech clause* (instead of the free exercise clause) whenever possible.

82. Although it is interesting to observe what the court identifies as "coercion." See Gedicks, 118. Professor Gedicks contrasts the level of "coercion" inherent within many of the court's free exercise cases, e.g., *Lyng v Northwest Cemetary Protective Association*, 485 U.S. 439 (1988), and some of its establishment clauses cases, e.g., *Lee v Weisman*. With respect to what really constitutes coercion, Gedicks asks:

> How does one explain a jurisprudence that finds it constitutionally unconscionable to require that high school students and their families sit quietly through forty five seconds of civil religious platitudes as a condition to participating in graduation ceremonies, while simultaneously finding constitutionally unobjectionable the destruction of an entire religious culture for something as mundane as a logging road?

83. Levy, 217–18.

84. See J. Brent Walker, "Utah's Rosa Parks," *Liberty* (May/June 1996) 22.

85. In fact, Ms. Bauchman sued the school to keep the two songs off the program. The federal district court in Salt Lake City refused to stop the singing of the songs, so Ms. Bauchman filed an emergency appeal with the Tenth Circuit Court of Appeals in Denver. The Tenth Circuit prohibited West High from singing the two songs at the graduation ceremony, and the choir actually prepared two replacement songs. However, at the graduation ceremony, a graduating senior took hold of a microphone and urged the audience to sing "Friends." J. Brent Walker, id., reports that "the choir and the audience belted out 'Friends' with gusto. The crowed jeered as Rachael left in tears." Several months later, the Utah Federal District Court ruled against Ms. Bauchman. Her appeal was argued recently before the Tenth Circuit. See "Six Religious Groups Join Appeal," *Ogden Standard Examiner* (August 22, 1996) 7B.

86. Walker, 22.

87. Id.

88. For an alternative perspective, see Mona Charen, "Bauchman's Rights Not Endangered," *Ogden Standard Examiner* (November 17, 1995) 14A.

89. The same thing is true in the widely reported, ongoing struggle of Lisa Herdahl—a mother of six children in Mississippi who has challenged her school district's policy of student-initiated intercom prayer and their inclusion of a course in biblical history. See Laurie Lattimore, "The Herdahl Family's Hurdle," *Liberty* (May/June 1996) 17.

90. The persecution seems to cut across geographical boundaries, denominational lines, and appears just to go on and on. See Richard Foltin, "Horror Stories," *Liberty* (March/April 1996) 6. In addition to reporting the Herdahl's story in Mississippi, Foltin observes:

> In Virginia an elementary school allowed missionaries to enter the premises in order to recruit children and pressured children to attend the classes. In Texas, a 12-year-old girl was called "a little atheist" by her teacher, and had fellow students ask "Isn't she a Christian?" when she did not participate in prayers at school events. In South Carolina a Jewish high school senior complained that he was harassed by fellow students, who called him a "Satan worshiper" after he challenged the inclusion of prayer in graduation ceremonies. And these are only a few of the reported cases. No one knows how many other examples of officially sanctioned sectarian prayer and proselytization take place across the country, yet no one openly complains because few are willing (and who can blame them?) to undergo the kind of harassment and ostracization that Lisa Herdahl and her children have faced.

91. See *Grand Rapids v Ball* and *Aguilar v Felton* discussed above, and Gedicks, 59. As I indicated at supra note 11, the court has recently paved the way for parochial students to receive remedial programs on campus rather than in an off-campus facili-

ty. Too, the court suggested that the after-school programs that were terminated in Grand Rapids might well be constitutional.

92. See *Board of Education v Mergens*, discussed above. Also, see Nat Hentoff, "A Bible Study in a Public School?," *The Washington Post* (March 14, 1989), A-27. Jay Sekulow, lead counsel for the American Center for Law and Justice, observed in *Casenote* (May 1995), 3, that "in Wisconsin, Texas, and Michigan our lawyers went to bat for high school Bible clubs who were being denied equal access for their clubs." Ongoing litigation involving student-initiated prayers during public school graduations, and whether or not local churches can rent or otherwise use public school facilities for worship services, suggest that several Supreme Court cases, including *Lee v Weisman*, 112 S.Ct. 2649 (1992), and *Lamb's Chapel v Center Moriches School District*, 113 S.Ct. 2141 (1993), have yet to be fully fleshed out. See Sekulow, *Casenote* (June 1994), and *Casenote* (February 1995), 3.

93. Hentoff, "James Gierke's Right to Read His Bible," *The Washington Post* (June 10, 1989), A-19.

94. Id.

95. Id.

96. Id.

97. Id. A very similar story is reported by Cynthia Force Neal in "Silencing the Lamb," *Liberty* (May/June 1995) 6. She describes the case of Kenny Haller, an eight-year-old boy who started to read the Bible in class during a period when students were encouraged to bring books from home and read them aloud. He was told by the teacher to "put it away right now!" The difference in the two cases is that, while Gierke was contending for the right to bring his Bible to school and read it silently, Haller wanted to read aloud. Neal notes, "Earlier in the school term Kenny read from *The Foot Book* by Dr. Seuss. The children laughed and howled at the story. The next time Kenny stood up to read, however, the reaction wasn't so favorable." Foltin, 8, reports of a suit in Florida in which the plaintiffs assert that a child was persecuted for reading his Bible silently in class. Foltin says that the child was reprimanded, his Bible was confiscated, and "he was forced to sit in the corner."

98. *Roberts v Madigan*, 921 F. 2d 1047 (1990).

99. Jay Sekulow, *Casenote* (May 1995) 3, and *Casenote* (October 1994).

100. "Defending and Restoring Religious Freedom Nationwide," *The National Legal Foundation Minuteman* (Winter 1987 to 1988) 1.

101. Id.

102. Id.

103. Sekulow, *Casenote* (February 1994) 2.

104. Sekulow, *Casenote* (April 1995) 3.

105. Sekulow, *Casenote* (January 1994) 3.

106. Sekulow, *Casenote* (May 1995) 2. Foltin, 8, tells of a sixth-grade student in California who was ordered to stop singing at a talent show "because he mentioned the name 'Jesus.' Right in the middle of his song, school officials turned off his music and asked the child to get off the stage."

107. Id., 6.

108. Id., 8.

109. Lines, 553–54. See Robert DuPuy, "Religion, Graduation, and the First Amendment: A Threat or a Shadow?," 35 *Drake L. Rev.* 323 (1985 to 1986), and Colson, 205–10 for other examples.

110. Sekulow, *Casenote* (August 1994), 2–3.

111. Sekulow, *Casenote* (September 1994).

112. Sekulow, *Casenotes* (May 1995), 3.

113. Carter, 12.

114. Sekulow, *Casenote* (April 1995) 2.

115. Id.

116. Molly Ivins, address presented at the University of California, Davis, February 23, 1995, recorded by *C-span*.

CHAPTER SIX

1. 330 U.S. 1 (1947).

2. 402 U.S. 603 (1971).

3. Jesse Choper, *Securing Religious Liberty* (1995), and Steven Smith, *Foreordained Failure* (1995).

4. See chapter 1, footnote 15.

5. 472 U.S. 38 (1985).

6. Id., 76.

7. See the discussion of Justice O'Connor's endorsement test in Frederick Mark Gedicks, *The Rhetoric of Church and State* (1995), 73.

8. Id.

9. Id.

10. *Allegheny County v ACLU*, 492 U.S. 573 (1989).

11. Id.

12. Id.

13. Id.

14. Id.

15. Note the similarities between Justice Kennedy's position and the case for "religious communitarian" discourse advanced by Professor Gedicks, 11 and 95. Is one consequence of Kennedy's noncoercion test the repression of religious minorities? No. See Gedicks, 122, and Kent Greenawalt, *Private Consciences and Public Reasons*, 95.

16. Justice Rehnquist's chagrin with *Lemon* was always fairly pronounced. It might well be exceeded by Justice Scalia's antipathy toward the 1971 decision. Note the venom in Scalia's concurring opinion in *Lambs Chapel v Center Moriches School District*, 508 U.S. 384 (1993) 398:

> As to the Court's invocation of the *Lemon* test: Like some ghoul in a late-night horror movie that repeatedly sits up in its grave and shuffles abroad, after being repeatedly-killed and buried, *Lemon* stalks our Establishment Clause jurisprudence once again, frightening the little children and school attorneys of Center Moriches Union Free School District. . . . Over the years, however, no fewer than five of the currently sitting Justices have, in their opinions, personally driven pencils through the creature's heart. . . . The secret of the *Lemon* test's survival, I think is that it is so easy to kill. It is there to scare us (and our audience) when we wish it to do so, but we can command it to return to the tomb at will. . . . Such a docile and useful monster is worth keeping around, at least in a somnolent state: one never knows when one might need him.

17. Id., 110.

18. Id.

19. Id.

20. Compare this list with Ronald Thiemann's breakdown of the court's positions in *Religion in Public Life* (1996), 46.

21. 333 U.S. 203 (1948).

22. 370 U.S. 421 (1962).

23. 343 U.S. 306 (1952).

24. 374 U.S. 203 (1963).

25. See Norman Redlich, "Separation of Church and State," 60 *Notre Dame L. R* 1094 (1985); Mark Tushnet, *Red, White, and Blue* (1988); Gerard Bradley, *Church State Relationships in America* (1987); and Francis Lee, *Wall of Controversy* (1986); Stephen Carter, *The Culture of Disbelief* (1993); Gedicks, and Thiemann.

26. Neither, however, is new to the debate. Before *Foreordained Failure*, Smith authored several articles on religious freedom in legal periodicals including in the *University of Pennsylvania Law Review*, the *Texas Law Review*, and the *Michigan Law Review*. Professor Choper's *Securing Religious Liberty* is the culmination of more than three decades of substantial scholarship on the religion clauses. See the joint review of

these books by Christopher Eisgruber and Lawrence Sager in 74 *Tex. L. Rev.* 577 (1995), and by Frank Guliuzza, 58 *Rev. Pol.* 398 (1996).

27. He wants to harmonize the church-state debate with his larger theory of judicial review offered previously in his prominent work *Judicial Review and the National Political Process* (1980). "This book," he notes, 1, "articulates a comprehensive thesis for adjudicating all significant issues that arise under the Religion Clauses of the Constitution." Thus, he ties his religious liberty argument securely to the moorings of his general theory that the court should "protect personal liberty, especially for minorities who do not receive vigorous representation in the political process." Since most of the threats to religious freedom are made against religious minorities, Choper believe an energetic role for the court is warranted. "The dominant theme of the religion clauses," argues Choper, 9, "is to "protect religious liberty and the integrity of individual conscience, and that *judicial enforcement of these provisions should be confined to securing those freedoms.*"

28. Choper, 35–40.

29. 494 U.S. 872 (1990).

30. Choper, 41–42.

31. Id., 49–52. See 113 S. Ct. 2217 (1993).

32. Choper, 54.

33. Id., 65–94.

34. Id., 97.

35. Id., 118. Note the similarity between Professor Choper's proposal and Justice Kennedy's coercion test. Choper does. He notes, 34 n.135, "The contours of Justice Kennedy's 'coercion' approach—unfortunately titled, in my view . . .—are probably not yet amplified enough to be helpfully considered; in any event, since its basic thrust appears to come quite close to my thesis, it will be reviewed indirectly throughout the book."

36. Id., 160.

37. Id., 36–38.

38. Id., 186–87.

39. Lee, 6.

40. Choper, 189.

41. Id., 190.

42. Smith, v-vii.

43. Id., 4-5.

44. Id., 6–11.

45. Id., 12–14.

46. Id., 17–18.

47. Id., 19.

48. Id., 18–26.

49. Id., 17–43.

50. Id., 49.

51. Id., 63.

52. Id.

53. Id., 68–117.

54. Id., 122.

55. Id., 125–127.

56. Id., v.

57. See Leonard Levy, *The Establishment Clause* (1986); Gerard Bradley, *Church-State Relationships in America* (1987).

CHAPTER SEVEN

1. 330 U.S. 1 (1947).

2. 403 U.S. 602 (1971).

3. Rehnquist's position is articulated in his dissenting opinion in *Wallace v Jaffree*, 472 U.S. 38 (1985), and was discussed in chapter 6. Nonpreferential accommodation has been rejected by a number of scholars primarily because Rehnquist based the alternative upon a particular understanding of history—one that has not found favor with his opponents. See Leonard Levy, *The Establishment Clause* (1986); Derek Davis, *Original Intent* (1991). Professor Douglas Laycock, in "'Noncoercive' Support for Religion: Another False Claim about the Establishment Clause," 26 *Val. L. Rev.* 37 (1991) offers a more complete critique of nonpreferentialism.

4. Jesse Choper, in *Securing Religious Liberty* (1995) 19–33, notes that there are basically three alternative perspectives from which to view the establishment clause offered by the court and in the scholarly literature: neutrality (Philip Kurland's prominent conceptualization of neutrality), divisiveness, and endorsement. He rejects all three as inadequate.

5. 343 U.S. 306 (1952).

6. 374 U.S. 203 (1963).

7. See the criticisms leveled at the "wall of separation" metaphor by Justice Reed in *McCollum v Board*, 333 U.S. 203 (1948). "A rule of law," argued Reed, 247, "should not be drawn from a figure of speech." Although Justice Reed was the lone dissenter in an 8-1 decision, F. William O'Brien, in *Justice Reed and the First Amendment* (1958), notes that his position was eventually vindicated in *Zorach*.

8. 333 U.S. 203 (1948).

9. 370 U.S. 421 (1962).

10. *Webster's New Collegiate Dictionary* 772–73, 1056 (3rd. ed., 1975).

11. *Black's Law Dictionary* 1193, 1530 (4th. ed., 1968).

12. Several scholars argue that there was an established/quasi-established relationship between "state" and "Protestant Christianity" including: Mark Dewolfe Howe, *The Garden and the Wilderness* (1965); Harold Berman, "Religion and Law: The First Amendment in Historical Perspective," 35 *Emory L. Rev.* 777 (1986); Gerard Bradley, *Church-State Relationships in America* (1987); Kenneth Wald, *Religion and Politics* (1987); Frederick Mark Gedicks, *The Rhetoric of Church and State* (1995); Ronald Thiemann, *Religion in Public Life* (1996). Leonard Levy, in *The Establishment Clause* (1986), argues, 9:

> Granted, religion was then virtually synonymous with Christianity, indeed, in most of America, with Protestantism. In Europe a state church meant exactly what the term denotes: the church of one denomination, not of Christianity or Protestantism. Christianity or Protestantism may signify one religion in contrast with Judaism, Islam, or Hinduism; Protestantism may, more dubiously, be one religion in contrast with Roman Catholicism. But nowhere after the sixteenth century had Christianity or Protestantism been the solely established religion except in America.

Thus, the court could have well held, in *Everson*, that the establishment clause requires, first, the separation of "church," in this case Protestant Christianity, from state, and then, second, described some postseparation follow-up relationship between state, church, and all those who had previously been outside the preferred relationship.

13. Back in 1958, Professor Loren Beth rejected "total separation" as a wholly ineffective means of protecting religious liberty primarily because it is purely a theoretical idea. Beth argued, in *The American Theory of Church and State* (1958), 126, "No state has ever achieved it, nor will any." In 1995, President Clinton expressed similar sentiments in his celebrated speech at James Madison High School in Vienna, Virginia. See "Clinton Speech Outlines Rights," *N.Y. Times* (July 13, 1995) A1. I will discuss the president's address more fully in chapter 8.

14. See John Swomley, *Religious Liberty and the Secular State* (1987) 85–86.

15. Again, by "neutrality," I do not mean the classic definition of strict neutrality offered by Professor Philip Kurland thirty-five years ago. Kurland, in *Religion and the Law* (1962), observed, 18:

> The thesis proposed here as the proper construction of the religion clauses of the first amendment is that the freedom and separation clauses should be read as a single precept that government cannot utilize religion as a standard for action or inaction because these

clauses prohibit classification in terms of religion either to confer
a benefit or impose a burden.

As I indicated in chapter 5, and will discuss below, Kurland's neutrality dramatically favors this other realm generally termed "nonreligion" over religion. Of course
one is not limited to Kurland's definition of neutrality. See Paul Weber, *Equal
Separation* (1990); Laurence Tribe, *American Constitutional Law* (1988) 1188.
Professor Weber notes, 151:

> Unfortunately, the term "neutrality" has now become so generic
> that in responding to the various critics I realized it was necessary
> to shift terminology and begin to use the term "equal separation."

My definition of neutrality is much more consistent with that described by
Gedicks, 59, and Stephen Monsma's approach delineated in "The Neutrality Principle
and a Pluralist Concept of Accommodation," in Weber, 73 and outlined fully in
Positive Neutrality (1993). I like Professor Monsma's approach very much. I debated
Dr. Monsma regarding our respective positions during the round table, "Is Positive
Neutrality the Answer?," at the 1997 National Conference of Christians in Political
Science.

16. I think the court's activism in interpreting the establishment clause is clearly a concern of Professor Steven Smith, in *Foreordained Failure* (1995), and of Professor
Choper. Choper wants the court to actively protect the religious liberty clauses, but he
wants their constitutional review to be principled. "The dominant theme of the religion clauses," notes Choper, 9, "is to protect religious liberty and the integrity of individual conscience, and that judicial enforcement of these provisions should be confined
to securing those freedoms." Professor Smith holds that the court continues tinkering
with the establishment clause in the hope that it might, finally, discover a single principle from which to interpret the clause. "Judicial intervention under the Constitution
into matters of religious freedom is illegitimate and unjustified," notes Smith, 125. He
concludes, 127, by arguing that the myriad discussions about religious freedom will be
more fruitful when scholars ease their fixation with judicial review and "relinquish their
accompanying demand that the meaning of religious freedom be cabined within the
narrow confines of constitutional 'principle'."

17. The nexus between Christianity and the government was not always an economic one, but was, nonetheless, an understandably unacceptable one to separationists,
Swomley, 85–86, notes:

> The so-called Christian era is marked by an alliance between
> church and state. This does not refer to contemporary government
> subsidies to church hospitals, schools, and colleges or other reli-
> gious programs, which mark the church as another social institu-
> tion competing for government funds. Rather, the alliance
> between church and state in the Constantinian sense meant that

the church participated in the formal direction of society, sanctify-
ing and blessing economic, political, and military structures so
long as those structures verbally acknowledged the Christian tradition and gave the church a position of special recognition.

18. See Justice Douglas' argument in *Zorach*, 312–15.

19. See the lengthy list of examples in Frank Guliuzza, "The Practical Perils of
an Original Intent-Based Judicial Philosophy: Originalism and the Church-State Test
Case," 42 *Drake L. Rev.* 343 (1993) 356n., 77, and n. 78.

20. See Judge Noonan's dissent in *EEOC v Townley Engineering & Mfg Co.*, 859
F.2d 610 (9th Cir. 1988), and Richard Baer, "American Public Education and the
Myth of Value Neutrality," in Richard John Neuhaus (ed.) *Democracy and the Renewal
of Education* (1987). Both men indicate that those philosophical presuppositions that
lead one to reject religious truth claims, or that would be characterized by the court as
"nonreligion" are, in fact, competing religious arguments.

21. Although he is no traditional separationist, this is Professor Choper's position regarding financial support. See Choper, 15–19.

22. That is what seems to me to be the problem with Professor Kurland's "neutrality." See Philip Kurland, "Of Church and State and the Supreme Court," 29 *Chi.
L. Rev.* 1 (1962).

23. The court's current approach produces a situation remarkably similar to that
addressed in *Larkin v Grendel's Den*, 459 U.S. 116 (1982). In *Larkin*, the court struck
down a statute that granted religious bodies veto power over the application of liquor
licenses for establishments located within 500 feet of a church or synagogue. The court
held that the statute fostered a fusion of government and religion, and actually dele-
gated important government powers to religious bodies. See Justice Souter's application of *Larkin* in *Board of Kiryas Joel Village School District v Grumet*, 114 S. Ct. 2481
(1994). Too, see Justice Scalia's scathing dissent. My contention is that, as in *Larkin*,
the court's current establishment clause jurisprudence gives the same unconstitutional
veto power to "nonreligion."

24. See Gedicks, 57.

25. See Kent Greenawalt, *Private Consciences and Public Reasons* (1995), 58 for
an illustration. I do like the alternative approach recently advanced by law professor
Carl Esbeck in "The Establishment Clause as a Structural Restraint on Government
Power," 84 *Iowa L. Rev.* 1,4 (1998). Professor Esbeck argues that the esablishment
clause should be conceptualized "as a structural restraint on the government's power to
act on certain matters pertaining to religion." Hence, the establishment clause would
serve as a prophylactic, or as a stiff-arm, to government action that is unequivocally
religious. Esbeck's approach makes the "purpose" prong of the Lemon test vital, but
would jettison the remainder of the unfortunate test. If there is no clear secular purpose, then government action will not survive constitutional scrunity.

26. Like the New Jersey program upheld in *Everson*.

27. See *Board of Education v Allen*, 392 U.S. 236 (1968).

28. See *Mueller v Allen*, 463 U.S. 388 (1983).

29. See *Committee for Public Education v Nyquist*, 413 U.S. 756 (1973).

30. See *Witters v Washington Department of Services*, 474 U.S. 481 (1986).

31. See *Zobrest v Catalina Foothills School District*, 113 S.Ct. 2462 (1993).

32. Like those struck down in *Lemon*.

33. See *Meek v Pittenger*, 421 U.S. 349 (1975).

34. See *Wolman v Walter*, 433 U.S. 229 (1977).

35. See *Grand Rapids School District v Ball*, 473 U.S. 373 (1985).

36. See *Aguilar v Felton*, 473 U.S. 402 (1985). Of course the court did modify substantially the Aguilar decision in *Agostini v Felton*, 117 S. Ct. 1997 (1997). See R. Collin Mangrum, "State Aid to Students in Religiously Affiliated Schools: *Agostini v Felton*," 31 *Creighton L. Rev.* 1155 (1998). Although not directly related, one interesting possibility for accommodation includes financial support for school choice. See Suzanne Bauknight, "The Search for Constitutional School Choice," 27 *J.L. and Educ.* 525 (1998); Christopher Pixley, "The Next Frontier in Public School Finance Reform: A Policy and Constitutional Analysis of School Choice Legislation," 24 *J. Legis.* 21 (1998); Michael Vaccari, "Public Purpose and the Public Funding of Sectarian Educational Institutions: A More Rational Approach After *Rosenberger* and *Agostini*," 82 *Marq. L. Rev.* 1 (1998).

37. See *Bradfield v Roberts*, 175 U.S. 291 (1899).

38. See *Tilton v Richardson*, 403 U.S. 672 (1971).

39. Note the distinction between diagnostic testing and therapy in *Wolman* discussed in chapter 5.

40. *Walz v Tax Commission*, 397 U.S. 664 (1970).

41. See *Bowen v Kendrick*, 487 U.S. 589 (1988).

42. I am mindful of the more than thirty years of serious scholarly study that Professor Choper devoted to the area of religious liberties before publishing *Securing Religious Liberties* in 1995. He started working in this area several years before I entered first grade.

43. See *Zorach* and *McCollum*.

44. See *Marsh v Chambers*, 463 U.S. 783 (1983).

45. And like the one struck down in *Jaffree*. See Roger Newman, "School Prayer and the Ten Commandments in Alabama," 28 *Cumb. L. Rev.* 1 (1997).

46. See *Sherbert v Verner*, 374 U.S 398 (1963), and *Wisconsin v Yoder*, 406 U.S. 205 (1972).

47. See *Widmar v Vincent*, 454 U.S. 263 (1981); *Board of Education v Mergens*, 496 U.S. 226 (1990); *Lamb's Chapel v Center Moriches Union Free School District*, 113 S. Ct. 2141 (1993).

48. See *Stone v Graham*, 449 U.S. 39 (1980).

49. See *Lynch v Donnely*, 465 U.S. 573 (1984); *Allegheny County v ACLU*, 492 U.S. 573 (1989).

50. See *Lee v Weisman*, 112 S. Ct. 2649 (1992).

51. See *Braunfeld v Brown*, 366 U.S. 599 (1961).

52. See *Edwards v Aguillard*, 482 U.S. 578 (1987).

53. I was more than a little surprised to find out how much attention is given to this issue by some very prominent constitutional scholars. For instance, Professor Choper, 145–46, 189, really wrestles with how to deal with cases involving evolution and creation science. Professor Stephen Carter, in *The Culture of Disbelief* (1993), 156–82, devotes a whole chapter to the issue. In order to be constitutional, creationist societies would likely have to demonstrate that one of two situations existed. First, they must prove that evolution is prominently featured in the public school curriculum in order to foster "secularism" or "humanism" and not because the scientific community is nearly unanimous in embracing it. That would be an enormously difficult task because creationist societies would not only have to successfully call evolution into question as a scientific model, but more important, they must also discredit the motivation of those educators requiring evolution in science classes. Second, if they cannot prove that secularists are overtly or covertly using evolution as a vehicle to establish their religious faith, creationist societies must at least show that creation science is, in fact, very good science. They must demonstrate that it is a legitimate scientific explanation for the earth's origin, one that leaves serious science students impoverished without its teaching, and also, that to ignore creation science, whether done intentionally or not, undermines religious neutrality. Although still quite difficult to prove, the latter situation has greater possibility for supporters of scientific creation. Therefore, it is imperative that legislation supporting creation science be drafted without a hint of discrimination. Further, since it is exceedingly more difficult to demonstrate that evolution is taught in classrooms as part of an intentional effort to establish secularism, and not because it is the dominant scientific explanation of the earth's origin, the language in the legislation, and the legislative history accompanying the law, should emphasize the scientific merits of creation science; it should not make reference to the promotion of religious doctrine. To do so would undercut the intentions of those who have a "secular purpose" in promoting creation science; it would also render any such legislation unconstitutional.

54. For a good example of this argument, see Peter Marshall and David Manuel, *The Light and the Glory* (1977).

CONCLUSION

1. *Pub. L.* 103–41 (1993).

2. In particular, I mean *Westside Community Schools v Mergens*, 496 U.S. 226

(1990), *Lamb's Chapel v Center Moriches Free Union School District*, 113 S.Ct. 2141 (1993), and *Rosenberger v Rector*, 115 S.Ct. 2510 (1995).

3. "Clinton Speech Outlines Rights," *N.Y. Times* (July 13, 1995) A1.

4. See *Boerne v Flores* (no. 95-2074) 65 LW 4612 (6/24/97).

5. That is what is so attractive about Professor Jesse Choper's book, *Securing Religious Liberty* (1995). He endeavors to deal with all issues that arise under the establishment clause *and* the free exercise clause.

6. See Frank Guliuzza, "The Practical Perils of an Original Intent-Based Judicial Philosophy: Originalism and the Church-State Test Case," 42 *Drake L. Rev.* 343, 356 n. 78 (1994).

7. See *Reynolds v United States*, 98 U.S. 145 (1879), and *Employment Division v Smith*, 494 U.S.872 (1990).

8. This hierarchy holds true whether the government participates in "ideological" accommodation, e.g., *Engel v Vitale*, 370 U.S. 421 (1962), *Abington Township v Schempp*, 374 U.S. 203 (1963), *Wallace v Jaffree*, 472 U.S. 38 (1985), or financial accommodation, e.g., *Grand Rapids v Ball*, 473 U.S. 373 (1985), *Aguilar v Felton*, 473 U.S. 402 (1985). The one area where the court tends to minimize the establishment clause claim is when government support goes directly to individuals. See *Everson, Board of Education v Allen*, 392 U.S. 236 (1968), *Witters v Washington*, 474 U.S. 481 (1986), and *Zobrest v Catalina Foothills School District*, 113 S.Ct. 2462 (1993). In June 1994, the court declared unconstitutional a public school district created by the New York state legislature for the welfare of a village of Orthodox Jews. In the decision, *Board of Education of Kiryas Joel v Grumet*, 114 S.Ct. 2481 (1994), Justice Souter argued that the state went beyond a legitimate accommodation of the group's religious needs. Souter hinted rather strongly, however, that perhaps the court should reconsider the *Grand Rapids* and *Aguilar* decisions. See the analysis of the *Kiryas Joel* decision in Linda Greenhouse, "High Court Bars School District Created to Benefit Hasidic Jews," *N.Y. Times*, (June 28, 1994), A1, D21. *Aguilar* and *Grand Rapids* were finally overturned in *Agostini v Felton*, US SupCt, no. 96-552 (6/23/97).

9. M. Glenn Abernathy, *Civil Liberties under the Constitution* (1968) 284–85. Abernathy's discussion of the religion clauses was extremely helpful in providing the analytical categories that I set up below.

10. The proliferation of free exercise and establishment clause cases correlates with the court's decisions incorporating the two religion clauses of the first amendment, *Cantwell v Connecticut*, 310 U.S 296 (1940), and *Everson v Board*. See Rossum and Tarr, *American Constitutional Law* (1987) 387.

11. 98 U.S. 145 (1879).

12. Id., 161.

13. Id., 166–67.

14. Id., at 167. In *Davis v Beason*, 133 U.S. 333 (1890), the court applied and expanded the *Reynolds* caveat in a case involving a man who, as a matter of religious

faith, believed in polygamy, and was convicted for simply wishing to vote. In Idaho prospective voters had to swear that they were not criminals, their allegiance to the Constitution, and that:

> I am not a bigamist or polygamist; that I am not a member of any order, organization or association which teaches, advises, counsels or encourages its members, devotees or any other person to commit the crime of bigamy or polygamy; . . . that I do not and will not, publicly or privately, or in any manner whatever, teach, advise, counsel or encourage any person to commit the crime of bigamy or polygamy, or any other crime defined by law, either as religious duty or otherwise. . . .

Davis registered to vote, was convicted of "conspiracy to unlawfully pervert and obstruct the due administration of the Laws of the Territory," and was sentenced to pay a fine of $500 and a jail term of 250 days. On appeal, the court held that the free exercise clause was never intended to trump the criminal law. Since, they reasoned , Idaho has the authority to set its own voter registration standards, and the law was generally applicable, the court affirmed Davis' conviction. Note that Davis was not a bigamist or polygamist. He simply believed that God permits and encourages plural marriage, and he wanted to vote. *Davis* blurs the belief-action dichotomy articulated in *Reynolds* by permitting the government to come very close to criminalizing belief.

15. 310 U.S. 296 (1940).

16. Id., 303–4.

17. See C. Herman Pritchett, *The American Constitution* (1968) for a thorough explanation of the valid regulation test.

18. See, for example, *Jacobson v Massachusetts*, 197 U.S. 11 (1905), *Prince v Massachusetts*, 321 U.S. 158 (1944), and *Bob Jones University v U.S.*, 461 U.S. 574 (1983).

19. Of course the court had bolstered free exercise dramatically, even if perhaps indirectly, in the landmark decision, *West Virgina v Barnette*, 319 U.S. 624 (1943). *Barnette* is primarily a free speech case, but in the decision the majority held that one cannot be compelled into expression that violates one's beliefs. In this case, Jehovah's Witnesses were reacting to state regulations requiring them to pledge allegiance to the flag in violation of their religious beliefs.

20. 374 U.S. 398 (1963).

21. Id., 399–400.

22. Id., 404–9. Justice Brennan, 404, stated, "The ruling forces here to choose between following the precepts of her religion and forfeiting benefits on the one hand, and abandoning one of the precepts of her religion in order to accept work on the other hand. Governmental imposition of such choices put the same kind of burden upon the free exercise of religion as would a fine imposed against appellant for her Saturday worship."

23. Stephen Pepper, "Taking the Free Exercise Clause Seriously," 1986 *B.Y.U. L. Rev.* 299 (1986) 300–301.

24. Id.

25. Id.

26. 406 U.S. 205 (1979).

27. Id., 216.

28. Pepper, 310–11. See John Baker, "Belief and Action: Limitations on Free Exercise of Religion," in Robert Alley (ed.), *James Madison on Religious Liberty* (1985) 275. Baker argues that:

> In *Yoder* can be found a three part test: (1) the court must deter-
> mine whether or not a legitimate religious belief is held and
> whether the activity affected by state action is pervasively religious;
> (2) the court must inquire as to whether the state action places a
> burden or inhibition on free exercise rights; (3) assuming an affir-
> mative response to these two, the court must decide if the burden
> is justified by a compelling state interest which cannot be served
> by less restrictive means.

29. See David O'Brien, *Constitutional Law and Politics*, vol II (1995) 1247–50. Professor O'Brien illustrates what has, in fact, become a three-tiered test for applying the equal protection clause: an upper tier applying a strict scrutiny test, an intermediate tier applying an exacting scrutiny or strict rationality test, and a lower tier applying a rational basis test.

30. *Yoder*, 406.

31. Id.

32. 455 U.S. 252 (1982).

33. Id., 257.

34. Id.

35. 461 U.S. 574 (1983). In *Bob Jones*, the court upheld the right of the IRS to withhold tax exemptions to private schools that practice racial discrimination—even if the discrimination emerged from sincerely held religious beliefs. Chief Justice Burger noted, 604, "the Government has a fundamental, overriding interest in eradicating racial discrimination in education which substantially outweighs whatever burden denial of tax benefits places on petitioners' exercise of their religious beliefs."

36. 475 U.S. 503 (1986). The case involved the right of an Orthodox Jew (and ordained Rabbi) to wear a yarmulke while in uniform and on duty as an Air Force officer.

37. Pepper, 322–25. See Ira Lupu, "Where Rights Begin: The Problem of Burden on the Free Exercise of Religion," 102 *Harv. L. Rev.* 933 (1989).

38. See *Lyng v Northwest Indian Cemetery Protective Association*, 485 U.S. 439 (1988).

39. See *Jimmy Swaggart Ministries v Board of Education*, 493 U.S. 378 (1990).

40. See William Marshall, "The Concept of Offensiveness in Establishment and Free Exercise Jurisprudence," 66 *Ind. L. J.* 1351 (1991) 354.

41. Id., 699–701.

42. Id., 692.

43. Id., 694.

44. Id. Note the court's recent decision, *Church of the Lukumi Babalu Aye v City of Hialeah*, 113 S.Ct. 2217 (1993) that struck down Hialeah, Florida's, restrictions on animal sacrifice. The court held that the ordinance was not neutral on its face, that the community had, indeed, targeted a particular church, and, therefore, the majority maintained its reliance upon *Smith*.

45. Id.

46. Id.

47. See, for example, Ellis West, "The Case Against a Right to Religion-Based Exemptions," 4 *Notre Dame J. L., Ethics and Pub. Pol'y* 591 (1990). Professor William Marshall has also argued forcefully against religion-based exemptions in several places including "Solving the Free Exercise Dilemma: Free Exercise as Expression," 67 *Minn. L. Rev.* 545 (1983); "The Case Against the Constitutionality of Compelled Free Exercise Exemptions," 40 *Case W. L. Rev.* 357 (1990); "In Defense of *Smith* and Free Exercise Revisionism," 58 *U. Chi. L. Rev.* 308 (1991). Professor Mark Tushnet, quite apart from the question of religious exemptions, generally, offers a defense of the court's holding in *Smith* in "The Rhetoric of Free Exercise Discourse," 1993 *B.Y.U.L.Rev.* 117 (1993).

48. See Douglas Laycock, "Watering Down the Free-Exercise Clause," *The Christian Century*, May 16–23, 1990, 518; Laycock, "The Remnants of Free Exercise," 1990 *Sup. Ct. Rev.* 1 (1990); Richard Neuhaus, "Church, State, and Peyote," *Nat'l Rev.*, (June 11, 1990), 42; Michael McConnell, "Free Exercise Revisionism and the Smith Decision," 57 *U. Chi. L. Rev.* 1109 (1990); McConnell, "Religious Freedom at a Crossroads," in Geoffrey stone, Richard Epstein, and Cass Sunstein (eds.), *The Bill of Rights in the Modern State* (1992), 139–40; Jesse Choper, "The Rise and Decline of the Constitutional Protection of Religious Liberty," 70 *Neb. L. Rev.* 651 (1991).

49. See Frank Guliuzza in "The Supreme Court, the Establishment Clause, and Incoherence," in Luis Lugo (ed.), *The Role of Religion in American Public Life* (1994) 115. See also the discussion of the Court's usage of separation and neutrality in Chapters Four and Seven of this work.

50. Id., 132–36. Several examples are discussed in chapter 5.

51. Pub. L. 103–41, 107 Stat. 1488 (1993). See Laycock, in "Free Exercise and the Religious Freedom Restoration Act," 62 *Fordham L. Rev.* 883 (1994), hereafter "Free Exercise," offers some examples of specific cases. Also see Laycock, "The

Religious Freedom Restoration Act," 1993 *B.Y.U. L.Rev.* 221 (1993), hereafter "RFRA"; John Whitehead and Alexis Crow, "The Religious Freedom Restoration Act: Implications for Religiously-Based Civil Disobedience and Free Exercise Claims," 33 *Washburn L. J.* 383 (1994), 391; and Mary Schnabel, "The Religious Freedom Restoration Act: A Prison's Dilemma," 29 *Willamette L. Rev.* 323 (1993), 337.

52. Former New York Representative Stephen Solarz introduced RFRA on July 26, 1990. See Whitehead and Crow, 391.

53. See Peter Steinfels, "Clinton Signs Law Protecting Religious Practices," *N.Y. Times* (November 17, 1993), A18.

54. Laycock, "Free Exercise," 896.

55. Laycock, in "RFRA," 233–45, looks at several objections raised by those who are, essentially, proponents of the legislation, and those compromises that were effectuated to pass the bill.

56. Laycock, "Free Exercise," 895–97.

57. See Whitehead and Crow, 388.

58. This is especially true since, argues Laycock, in "Free Exercise," 892–95, the court, when interpreting the free exercise clause, has a less than stellar record in defending religious liberties claims.

59. Laycock, "RFRA," 230.

60. The critique of RFRA has been pretty wide-ranging both from those who oppose the kind of religious-based exemptions RFRA would seem to permit, discussed above, and even from supporters of RFRA. For example, Scott Idleman, in "The Religious Freedom Restoration Act: Pushing the Limits of Legislative Power," 73 *Tex. L. Rev.* 247 (1994) argues that RFRA might violate the establishment clause and gives unconstitutional authority to Congress. Too, note the criticisms of RFRA raised in: Thomas Berg, "What Hath Congress Wrought? An Interpretive Guide to the Religious Freedom Restoration Act," 39 *Vill. L. Rev.* 1 (1994); Marci Hamilton, "The Religious Freedom Restoration Act: Letting the Fox into the Henhouse Under Cover of Section 5 of the Fourteenth Amendment," 16 *Cardozo L. Rev.* 357 (1994); Christopher Eisgruber and Lawrence Sager, "Why the Religious Freedom Restoration Act is Unconstitutional," 69 *N.Y.U. L. Rev.* 437 (1994); Stanley Ingber, "Judging Without Judgement: Constitutional Irrelevancies and the Demise of Dialogue," 46 *Rutgers L. Rev.* 1473 (1994); Jay Bybee, "Taking Liberties With the First Amendment: Congress, Section 5, and the Religious Freedom Restoration Act," 48 *Vand. L. Rev.* 1539 (1995); Daniel Conkle, "The Religious Freedom Restoration Act: The Constitutional Significance of an Unconstitutional Statute," 56 *Mont. L. Rev.* 39 (1995); Eugene Gressman and Angela Carmella, "The RFRA Revision of the Free Exercise Clause," 57 *Ohio St. L.J.* 65 (1996). See also Laycock, "RFRA, Congress, and the Ratchet," 56 *Mont. L. Rev.* 145 (1995); and Bonnie Robin-Vergeer, "Disposing of the Red Herrings: A Defense of the Religious Freedom Restoration Act," 69 *S. Cal. L. Rev.* 589 (1996).

61. Laycock, "Free Exercise," 886–95.

62. It is noteworthy that Laycock raised this fear in 1990—just after *Smith*. See Laycock, "Watering Down the Free Exercise Clause," *The Christian Century* (May 16–23, 1990), 519. He does concede the possibility that Congress could scuttle the religious liberties of political and religious minorities. One consequence of RFRA, notes Laycock, "RFRA," is that, "Religious liberty was committed into the hands of shifting political majorities precisely to the extent that the Court withdrew judicial protection under the Constitution." Although he acknowledges this possibility, he believes it unlikely. Id., 254–56, and Laycock, "Free Exercise," 899–900.

63. Laycock, "Free Exercise," 901. Laycock, a staunch proponent of RFRA, acknowledges that the possibility of watering down the compelling interest test represents the principal danger to the act. "The Supreme Court has been very inconsistent on what it means by compelling state interest," Laycock observes. "There is no government bureaucrat in America who doesn't believe that his program serves a compelling interest in every application." Laycock, Id., cites the animal sacrifice case, *Church of the Lukumi Babalu Ave, Inc. v. City of Hialeah* (508 U.S. 502 (1993)—a case that he argued before the court—as a "clear example of how weak the compelling interest test can become in the hands of a judge who doesn't want to grant the claim." At the trial court level, the judge equated the concepts of compelling interest, rational interest, and legitimate interest. Protecting animals is a legitimate power of the state. Moreover, it is clearly a rational interest of the state of Florida. That a city ordinance restricting animal sacrifices is legitimate and rational does not, however, make it "compelling" in the face of a first amendment free exercise claim; and, that the trial judge could equate these related—but hardly synonymous—legal ideas, illustrates the very real potential that federal judges, many of whom are inclined to defer to legislatures and bureaucratic bodies, could scuttle the act.

64. Whitehead and Crow, 394.

65. *Sherbert*, 404.

66. Whitehead and Crow, 394–95.

67. Id., 394.

68. Public Law, 103–41, Sec. 7 (1993).

69. 112 S.Ct. 2649 (1992).

70. Whitehead Crow, 399.

71. 114 S.Ct. 2481 (1994).

72. Id.

73. *Boerne v Flores*, 4613.

74. Id., 4614–15. The court's repudiation of RFRA prompted a significant response in the academic literature regarding the future of the free exercise clause. See, for example, Frederick Gedicks, "An Unfirm Foundation: The Regrettable Indefensibility of Religious Exceptions," 20 *U. Ark. Little Rock L.J.* 555 (1998); Marci Hamilton, "The Constitutional Rhetoric of Religion," 20 *U. Ark. Little Rock L.J.* 619 (1998); Daniel Conkle, "Congressional Alternatives in the Wake of *City of Boerne v*

Flores: The (Limited) Role of Congress in Protecting Religious Freedom from State and Local Infringement," 20 *U. Ark. Little Rock L.J.* 633 (1998); Teresa Stanton Collett, "Heads, Secularists Win; Tails, Believers Lose—Returning Only Free Exercise to the Political Process," 20 *U. Ark. Little Rock L.J.* 689 (1998); Thomas Berg, "The Constitutional Future of Religious Freedom Legislation," 20 *U. Ark. Little Rock L.J.* 715 (1998); John DiPippa. "The Death and Resurrection of RFRA: Integrating *Lopez* and *Boerne*," 20 *U. Ark. Little Rock L.J.* 767 (1998); Garrett Epps, "What We Talk About Free Exercise," 30 *Ariz. St. L.J.* 563 (1998).

75. 343 U.S. 579 (1952).

76. Id.

77. *Boerne v Flores*, 4615–18. Note the impact of the court's decision—a full-fledged triumph for judicial supremacy/finality. Contrast Justice Kennedy's decision with those constitutional scholars who argue for departmentalism, or coordinate constitutional review. See John Agresto, *The Supreme Court and Constitutional Democracy* (1984); Louis Fisher, *Constitutional Dialogues* (1988); Susan Burgess, *Contest for Constitutional Authority* (1992).

78. See, for example, *Cantwell v Connecticut*, 310 U.S. 296 (1940); *Murdock v Pennsylvania*, 319 U.S. 105 (1943); *West Virginia State Board of Education v Barnette*, 319 U.S. 624 (1943).

79. They were not always successful, however. In some cases, e.g. *Prince v Massachusetts*, 321 U.S. 158 (1944), the court employed free exercise clause analysis to affirm the state's authority to protect children. In other cases, e.g., *Cox v New Hampshire*, 312 U.S. 569 (1941); *Minersville v Gobitis*, 310 U.S. 586 (1940); and *Jones v Opelika*, 316 U.S. 584 (1942), the court considered the free speech claims of the Witnesses, but held for the government.

80. See Ted Jelen and Clyde Wilcox, "Preaching to the Converted: The Causes and Consequences of Viewing Religious Television," in David Leege and Lyman Kellsted (eds.), *Rediscovering the Religious Factor in American Politics* (1993) 255.

81. See, for example, Laurence Barrett, "Fighting for God and the Right Wing," *Time* (September 13, 1993), 58; Howard Fineman, "God and the Grass Roots," *Newsweek* (November 8, 1993), 42; Alan Hertzke, *Echoes of Discontent* (1993); David Leege and Lyman Kellstedt, *Rediscovering the Religious Factor in American Politics* (1993); Michael Cromartie, *No Longer Exiles* (1993); Gerry O'Sullivan, "Against the Grain," *The Humanist* (November/December 1992), 37. Richard Berke, in "Religious Right Gains Influence and Spreads Discord in G.O.P.," *N.Y. Times* (June 3, 1994), A1, writes that:

> Christians who cleave to a strict interpretation of the Bible have effectively taken over the Republican parties in Texas, Virginia, Oregon, Iowa, Washington, and South Carolina, and have made significant advances in several states including Florida, New York, California, and Louisiana.

Further, Berke notes that the rise of evangelical Christians as a force in the Republican Party has grown substantially since Pat Robertson ran for president in 1988. He observes that religious conservatives push the party to adopt more conservative platforms; they are getting elected to local offices, "and are beginning to have an influence on higher offices." Berke, "As Christians Pull the G.O.P to the Right, Its Leaders Argue Over Holding the Center," *N.Y. Times* (June 27, 1994), A12.

82. Hubert Morken, "The Evangelical Legal Response to the ACLU: Religion, Politics, and the First Amendment," presented at the 1992 annual meeting of the American Political Science Association, Chicago, September 3–6, 1992; Roy Rivenburg, "Litigating for a 'Godly Heritage,'" *L.A. Times* (December 30, 1992), E1; and Tim Stafford, "Move Over ACLU," *Christianity Today* (October 25, 1993), 20.

83. There are several other groups not discussed in Morken's paper, e.g., the Rutherford Institute headed up by attorney John Whitehead. Morken, supra, note 147, 3, acknowledges that his work does "not exhaust the supply." He indicates that, in the future, he intends to examine other evangelical legal organizations. See William Martin, *With God on our Side* (1996), 361.

84. Id., 20, Stafford, supra, note 147, 20.

85. Id., 29.

86. Id., 30.

87. Rivenburg, E1.

88. Id.

89. Id.

90. 496 U.S. 226 (1990).

91. Morken, 20.

92. 506 U.S. 263 (1993).

93. O'Brien, 236–37.

94. 508 U.S. 384 (1993).

95. Rivenburg, supra, note 147, E1, and Morken, supra note 147, 21, 25–28. Morken, 21–28, presents a brief biographical sketch of Sekulow and his career in private corporate practice and as an attorney for public interest groups. So does Rivenburg, E5. Although he is chief counsel for the ACLJ, Morken hints that Sekulow might be bothered by the structure of the organization—one that relies heavily upon a large staff of attorneys.

96. Morken, 25–28.

97. Jay Sekulow, *From Intimidation to Victory* (1990), 20.

98. Rivenburg, E5.

99. Id.

100. 20 U.S.C. ss 4071–74.

101. *Mergens*, 247.

102. Id., 248–51.

103. Id.

104. Id.

105. Levy, 129.

106. *Mergens*, 226. They spend several pages distinguishing *Mergens* from Widmar. While they came close to ruling that the EAA, especially because it is applied at the secondary school level, is an endorsement of religion, they nonetheless struck the balance in favor of free speech. The same cannot be said for Justice Stevens. He rejected the court's definition of a "noncurriculum" related club, and held that, in this case, the establishment clause prevailed because the free speech argument is not as strong at the high school level.

107. *Lamb's Chapel*, 2688–90.

108. Id., 2685.

109. Id., 2688.

110. Id.

111. Id., 2689.

112. Id., 2690.

113. Jay Sekulow, letter to school superintendents, December 3, 1993.

114. "Denial of Bible Clubs in Schools is Challenged," *Ogden Standard Examiner* (February 17, 1994), 9A. It is important to note, however, that the strategy depends upon the court's robust defense of free speech. According to Sekulow, *Madsen* was "a devastating blow" not only to the prolife movement, but for proponents of free speech period. Matthew Staver, who argued for Madsen, maintains that "this injunction, instead of using a surgeon's scalpel, cuts with a butcher's knife." David Van Biema observes that constitutional scholars as far ranging as Antonin Scalia and Laurence Tribe have expressed their concern, following the announcement of *Madsen*, for potential damage that might be done to the free speech clause. Van Biema, "Keep Your Distance," *Time* (July 11, 1994), 25.

115. Aaron Epstein, "High Court Takes On Church-State Issue," *Duluth News-Tribune* (November 1, 1994), 3A.

116. Id.

117. Id.

118. Mark Tushnet, "The Constitution of Religion," 50 *Rev. Pol.* 628 (1988), 635–39. Hereafter, Tushnet, "Constitution of Religion."

119. Id.

120. Id., 639–41.

121. 454 U.S. 263 (1981).

122. Id., 265–66.

123. Id., 271–72.

124. Id., 273–74.

125. Id., 276.

126. Id., 271–76.

127. Tushnet, "Constitution of Religion," 652, n. 44.

128. 454 U.S. 263, 269.

129. Id., 284.

130. Tushnet, "Constitution of Religion," 653 n. 54.

131. 454 U.S. 263, 284.

132. See "President's Memorandum on Religious Expression in Schools," *N.Y. Times* (July 13, 1995) B10.

133. Id.

134. Id.

135. Id.

136. Id. Note that President Clinton has recently "issued guidelines requiring government supervisors to respect individual expressions of faith by federal employees."

Index

Skinner, B. F., 32
Slagstad, Rune, 173n, 174n
Smidt, Corwin, 156n
Smith v School Board of Mobile City
    (1987), 171n, 172n
Smith, Alfred, 133
Smith, Rodney, 153n
Smith, Steven, 102–105, 150n, 152n,
    154n, 197n
Smolin, David, 150n, 176n
Social Gospel, 155n
Solomon, King (in 1 Kings 4), 122
Southern Baptists, 33, 135
Stafford, Tim, 157n, 208n
Staver, Matthew, 209n
Steffey, Matthew, 153n
Steinberg, David, 173n
Steinfels, Peter, 205n
Stephenson, D. Grier, 152n
Stevens, John Paul, 54–56
Stewart, Don, 160n
Stiver, Athena, 86–87, 89
Stiver, Theda, 86–87, 89
Stokes, Anson, 151n
Stone, Geoffrey, 168n, 180n, 184n
Stone v Graham (1980), 200n
Sullivan, Kathleen, 53, 153n 173n, 174n
Sullivan William, 175n
Sullivan, Winnefred, 152n
Sunstein, Cass, 168n, 180n, 184n, 204
Swanson, Donald, 6, 151n
Swindler, Ann, 175n
Swomley, John, 30, 34, 35, 36, 52, 53

Taney, Roger, 45
Tarr, G. Alan, 152n
Tennessee v. John Scopes (1925), 155n
Thiemann, Ronald, 3, 49, 149n, 150n,
    174n, 175n, 176n, 181n, 183n,
Thomas, Oliver, 12, 26, 167n
Tillich, Paul, 35, 36
Tipton, Steven, 175n
Tocqueville, Alexis de, 9, 154n

Torcaso v Watkins (1961), 169n, 172n
Tracy, David, 16
Tracy, Spencer, 35
Tribe, Laurence, 197n
Turque, Bill, 163n
Tushnet, Mark, 12, 77, 83, 84, 144–145,
    204n, 209n

Ultimate concern, 35
U.S. v Ballard (1944), 172n
U.S. v Lee (1982), 133
U.S. v Seeger (1965), 35, 172n
University of Notre Dame, 26–27

Vaccari, Michael, 199n
Van Biema, David, 209n
Vitz, Paul, 12, 80, 81, 187n

Wacker, Grant, 155n, 157n
Waite, Morrison, 131
Wald, Kenneth, 3, 9, 12, 16, 17, 26,
    149n, 156n, 158n, 164n
Walker, Graham, 161n
Wallace v Jaffree (1985), 55, 94–95, 145,
    186n, 199n, 201n
Walz v Tax Commission (1970), 65, 67,
    181n, 183n, 199n
Washington, James Melvin, 167n, 179n
Wax, Darold, 6, 151n, 151n
Weber, Paul, 164n, 169n, 183n, 197n
Weber, Max, 38, 170n
Webster v Reproductive Health Services
    (1989), 54, 56
Weeks, David, 155n
Weiner, Merle, 149n, 175n
Weiss, Wallace, 85, 88
Wells, David, 156n
West Virginia Board of Education v
    Barnette (1943), 202n, 207n
West, Ellis, 172n, 203n
Westside Community Schools v Mergens
    (1990), 140–143, 191n, 199n, 209n
White, Byron, 65, 142, 145